Fever & Thirst

An American Doctor Among the
Tribes of Kurdistan, 1835–1844

Gordon Taylor

ACADEMY CHICAGO PUBLISHERS

Academy Chicago Publishers
363 West Erie Street
Chicago, Illinois 60610

© 2005 Gordon Taylor
Introduction © 2008 John Agresto

First published 2005
Second printing 2008

Printed and bound in the U.S.A.

Library of Congress Cataloging-in-Publication Data
on file with the publisher.

For Noel and Margaret Taylor

Contents

INTRODUCTION

EVERYTHING SEEMS SO DIFFERENT now. From my room here in Sulaimani, in Kurdish Iraq, I can look down the street to the dilapidated green domed Shiite mosque and, from there, to the more prosperous Sunni mosque not too far behind it. Up the street is the Kurdish Cultural Center next to the Chaldean Catholic church, next to the headquarters of the Communist Party. Overlooking it all is a heavily treed compound that everyone says is the CIA headquarters. No one seems to think twice about any of this; religion, tribe, sect, nationality, politics . . . in this part of Kurdistan they all seem to coexist peacefully, even happily, together.

Compared to the world described in this extraordinary book, things seem different, things are different. The Kurds of Iraq, once surely one of the most ferocious people anywhere, have calmed down a good bit. Getting a job, owning a Nissan dealership, visiting Europe, flirting and being flirted with . . . all these are more important these days than cutting off your neighbor's ear. Commerce, trade, and money-making have worked their wonders on this part of the world, and turned peoples' attention to less sanguinary pursuits. Islam—never as fanatical here as in other parts of the Middle East—remains a mildly cohesive rather than a divisive element. And nationalism, Kurdish nationalism, exercises an attractive force that erodes, dissolves, many of the petty differences that only recently separated tribe and village and family.

Beyond politics and nationality, even the ancient religious landscape seems to have been erased by time. Asahel Grant, M.D., the great protagonist of this book, went to minister to the "Nestorians." But even among serious Christians, who these days knows anything about the Nestorians? No matter that these Christians were the offshoot of the first great and lasting divide in Christendom, dating back to 431 AD, when the Church of the East separated itself from the rest of Christianity. No matter that, for a while, these Nestorians— "Assyrians" as we refer to their remnant today—might even have been Christianity's dominant branch, with Nestorian churches thriving as far away as China, India, Japan and Tibet. But that was then, and surely times have changed.

So maybe everything is different now, and maybe Gordon Taylor's book is simply a beautifully written, impeccably researched, compellingly told historical curiosity. But . . . why do I have this odd feeling this book is more than that?

Perhaps, as the French might say, the more things change the more they remain the same. Look again at the Kurds. It wasn't all that long ago that half the Kurds of Iraqi Kurdistan, under the banner of the Kurdistan Democratic Party, called upon their arch-enemy, Saddam Hussein, to help them exterminate their political rivals in the Patriotic Union of Kurdistan. Not to be outdone, the PUK, in turn, called upon the hated Iranians to help them in destroying the KDP. And now, fifteen years later, a political alliance brings both parties together, based, as always, on newly-perceived shared interest. And the cycle called History rolls on. More importantly, perhaps Americans haven't changed much, either. Look at Asahel Grant—physician, missionary, and educator—improver of the body, the soul, and the mind. Asahel Grant epitomizes everything admirable, everything naive, and everything almost incomprehensible to the rest of the world, about the American spirit.

In some ways, the Kurds of this book are unremarkable. Tribesmen warriors, with all the brutality of the unconquered world in which they live, they display all the virtues and all the many vices that are catalogued in all stories, travelogues, and histories since the start of writing. Perhaps the amazing thing about the Kurds is not the ferocious picture of them in this book, but what they seem to have become of late.

Nor, perhaps, should we be too surprised by the character of the Nestorians, even though Asahel Grant, in his most American naiveté, was initially taken aback by their un-Christian like natures. (How else to describe a sect so rife with murderers, thieves, swindlers, and extortionists?) Even though most of us would like to think otherwise, it is a fact of life that there are serious religions and serious religious sentiment without a shred of morality.

No, for me at least, the most amazing thing about this more than amazing book is Asahel Grant, the American. We meet the good doctor with a swollen face, bleeding himself with a lancet. We meet him in the sixth year of his sufferings. He has already lost his wife and two infant daughters to the ravages and diseases of Kurdistan. Yet he bleeds himself, and rides on. Why? Simple answer—To bring some semblance of literacy and education, some medical relief, and some moral support to an ancient Christian denomination that civilization seems to have passed by.

But, again, why? Why should Asahel Grant care so much about people he barely knows to lose his wife, his children, his health, and ultimately his life over them? In a world these days where we so easily talk about the common threads of our humanity, how all of us are really the same, why does

Asahel Grant, the American, seem so different? Why is he concerned about the health of—of all people!—Kurds? Why does he exhaust himself over the education of children not his own? Why does he care if these "Nestorians" fall under the sway of the pope or not? Why are their bodies, their minds and the freedom of their spirits of any concern to him? To be sure, not one of the people he ministers to would have given up all they possessed to cross the ocean and climb the hills to minister to Asahel Grant. So why? Why does he do it?

This is hardly an idle or academic question in my life. When I look out my window here in Kurdistan I see more than buildings. Not missionaries exactly, but I do see Americans setting up schools, starting clinics, laying sewer pipe, helping to build roads. . . . All with lives elsewhere, all with families left behind. Like Asahel Grant, none of them is here for money or oil or politics or honor or acclaim. What's the idea or the idealism that drives them? Is it the same vision of Humanity that drove Grant? I think it is, though I'm not sure what to call it. Nor do I fully know exactly why it's there.

Perhaps the Kurds are changed from what they were in 1840. For sure the Nestorians are pretty much gone. But Asahel Grant seems still to be around, with all his idealism, all his boundless energy, all his up-to-date technology, all his mistakes, and, all too often, all the failures that come from his misplaced good intentions. *Fever and Thirst*, like any great book of biography and history, is hardly a book just about the past, hardly a curiosity at all.

In saying that, I have only touched on one of the wide-ranging themes of this book. Yet, even if we resist succumbing to any of the grand and perplexing themes of the book, the fascinating thing about *Fever and Thirst* is that we can easily take in its hundreds, its thousands of wonderful details. "Phlebotomy"? Here it is. Ever wonder what the sweet that Kurds and Arabs call Manna from Heaven is made of?

That's right . . . aphid secretions. (Sorry to say, I read it here after I had eaten it.) Need to know about gallnuts or mercury poisoning or the proper use of leeches? No worry; they're all here. Or perhaps you had forgotten that lions roamed Iraq until the 1920s? From philosophy to botany to politics, religion and medicine—I now know how the first reader must have felt upon opening Diderot's Encyclopedia.

John Agresto
Sulaimani, Iraq
March 2008

And there are some, whom a thirst
Ardent, unquenchable, fires,
Not with the crowd to be spent,
Not without aim to go round
In an eddy of purposeless dust,
Effort unmeaning and vain . . .
We, we have chosen our path—
Path to a clear-purposed goal,
Path of advance! but it leads
A long, steep journey, through sunk
Gorges, o'er mountains in snow!

—MATTHEW ARNOLD, "RUGBY CHAPEL" (1857)

This is the patent age of new inventions
For killing bodies, and for saving souls,
All propagated with the best intentions.

—BYRON, *DON JUAN*, CTO. I, ST. 132

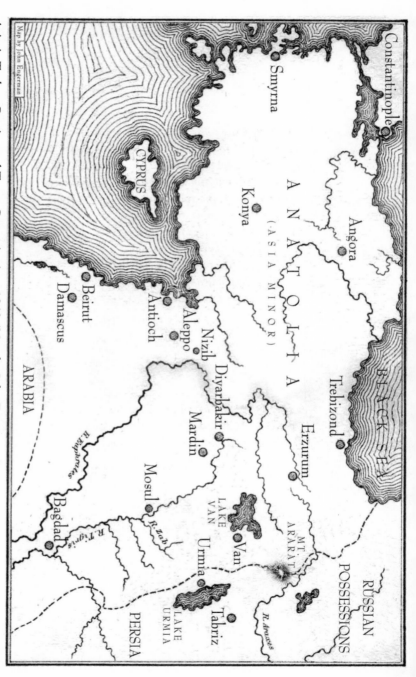

Asiatic Turkey, Persia, and Trans-Caucasia circa 1840 (*Map by John Engerman*).

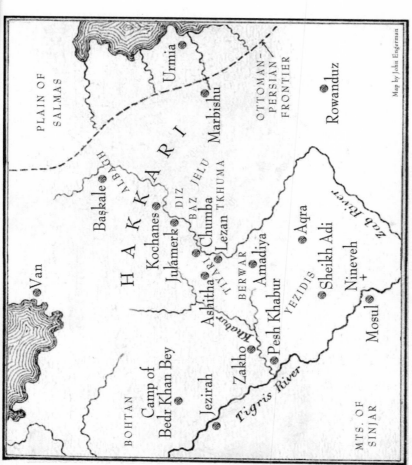

Hakkari and Central Kurdistan (*Map by John Engerman*).

The Remedy

"To the place where the sun doesn't come, comes the doctor."
—*Turkish proverb*

ON AUGUST 14, 1842, a man woke at dawn to find his face swollen into a bubble of pain. His beard, grown thick after months of mountain travel, probably masked the worst of the swelling; still, for one so lean of countenance this must have been a shock. A modern physician might name a dozen reasons, from food allergies to insect bites, why this could have happened; but the man had been ill for such a long time—six years, on and off, a recurrent round of vomiting and fever, broken by occasional spells of relief—that to him any new complaint must have seemed simply an extension of the old. He was not elderly—his thirty-fifth birthday was only days away—nor was he sickly by nature. Back in the United States, before he set sail for this remote corner of the Middle East, he had enjoyed the vigorous health of one raised to hard work on the family farm. But within a year after his arrival in Urmia, the town in northwest Persia where he first made his home, he had fallen ill. Only in the mountain air could he find a measure of relief.

When he felt the swelling, he identified the source immediately. That night he had slept in Chumba, a village on the river Zab, very close to what is now the border between Turkey and Iraq. His host, Malek Ismael, the chief of this Christian village, had given him the use of an *arzaleh* upon which to sleep. These structures, ten to fifteen feet high, were a common feature of life in the villages, where mosquitoes hatched in summer to supplant the winter's crop of fleas. With the *arzaleh,* a sleeping platform set upon a framework of poles, the people sought refuge from the worst of the insects. The villages of this area abounded in water, which fed their terraced fields with torrents of melted snow falling from the mountains above. This particular *arzaleh* had been erected so close to such a stream that when the American climbed its rude ladder and lay down, his head rested only a few feet from a roaring cataract. The long-suffering traveler did not get wet; still, it was the proximity to dampness, he felt, that had brought on the swelling. This was no idle opinion, for the man was a physician.

Asahel Grant, M.D., a general practitioner from Oneida County, New York, was traveling in this wild border region between the Ottoman and Persian Empires under the auspices of the American Board of Commissioners for Foreign Missions. In May 1835, aged 27 years, he had sailed from Boston with his bride, Judith, to teach the unlettered, preach the gospel, and heal the sick. Since then he had worked ceaselessly, traveling alone through mountains where the people lived in a constant state of feuding, robbery, and war. His character impressed everyone who met him, but his presence had changed this human cockpit not a jot. In fact, there is ample reason to believe that he had made matters worse. By January 1840, Grant's wife Judith and twin baby girls—three-fifths of his family—lay buried in the mission graveyard in Urmia. Every year saw new deaths among the missionaries, some of whom were already dying when they arrived. And yet, faced by these and other losses, despite threats of robbery and murder, Grant rode on. He had not come to Hakkari, this untamed corner of Turkish Kurdistan, to allow something so trifling as a swollen face, or even so discouraging as a death, to hold him back.

On that Sunday morning Grant faced a five-hour climb to the *zozan*—the summer pastures—of Chumba, where Mar Shimun, patriarch of the "Nestorian" Church of the East, awaited his visit. Grant needed the patriarch's friendship and approval; it was impossible to overstate the importance of this connection. The doctor had wearied of long marches through the mountains, so it was in the village of Asheetha, the center of a populous valley to the south, that he wanted to build a permanent home, a large house with many rooms where he and his missionary colleagues could teach and minister for the rest of their days. Through their efforts and with the patriarch's support, the Church of the East, a tiny relic from the dawn of Christianity, would flourish again. Even the Kurds, Grant believed, might some day throw off the delusions of the False Prophet and receive the word of Jesus Christ.

When he arrived at the *zozan*, Grant found acres of sheep grazing amid alpine splendor. Most of the people of Chumba had retired to this summer camp in the high pastures with its invigorating air; they took shelter in crude huts made of branches or slept in the open on felt cloaks. The patriarch Mar Shimun, who occupied the only tent, gave a warm greeting to Dr. Grant, who had brought with him copies of the Psalms, printed in modern Syriac at the American mission in Urmia, the first of their kind ever produced. Mar Shimun accepted them with gratitude, and on that Sabbath afternoon he read the new books aloud as flocks grazed about them, shepherds kept watch for bears, and last winter's snows seeped into the earth.

For six days of the week, armies of the sick and lame followed the doctor wherever he went; on this Sabbath he took time to minister to himself. We can only imagine the misery that beset him. His face remained swollen and painful; intermittent malaria drained his strength. Since 1836, when he had

barely survived an attack of cholera, his stomach could retain
food only fitfully. Now as a doctor, he knew one ultimate remedy for the swelling of his face.

This was neither a drug nor brandy, and certainly not a poul-
tice or a salve. From his black bag Dr. Grant drew an object that,
although no bigger than a pen, was the most potent weapon in
the physician's arsenal, used to attack all diseases, including diphtheria, malaria, and yellow fever, as well as childbirth, female
disorders, and broken bones. This instrument took such prece-
dence in the fight against disease that even today the journal of
the British Medical Association bears its name. The lancet, as its
name implies, resembled a tiny spear, with a double-edged blade
tapering to a sharp point. It was used with small bowls to catch
the blood. And surely that night, in the privacy bestowed by darkness, blood flowed freely. For his swollen face, says his biographer, Grant found relief "only by a desperate plunge of his lancet
into the very roots of his teeth." The blade, Grant admits, had
struck so deeply into his gums that the labial nerve was severed,
leaving his upper lip numb for nearly two weeks.

This was not the act of a madman or a quack. Grant was a
competent and conscientious physician, a man who never acted
with anything but the best of intentions. No one can read about
his desperate thrust of the lancet without the queasy realization
that little had changed since alchemists stalked the earth. In
some parts of the United States, doctors continued to draw blood
up to the beginning of the 20th century, and the potions they
dispensed lingered even longer in their black bags and in
apothecaries'chests. Such was the staying power of an illusion;
such was the world of Asahel Grant.

2

Utica and Beyond

"And I would never travel among Christians. Christians are so slow, and they wear chimney-pot hats everywhere. The further one goes from London among Christians, the more they wear chimney-pot hats. I want Plantagenet to take us to see the Kurds, but he won't."

"I don't think that would be fair to Miss Vavasor," said Mr. Palliser, who had followed them.

"Don't put the blame on her head," said Lady Glencora. "Women always have pluck for anything. Wouldn't you like to see a live Kurd, Alice?"

"I don't know exactly where they live," said Alice.

"Nor I. I have not the remotest idea of the way to the Kurds . . . But one knows that they are Eastern, and the East is such a grand idea!"

—Anthony Trollope, *Can You Forgive Her?* (1865)

It began with a child's desk drawer, a wayward axe, and a life of hard work and Puritan religion. At the turn of the nineteenth century Asahel Grant's parents, Thomas and Rachel Grant, had migrated west to New York from Litchfield County, Connecticut, an area known, wrote Rev. Thomas Laurie, Grant's biographer, for "pure revivals" and the "sterling, intelligent type of its piety." In Oneida County, atop an eminence known as "Grant's Hill," on the road between Waterville and Clinton, they built the Grant family homestead.

There on August 17, 1807, Asahel ("made by God" in Hebrew) was born, and there, in a youthful accident, he disqualified himself from a life of farming by slicing his foot with an axe. As if to compensate, he displayed an early interest in medicine, keeping an assortment of ingredients in a desk drawer for his own study and use. After a time teaching in a country school, Grant studied medicine in Clinton with Dr. Seth Hastings, after whom he named his eldest son. Later he audited a chemistry course at Hamilton College in the same town and attended medical lectures in Pittsfield, Massachusetts. As was typical of the time, Grant never received a formal college degree. Despite a proliferation of medical schools, most physicians learned their trade through apprenticeship with other doctors, without attending even a single course of medical lectures. Eventually Grant ended up in Utica, New York, where he studied surgery with a local doctor and married Electa Loomis, daughter of another pious Connecticut family. Most important, it was in Utica that he found missionary Christianity.

The "call" came on October 8, 1834, when the American Board of Commissioners for Foreign Missions convened its twenty-fifth annual meeting at the Dutch Reformed Church in Utica. By then, at age 27, Grant was well established both as a physician and an elder in the First Presbyterian Church. After receiving his medical diploma, he had set up his first practice in what is now Laceyville, Pennsylvania. Upon Electa's death in 1831, Grant returned to Utica to seek help in caring for his two sons, and set up a practice there with another physician, who eventually had to flee the town because of a financial scandal. Grant inherited the entire practice and prospered in Utica, a newly incorporated, rapidly growing city on the Erie Canal. In 1830, Utica had a population of "4,135 males, 3,968 females, and 183 colored." The young doctor exhibited great courage and energy during the epidemic of Asiatic cholera which swept through Utica in 1832, causing some 3,000 people to flee the city.

By the time the American Board convened its meeting, Asahel Grant had become imbued with that devoutness so characteristic of 19th-century New Englanders. Rev. Thomas Laurie writes, "His piety was not of that spongy character that is dry and hard save as it absorbs moisture from without, and then refuses to impart it except under pressure. It was like the fountain, ever filled from the fulness there is in Christ, and ever imparting what it had to others." In short, the man overflowed with energy, religious ardor, and idealism. "I cannot," Grant wrote to a friend, "I dare not go up to judgment, till I have done the utmost God enables me to do to diffuse his glory throughout the earth."

Part of the American Board's 1834 convention dealt with reports of missions in the field, and one of these came from northwest Persia, where Rev. Justin Perkins, of Springfield, Massachusetts, and his wife, Charlotte Bass Perkins, had gone to open a mission to the local Nestorian Christians. At that point they had done little but survive the journey, which involved a long internment by thuggish Russian officials. Above all, they needed colleagues. "The Committee have sought in vain," said the Annual Report, "for a pious and competent physician, able and disposed to go forth as an associate with Mr. Perkins . . . Such a man is exceedingly needed." Confronted with this plea, Grant felt the call to service. For many weeks, he wrestled with his feelings. His two motherless sons would have to be left behind with foster parents; he had no wife to share his burdens; his practice in Utica was profitable, and his many friends implored him to stay. Yet such were his reverence and resolve that, one by one, the objections fell away. He found a good man willing to care for his children. The profits from his practice were nothing, he decided, compared to those that would accrue from God's work. And very quickly, a woman entered his life.

Judith Campbell, seven years younger than Asahel Grant, had been orphaned at an early age and adopted by an aunt and uncle. She read Latin and Greek, spoke French and was, if anything, even more pious than the doctor. Thomas Laurie tells us that at age seven, when a missionary couple from an adjoining town left for the Sandwich Islands, Judith was persuaded to donate her favorite mittens to a gift box assembled by the ladies of her church. Such climatic naïveté may seem absurd; but it should not be forgotten that girls like Judith Campbell and other Protestant women of New England were formidable human beings—so devout, so fervid in their desire for education, progress, and self-sacrifice, that they formed the core and conscience of the Abolitionist movement, as well as the movement for women's rights and suffrage.

Judith Campbell had already been accepted for missionary work when Dr. Grant met her, and in retrospect their union seems inevitable. By October 28, 1834, he had written to the Board asking to be accepted as a missionary, and as his plans matured over the winter, his relations with Judith matured as well. In February he wrote to a colleague, "You will rejoice to learn that a kind Providence has united with mine the heart of a young lady of most precious spirit, whose ardent piety, good health and highly cultivated intellect, fit her for extensive usefulness."

Here the good doctor might seem to be describing a new employee rather than a fiancée. "Usefulness," however, was high praise for someone of Grant's convictions. Being useful—in God's work—implied qualities of a far higher order than mere niceness or pleasantness. Grant could not have loved a woman who would not prove useful in the great labors ahead. For her part, in a letter to her brother dated March 10, Judith delivered a warmer assessment:

> You know, dear brother, how much I have thought of being a missionary, and how I have prayed to know my duty in the matter. Hitherto the way seemed hedged up; but a door is

now opened, and I am about to enter it. Yes, my dear, dear
brother, I expect soon to leave these loved familiar scenes for
Persia. The interesting ceremony that unites me with Dr. Grant
takes place on Monday, April 6 . . . I wish you could become
acquainted with Dr. Grant, for I am sure you would like him.
He has been an elder in Mr. Aikin's church three or four years,
and bears the character of *an eminent and devoted Christian.*

Judith Campbell and Asahel Grant were married on April
6, 1835. On May 11, aboard the brig *Angola,* they sailed from
Boston harbor for the shores of Turkey.

In 1835 the word "Turkey" was political shorthand, not an
official name. The Ottoman Empire, like Saudi Arabia today,
was named after a man, in this case Osman I, the Turkish *gazi,*
or warrior, who founded the dynasty in 1299. There were several sobriquets for the Empire and its sultan—"the Grand Turk"
and "the Grand Seigneur" among them—but commonly the
central government was referred to as the Sublime Porte, or
simply the Porte, after the gate which led into the inner reaches
of the Topkapi Palace in Constantinople. The Osmanlis, as the
Ottomans were also called, had once ruled a vast empire stretching from the Persian Gulf to the gates of Vienna, but by 1835
they were in retreat. In Iraq and the Arabian Peninsula, the Turks'
authority, loosely applied, remained, but in Egypt, nominally a
part of the Empire, an Albanian soldier-of-fortune named Mohammed Ali had taken power, established a de facto independence and, after aiding the sultan in the Greek War of Independence (1821–28), had extended his authority into the Ottoman
provinces of Palestine and Syria. When Mohammed Ali's troops
invaded Anatolia and routed the Ottomans at Konya in 1832,
only the intervention of the Russian fleet kept the Egyptians
from taking Constantinople. By the time the Grants arrived in
Turkey, everyone knew that another war between Mohammed
Ali and the Ottoman sultan, Mahmud II, was inevitable.

In the east, west, and north matters were even worse, for there the Turks faced the ever-growing power of the Russians. It had long been common knowledge that the czars were pushing south in search of a warm-water port, their obvious goal being Constantinople and the Straits. Between 1768 and 1878 the Turks and the Russians fought six major wars, and as these conflicts took their dismal course, the Turks' possessions fell steadily away. On the north shore of the Black Sea, the Russians took the Crimea from the Tatar Khans. They absorbed the Kingdom of Georgia and were waging a war of conquest against the Muslim tribes of the Caucasus. In Rumania, Bulgaria, and the Balkans, Russian power was growing every year.

When Judith and Asahel Grant landed in Turkey in 1835 and sailed east on the Black Sea, to take the caravan route to northwest Persia, they were the direct beneficiaries of a Russian victory over the Turks. Before 1829, when Turkey was forced to sign the Treaty of Adrianople, the Dardanelles and the Bosphorus—and thus the Black Sea—had been closed to foreign shipping by decree of the sultan. After Adrianople, Turkey was open again to travel and commerce. Thus, only two years after the peace, two American missionaries, Eli Smith and H.G.O. Dwight, were able to cross Anatolia from Constantinople to Erzurum, past Mt. Ararat and into Persia. There, after much sickness and hardship, they made contact with local Nestorian Christians in Urmia and obtained the shah's permission to open a school.

All of this brought joy to the American Board, who could now contemplate a push eastward in the same pioneering spirit that had sent their fellow New Englanders to the west. But in the Middle East, unlike America, the land sagged beneath its burden of history. (Even now, after 150 years of digging, archaeologists in Turkey have scarcely begun to work their way through the layers.) Then there was the political situation (hopeless), the military situation (ditto), the domestic blood feuds (infinite), and the religious suspicion (worse every year). In the

1830s the Ottoman Empire was spread across the Middle East like a vast cavern laced with side passages, each crowded with its pack of assassins sharpening their knives in the gloom. But with bright eyes, high spirits, and hopeful hearts, the Americans came—to establish the Kingdom of God and Jesus Christ on earth.

The Muslims, in the majority, were understandably skeptical. The bloody, strife-torn centuries had taught them caution, and they no doubt found it difficult to accept the idea that prosperous, smiling Christians would travel thousands of miles from an unknown land, with only benign motives. The Muslims knew what the European navies had done to the sultan's fleet at the Battle of Navarino, which ended the Greek War of Independence in 1827, and they knew what the Russians were up to. Every year Muslims from across the globe made their way to Mecca, and these assembled masses could not fail to discuss Islam's failing fortunes. The news would spread that the White Czar was threatening the sultan's power and driving the Faithful from their lands. And when a peace treaty following a Russian victory led to the arrival of missionaries who tended mostly to the Czar's Armenian allies, these arrivals could only spell trouble.

After a 44-day passage from Boston, with on-deck afternoon Bible classes for the crew, the Grants arrived in the Aegean port of Smyrna (now Izmir) at the end of June. There they exchanged their sailing ship for a new Austrian steamer, which carried them north to Constantinople (now Istanbul), where they rested for six weeks among the missionaries and Armenians. The great city, nicknamed Stamboul, proved more than welcoming to the young doctor. During his sojourn there, Grant had ample opportunity to practice medicine, and one of his patients, a rich Armenian, offered him a substantial sum of money to remain there. But at the end of the six weeks, the Grants boarded a schooner bound for Trebizond (now Trabzon) at the east end of the Black Sea. The schooner, American-built and English-owned, had formerly served in the slave trade—a grim fact which the couple did not fail to note. With the ship's arrival at Trebizond on August 30, their sea voyages came to an end, and the difficult part of their journey began.

In Trebizond, the Grants confronted Eastern reality. Here another American missionary, the Rev. T.P. Johnston, had established an outpost, but so strong was the prejudice against him and his family that they could scarcely step outside their house without being cursed or threatened. These ugly prejudices should have been expected. The Russian border lay close to Trebizond, and the Treaty of Adrianople had brought it closer. In the recent war, the Russian army had captured the fortress of Erzurum, the next major city on the caravan route to Persia, as well as Gümüşhane, a town just forty miles inland. The Russians had withdrawn only on the signing of the peace treaty in September 1829. Had the Treaty of Adrianople not been signed when it was, Trebizond would easily have fallen.

In all this fighting the local Armenians openly sided with the Russians, providing them with intelligence that proved vital in the final attack on Erzurum. After its capture, wrote Alexander Pushkin, who served in the Russian army, the city "presented an astounding picture. From their flat roofs the Turks were looking at us sullenly. Armenians were thronging noisily in the narrow streets. Their little boys ran in front of our horses, crossing themselves and repeating: 'Christians! Christians!'"

None of this could have produced good feelings between the two groups, especially since everyone knew that despite their withdrawal, the Russians would attack again soon. In his biography, Thomas Laurie ignores these facts, if indeed he ever considered them. He does not mention that even Urmia, the Grants' ultimate destination, had been occupied by the Russians in 1828. Laurie and Grant were missionaries, and from the Johnstons' isolation in Trebizond they drew their own lesson: if the American Board was to continue their work—and no one seriously expected them not to continue—they needed to send Christian physicians to provide needed services, and open doors for the preachers to come.

On September 17, 1835, after a long wait for horses, the Grants set forth. Any Turkish journey involves mountain travel, and this one was no exception. Such inns as existed were mere hovels, and so the couple slept in a tent, with armed guards posted and baggage stacked around them in a square. Five days into the journey they were met by Rev. Justin Perkins, who had ridden the 300 miles from Tabriz to offer his help. September 26 saw the party in Erzurum, and three days later, in a caravan of over 600 horses, they started for Persia.

Here, for the first time in the East, illness struck Asahel Grant. On the mountain pass of Dahar, he became so exhausted by vomiting that he had to lie down and rest, and when he woke the caravan had disappeared. It took several hours of hard riding to catch up with it. Grant soon recovered his strength, but in light of his later history, this first sickness is troubling. Equally ominous was an epidemic of cholera, which they encountered on October 15 when they reached Tabriz, the Turkish-speaking capital of Persian Azerbaijan. In Constantinople and Trebizond, they had already seen outbreaks of plague, but Asiatic cholera was fast supplanting that ancient scourge. Obviously, in their new homeland there would be no lack of disease. In Urmia, which the Grants reached on October 27, 1835, they would find a smorgasbord.

3

MIASMA

"And a river went out of Eden to water the garden; and from thence it was parted, and became into four heads. The name of the first is Pison: that is it which compasseth the whole land of Havilah, where there is gold; And the gold of that land is good: there is bdellium and the onyx stone."—*Genesis 2:10–13*

BOTH IN CLIMATE AND TERRAIN, Urmia resembles a city that did not then exist: Salt Lake City, in Utah. To the east, in the midst of high desert, lies Lake Urmia, a shallow lake ninety miles long by thirty-five miles wide, so saline that fish cannot live in it and swimmers floating upright can barely sink up to their shoulders. Lake Urmia is fed by fourteen rivers that fall from the great snow peaks rising to the west, the Kurd-inhabited mountains that form the frontier with Turkey. This border, stretching from the Persian Gulf to Mt. Ararat, was established by treaty in 1555, yet for most of its length no one knew exactly where it lay. Near Urmia the frontier followed, more or less, the drainage divide at the passes leading into Ottoman domains. In Turkish territory, the water flowed west and south into the tangled river systems feeding the Tigris. On the Persian side, the rivers fell to Lake Urmia.

Thousands of years before the Mormons arrived in Salt Lake, the residents of Urmia and the surrounding villages had turned its plain into a garden, where fruits, nuts, vegetables, and cereals grew in abundance. Trees and vegetation cloaked the villages, while poplars, sprouting in serried ranks, were cultivated for their timber. The cultivation of melons had developed into an art form, and cherries in season sold for twenty-five cents a bushel. The English traveler Isabella Bird visited the town, which she called Urmi, in autumn 1890:

> But beautiful Urmi, far as the eye can reach, is one oasis. From Turkman onwards the plain becomes more and more attractive, the wood-embosomed villages closer together, the variety of trees greater. Irrigation canals shaded by fruit trees, and irrigation ditches bordered by reeds, carry water in abundance all through the plain. Swampy streams abound. Fair stretches of smooth green sward rejoice the eye. Big buffaloes draw heavy carts laden with the teeming produce of the black, slimy, bountiful soil from the fields into the villages. Wheat, maize, beans, melons, gourds, potatoes, carrots, turnips, beets, capsicum, chilis, *bringals,* lady's fingers, castor-oil (for burning), cotton, madder, salsify, scorzonera, celery, oil-seeds of various sorts, opium, and tobacco all flourish. The orchards are full of trees which almost merit the epithet noble. Noble indeed are the walnuts, and beautiful are the pomegranates, the apricots, the apples, the peach and plum trees, and glorious are the vineyards with their foliage, which, like that of the cherry and pear, is passing away in scarlet and gold.

But these blessings came with a curse. Despite the altitude of 4000 feet, European travelers talked of the unhealthy "miasma" of the Urmia plain. No one knew what this miasma consisted of, but they knew that in the summer heat, when irrigation water lay about in puddles, the rice paddies were flooded, and gardens were bursting with life, the fevers came calling. When Rev. Horatio

Southgate, an American Episcopal missionary, visited the town in the summer of 1837, he noted the mud wall surrounding Urmia and its moat filled with stagnant water, which, he wrote, "is covered with a green slime and emits baleful odours." He did not of course connect this stagnant water with mosquito larvae, no doubt wriggling in it by the millions.

Fevers were only part of the problem: dysentery, cholera, and stomach complaints made their contribution as well. Urmia's water came from the mountains. It looked clear and tasted good, so people drank it: the stream might have passed through ten villages before it reached their lips, but that was not considered a problem. According to the Hadith, the collected sayings of Mohammed, any water that flowed nine feet could be considered clean. If the people got sick, they may have "caught a chill"; or, as with Dr. Grant's swollen face, had fallen victim to "the damp." Above all, they were cursed with the miasma: the bad air; the *mal aria*.

In this oasis city with its burbling watercourses and high mud walls, the dedicated Americans set busily to work. Setting up housekeeping was not easy. The missionaries' house was unfinished when they arrived, and they spent those first November nights sleeping on wood shavings left behind by the carpenters. When they lit fires, the heat caused the barley straw to sprout in the fresh mud of the walls. Besides homemaking, preaching, and teaching, there were languages to learn: the Syriac of the Christians, as well as the Turkish of the Muslim townsmen. Judith proved especially adept, learning Turkish quickly and eventually mastering both ancient and modern Syriac. From the first day Grant was overwhelmed with patients, and in addition to his medical practice he taught in the mission schools, to which the local children flocked for instruction. These became so popular that the doctor soon opened a school for Muslim children as well. Despite recurrent illnesses, these were heady times. Grant made a name for himself back home by writing "An Appeal to Pious Physicians," a widely-disseminated tract exhorting American doctors to devote themselves to missionary work. By 1837 Judith Grant was writing to friends that the previous two years had been the happiest of her life.

The missionaries' chief clients were Nestorian—known also as East Syrian or Assyrian—Christians, adherents of the Church of the East, which had been the predominant Christian sect of the ancient pre-Islamic Persian Empire. The Nestorians were the tiny remnant of a once-powerful church that had sent missionaries and traders as far as China and the Malabar Coast of India. Most of these Christian villagers, like the Muslim majority, lived as feudal subjects of the Muslim landowners who controlled the Urmia plain. In Ottoman territory to the west, in the high mountains of Hakkari, the Nestorian tribes lived independent of all authority. Nominally they owed allegiance to the Kurdish emir of Hakkari, but in practice they answered to no one but themselves.

The patriarch of their church called himself Mar Shimun: the patriarchate had been hereditary in the Shimun family since 1535, passing from uncle to nephew through the generations. The history of these patriarchs and their church could scarcely be more complicated. From century to century the patriarchate moved its seat among half a dozen places in Persia and Turkey. By the 19th century, Mar Shimun was living in the village of Kochanes, near Julamerk (now Hakkari). Some patriarchs yielded to the authority of Rome and split off; others returned to independence. A separate East Syrian church, generally known as Chaldean Catholic, acknowledged the supremacy of the pope. Most of these Chaldeans lived near Mosul in northern Iraq, where Arabic had largely supplanted the Syriac or 'neo-Aramaic' language spoken by Old Church Nestorians of the mountains.

"Nestorian" is a name now rejected by these people, who prefer to call themselves Assyrians or Aramaeans. Nestorius was a 5th-century bishop of Constantinople who objected to the orthodox term "Mother of God," then used to describe the Virgin Mary, and was denounced for his opinions by the Council of Ephesus in 431. These distinctions mattered a great deal in a time when no clear division existed between politics and theology, and the power brokers of the early church spilled large quantities of blood (and ink) in defense of their interpretations. The Church of the East still reveres Nestorius as an orthodox teacher, though his original heresy, grossly distorted by his enemies, has no place in their doctrines. In the middle of the 19th century the adherents of the Church of the East had no qualms about calling themselves "Nestorayé" Syrians, as distinct from Armenians, Chaldeans, Syrian Orthodox, and Catholics. It seems to have been simply a label of convenience. To Dr. Grant and his colleagues these members of the Church of the East were always "the Nestorians," and I will follow his example.

In the 1830s these Nestorians had only recently been discovered by the West. In the previous decade travelers had brought electrifying rumors of Christians, ferocious tribesmen, living in the highest, most remote mountains of Kurdistan and terrorizing their Muslim neighbors. No one had actually seen them, but this romantic image proved irresistible, especially to English-speaking Protestant missionaries who were eager to get to these ancient Christians before they were won over by the ever-diligent emissaries of the pope. In 1830 Eli Smith and H.G.O. Dwight had contacted the Nestorians on the Urmia plain, but when Asahel Grant arrived, no European had yet met Mar Shimun and traveled among the independent tribes of Hakkari. It seems likely, given Grant's energy and ambition, that nothing, not even the demands of a family, could have kept him away. As the doctor labored in Urmia, his eyes lifted to the hills. Their remote beauty was enticing, but danger lurked there. Everyone remembered what had happened to Friedrich Schultz in 1829.

Like a dark Wagnerian chord, this phrase echoes in travel books throughout the 19th century: "the murder of Schultz" was invoked as a warning to those who would venture into Hakkari. Everyone knew who had done this blatant, brutal deed, and they knew who had ordered it done. But it remained unpunished.

Friedrich Schultz of Giessen was a young German scholar who traveled in Turkey and Persia under the auspices of the Academy of Paris. He had come primarily to study cuneiform inscriptions on the citadel rock at Van, north of Hakkari, which he did by having himself lowered in a basket from the ramparts of the fortress. When local officials forbade this, he brought a telescope to the minaret of a nearby mosque and copied the remaining inscriptions from there. Fifty years later, when the inscriptions were finally translated, Schultz's efforts formed the basis of our knowledge of Urartu, that unknown country mistakenly called "Ararat" in the Bible. When Schultz left Van to cross into Persia, he spent time in Tabriz perfecting his knowledge of local languages and planning an expedition into the mountains of Hakkari. This plan was discouraged by everyone, including local diplomats as well as officials of the shah. The Kurds, they told him, were notorious robbers and murderers. But these warnings only hardened his determination. In October 1829, he set forth, accompanied by guides, muleteers, and two Persian officers.

The German's lust for knowledge, so guileless and open, aroused ill will against him in Hakkari. A scientist as well as a scholar, Schultz carried with him a complement of instruments for taking measurements, both geographic and atmospheric. He asked questions, measured castles and buildings, and took copious notes on natural history and minerals. He also traveled in lordly style (he needed seven pack horses for his equipment) and carried a good deal of money, which he apparently made no effort to conceal. This behavior, along with his conspicuous height—the Pasha of Van said that Schultz was the tallest man he had ever seen—augured disaster.

Schultz was also unlucky in his choice of emirs. In 1829 Hakkari was ruled by Nurullah Bey, the Kurdish emir of

Julamerk, whose name means "the Light of God." When he
met Nurullah ten years later, Dr. Grant described the emir as
"very affable," and "a man of noble bearing, fine, open countenance" who appeared to be about thirty years old. But the Light
of God seems to have been both distrustful and cunning. He
did not sit securely on his throne: he was eternally wary of his
nephew Suleiman, who was regarded by many as the man who
should rightly have become emir. (This Suleiman Bey, as we
shall see, had his own propensities for villainy.) Nurullah Bey
resented the Nestorians and especially Mar Shimun, who was
supposed to be his vassal but who had recently stopped paying
his customary annual tribute. Nurullah also wanted to remain
independent of the Ottoman Turks; like so many men who have
tasted power, he could never quite get enough of it. When Schultz
arrived in Julamerk, the "capital" of Hakkari, Nurullah was
not only attracted by the glitter of the German's scientific instruments and the obvious wealth that lay behind them; he was
also suspicious of possible threats to his control. In Schultz's
inquisitiveness he perceived such a threat.

The mountains of Hakkari have never yielded much in the
way of mineral resources. The Kurds and Nestorians worked small
mines for their own needs—iron for tools, lead for bullets, ni-
trates and sulphur for gunpowder—but none of these existed in
commercial quantities, with one minor exception. Even today
Hakkari holds one of the world's larger deposits of orpiment, a
mineral known to artists as "King's yellow." This substance, a
crystalline compound of arsenic and sulphur, is formed from the
sublimation—the direct condensation from gas to solid—of volcanic gases. Italians derived their orpiment supplies from the fu-
maroles of Mt. Vesuvius. Despite its high arsenic content, orpiment
was prescribed as a medicine by Hippocrates and the ancient
Greeks. But it is as a yellow pigment (the name is from Latin
auri-pigmentum, literally, yellow paint) that orpiment is best
known. Since the time of ancient Egypt it was used in painting

and dyeing; Renaissance artists used it extensively. To Nurullah Bey the orpiment mines of Julamerk probably provided a small but important income: his inability to collect taxes, coupled with a chronic need for gifts to buy the loyalty of the tribes—meant that he was always in debt.

Julamerk, a town high above the river Zab (Pison to the Nestorians), marked Schultz's deepest penetration into Hakkari. When the German arrived, he gathered samples of the orpiment mined there, just as he had taken mineral samples all along his route. The mineral's yellow color, however, seems to have proved a focus for the Kurds' latent suspicions. Why had he taken this cheap rock, which everyone knew was used in paint? The foreigner, they decided, had found gold in the yellow rocks, and when he showed it to his rulers, the Franks or the Turks, hungry for riches, would call up an army to take over the Kurdish lands. This, at least, was the story Dr. Grant heard from local people whose intelligence he respected. Others ascribed the death of Schultz to simple greed. Both explanations make sense, and both are probably true. Xenophobia, greed and the eternal Middle Eastern belief in conspiracies probably fed the sort of delusion that would have impelled Nurullah to commit murder.

For his return to Persia, Friedrich Schultz was given escorts by the emir. Their route took them northeast along the river Zab, first to Başkale, Nurullah's second capital, then toward the river's headwaters at a pass leading to the plain of Salmas, at the north end of Lake Urmia. It was near Başkale (it rhymes with "posh-Calais") that the guides provided by Suleiman, a nephew of Nurullah Bey, lured Schultz into a side canyon with the promise that he could see ruins that only they knew about. Once off the road into this secluded glen, Schultz was summarily shot. One of his servants, says Grant, escaped to Başkale, where he too was murdered. Schultz's other servants, along with the two Persian officers, were taken elsewhere and killed, to prevent them from talking. When Armenian peasants, who were forced to bury the bodies, told the story to their priests, the news filtered across the border into Persia.

Six years later, when the Grants arrived in Urmia, the memory of Schultz's murder still hung heavy in the air. In his castles at Julamerk and Başkale, Nurullah, the Light of God, lived on. Nothing was done to make him pay for the murders, though the Persians did force him to punish the man who did the actual shooting. Justin Perkins, Grant's colleague, opposed any early attempt to penetrate the mountains, as did Col. Justin Sheil of the British legation in Persia. But visiting Nestorians and Kurds assured Grant that, despite the area's evil reputation, if he were to travel in Hakkari he would be warmly welcomed. His fame as a great *hakim,* doctor, was growing. Every day patients came from the mountains looking for treatment, and every day they returned to sing his praises. One Kurdish chief, Dr. Grant reported, brought his ailing wife five days' journey from their home. Another, a blind Nestorian youth from the Tiyari district, took five weeks to get to Urmia, led by the hand through the mountains by a succession of guides. Grant was becoming so popular, reported Horatio Southgate in 1837, that on one occasion, when threatened by robbers, he had only to announce his identity to thwart the attempt. Grant felt with increasing conviction that the future of the American mission lay with the independent mountaineers, not with the feudal subjects of the Urmia plain.

There was an even more compelling reason for work in the mountains: Dr. Grant's health. Quite simply, the plain of Urmia was killing him. The fevers and malaria were bad enough, but even worse was the constant vomiting which made his life a misery. This, he says, was caused by intestinal damage sustained in a near-fatal attack of cholera. Only outside the town did his health improve. When, in February 1838, Grant retreated to Tabriz for relief, the resident British physician in that city, Dr. Riach, was horrified at the change in him since his arrival in

1835. In two long letters to the missionaries at Urmia, Riach expressed the gravest concern about his patient. "*We must not lose him,*" the doctor warned the missionaries. Grant's condition improved in Tabriz, and he even gained some weight, but he relapsed as soon as he returned to Urmia. When Riach heard this he wrote immediately to the mission, advising them that they should apply to the American Board for another physician. Riach also suggested that, since Grant's health improved in the mountains and he longed to work there, perhaps the Board should send him to Hakkari. The danger to him there could not be worse than in Urmia.

During this time Grant remained in constant touch—though the letters took many months to pass back and forth—with the American Board's Prudential Committee, which made the final decisions on budgets and deployments. As early as July 1836 he had urged the importance of a mission to the mountains. He now told them frankly of his continued ill health, and Justin Perkins, as the head of the mission, kept them informed as well. By the spring of 1838 the American mission in Urmia had opened twelve schools in surrounding villages with Dr. Grant as their superintendent. According to Thomas Laurie, Grant had ridden some 500 miles visiting these schools since his return from Tabriz, and he was "still vomiting, more or less, every day." In April 1838 Grant wrote to the Prudential Committee, telling them he did not think that he could survive much more than another year in Urmia's climate. "The most distressing and alarming effect of this constant vomiting," he wrote, "is the debility and lassitude which are occasioned by the want of necessary nutrition." Asahel Grant, in other words, was starving to death, an opinion in which Dr. Riach concurred. Still, Grant left his fate in the hands of the Committee.

By this time, after the Panic of 1837, the United States had gone into a depression. Money for the mission's activities were severely cut back: schools had to be closed; native teachers and assistants lost their jobs. Winter fuel, extremely expensive in a

land denuded of forests and over-grazed by goats, was rationed
to only one room per household. Grant was forced to neglect
himself in order to save medicines for others. In August 1838
the mission at Urmia passed a resolution and sent it to the Prudential Committee. Since, according to Dr. Riach of Tabriz, the
air in Urmia was so dangerous to Dr. Grant, the missionaries
urged that he should be given a new post in a more suitable
climate. On January 19, 1839, they went further and made a
formal request for a new physician. The timing of this request
is significant. In September the missionaries had made recommendations; now they made demands: only five days before
this formal appeal, the mission had taken a terrible blow.

Even in the context of Grant's turbulent life, the year 1839
seems impossibly crowded. Although Thomas Laurie provides a
faithful chronology, beginning with that awful January, the reader
soon becomes lost in the swirl of events. Grant prays at an open
grave, moves on through a blizzard, then to a blazing desert. He
goes here; he goes there; he climbs mountains and fords rivers: he
finds in that one year more hardship, danger, despair, and exhilaration than most humans experience in a lifetime.

We have talked little about Judith Grant, but if justice prevailed in this world she would have had a biographer of her own
and an old age crammed with grandchildren, love, and honors.
Her contemporaries describe her as the embodiment of grace and
loveliness, and it is fair to say that the people of Urmia had never
seen anything like her. Since her arrival she had toiled like some
superhuman being. She bore a son in the summer of 1836 and
twin daughters in 1838. She taught school, she learned Persian,
Turkish, and ancient and modern Syriac, she nursed the sick, she
made a home. When the Syriac scriptures differed from the King
James Bible, it was Judith who could turn to her copy of the
ancient Greek Testament to resolve the disparity. She was the
pioneer of female education in Persia, a woman who not only
taught her own domestics how to read but persuaded the local

Nestorians to allow their daughters to come to school. Like her husband, she bore cheerfully her many illnesses and showed with tortuous logic that these plagues were really God's blessings. By December 1838 an infection had left her blind in one eye, but in a letter to relatives in America she thanked the Lord for allowing her to retain sight in the other. These years in Persia, she told friends, had been the happiest of her life. She felt "unworthy" to have been given an opportunity to suffer for her Savior.

Unworthy or not, this remarkable woman was soon to suffer further. On January 3, 1839, Judith came down with a violent fever—probably malaria. She was already weak from previous illnesses, and from the very first, says Laurie, she did not expect to recover. Within days she became delirious. The Nestorians, who had come to love her, gathered from the surrounding villages and set up a vigil. One of the mission's resident Muslim helpers, a young Persian scribe, could not sleep and "wept like a child" at the thought of her death. On January 14, Judith Campbell Grant died. She was twenty-five years old.

Now, in the winter of 1839, Asahel Grant faced a future as blank as the mud walls of the town. He was thirty-one. His health had not improved: in fact, after Judith's death he sank much lower. Twice widowed, he had five motherless children to care for: two in New York and three in Urmia. His ambitions for missionary work in Hakkari were going nowhere. One thing was certain: his own death would benefit no one; and so, leaving his children to the care of missionary families in Urmia, Grant once again set off to see Dr. Riach in an attempt to regain his health. So it was in Tabriz, in February 1839, that he received the message which propelled him into the great effort of his life.

Dr. Grant had always expected to enter Hakkari directly from Persia, as Schultz had done in 1829. The Prudential Committee, it turned out, preferred an approach from the western side of the mountains, where they could also establish a new outpost in Mesopotamia. They sent instructions to the mission in Constantinople, to the Reverend Henry Augustus Homes, a Board missionary, who forwarded their orders to Grant. Homes and Grant, the letter told him, were to meet in Erzurum, the great caravan city inland from Trebizond. From there they would travel south to Mosul, where they would set up a station from which missions could be launched to the Nestorians of Kurdistan. When the station was ready, Grant could bring his family there.

With these orders the Prudential Committee, although ignorant of his recent tragedy, solved Grant's dilemma. He no longer had to peer through a haze of grief: the future had been decided for him. On April 1, 1839, only two and a half months after Judith's death, Asahel Grant set out for Erzurum.

He had ridden no farther than Salmas, at the north end of Lake Urmia, when he encountered another messenger from Constantinople. The previous letter had crossed paths with the sad news about Judith Grant; consequently in this new letter, the mission at Constantinople, assuming that grief would prevent Grant from coming, rescinded the previous order. Grant returned to Urmia to confer with his colleagues. He argued that this was a sign from Providence, making possible his original plan to enter Hakkari from Persia. The other missionaries, however, did not agree. The advice of the majority, which he had to obey, was to heed the first message and start at once for Constantinople.

We must pause to consider the conditions facing him. "Travel," says a Turkish proverb, "is a foretaste of hell," and no one could have known this better than the doctor. In the mountainous tangle of Anatolia, the wheel was useless for a journey of any length. Dynamite, so essential for road-building in rough terrain, had not yet been invented. In 1840, the cast-iron printing press for the Urmia mission had to be specially manufactured in smaller pieces, so that it could be crated and strapped to horses. A Steinway piano for the American girls' school in Bitlis, near Lake Van, was transported 400 miles from the Black Sea on the backs of forty men working in relays. Hotels did not exist. Travelers had to ride in the open and sleep on hard ground. If they found shelter in the winter it was often in an underground dwelling, thick with tobacco smoke and fleas, heated to suffocation by the belching and breathing of the owners' livestock. When we say, "Grant went here," or "he returned there," these are the realities of his life.

Once again, Grant left Urmia for the north. Over the border and past Mt. Ararat, the nightmare pass of Dahar blocked his journey to Erzurum. Here, where he had first fallen sick in October 1835, three travelers had perished shortly before his arrival. In February of 1835, the Scottish traveler and artist James Baillie Fraser had almost died at the same spot.

Rain, falling hard when Grant and his guide started up the mountain, soon turned to snow. The wind became a gale; Grant's guide lost his way; the horses could not move in the drifts. The party were in desperate straits when four villagers appeared out of the storm and agreed to guide them on, using long poles to find solid ground beneath the snow. This narrow escape was immediately followed by another. The next day, after the descent from Dahar, Grant's horse was swept from under him by a mountain torrent, one of the tributaries of the river Araxes, and both rider and mount came close to drowning. He rode for miles, says Grant, with his boots full of ice water. At last, on April 17, he reached Erzurum, where his friend Dr. Riach of Tabriz was temporarily in residence.

Here we might expect the doctor to pause and recuperate, but there was, it turned out, no need. Through all these perils and exertions, his health had actually improved. He was not vomiting nearly as often, and fever affected him only "two or three" days on the march. After only one night in Erzurum, Grant immediately pressed on through the mountains to Trebizond, and there on April 25 he boarded a steamer, part of the newly established service to Constantinople.

The Last Dreams of Mahmud

"The climate in Tiflis, they tell you, is unhealthy. The local fevers are awful; they are treated with mercury, which can be administered without harm because of the heat. The doctors feed it to their patients without any qualms."
—Alexander Pushkin, *A Journey to Arzrum* (1829)

IN THE CAPITAL, GRANT'S blooming health was reflected inversely by that of Sultan Mahmud II, who was weighed down with illnesses. By 1839 the sultan had sat on the Ottoman throne for thirty-one years. His mother was a French girl named Aimée Dubucq de Rivery, a blonde beauty of Norman descent who had been captured at age twenty-one by Algerian pirates and given to Mahmud's father, Sultan Abdulhamid I, as a gift for his harem. Legend said that Mahmud had begun his reign hiding on the rooftops of the Topkapi Palace while in the apartments below, his cousin, the deposed sultan Selim III, was being slaughtered by men who were hunting for Mahmud as well. Having narrowly escaped, Mahmud, with the help of his mother, spent the first decades of his rule building alliances within the court. He wanted to be a reformer like Mohammed Ali in Egypt, and, above all, to model himself on Napoleon Bonaparte—the military genius, the law-giver and rationalist, the great centralizer who knew what subjects French schoolchildren were studying simply by consulting his clock for the time of day. Mohammed Ali had imported French officers, Napoleonic veterans, to train and equip his armies; Mahmud hired Prussians. The Egyptian ruler had eliminated his opposition, the Mamelukes, a caste of Circassian-Turkish warriors, by inviting them to dinner at the citadel of Cairo and slaughtering them to a man. Mahmud's biggest threat, the Janissaries, received roughly the same treatment.

These Janissaries, once the elite of the Ottoman army, had degenerated into a crew who robbed the citizenry and unseated sultans at their whim. Since they controlled the fire brigades in Stamboul, a city packed with wooden houses, one of their most lucrative endeavors involved setting fires and then charging extra to put them out. In 1826, after decades of waiting, Mahmud made his move. Ottoman troops infiltrated the capital; artillery was brought in by night. Eventually the Janissaries, locked in their barracks and surrounded, were simply blasted to bits by cannon fire. This annihilation, which occurred on June 15, 1826, and became known thereafter as the "Beneficent Event," was Mahmoud II's greatest victory.

In virtually everything else, the sultan either failed or met with limited success. His desire to "reform" the Empire certainly did not involve any form of democracy; Mahmud wanted to create a centralized despotism, with a strong standing army supported by taxes. This, in the face of reaction and state bankruptcy, he could only begin to do.

The Ottoman armies, undisciplined, ill-equipped, and poorly paid, were, as one English observer noted, "a mob assembled" rather than a real military force. From 1806 to 1812 the Turks fought a war against the Russians and lost. Then in March 1821 the Greeks in the Peloponnese rebelled. As a rallying cry, one of the leaders, a Greek Orthodox archbishop, proclaimed "Peace to the Christians! Respect to the Consuls! Death to the Turks!" This was not an empty threat. At the beginning of March, 1821, some

25,000 Muslims lived and farmed in the Peloponnese; by Easter of that year there were none. When, after lengthy sieges, the Turks at Monemvasia, Navarino, and Tripolitsa surrendered, the residents were promised safe passage by the Greeks. In each case, despite the promises, all the surrendering Muslims were slaughtered, including the women and children. In Tripolitsa, a major town of the Peloponnese, the carnage was especially awful. Later in the summer of 1821, the same fate was visited upon the Turks who had taken refuge inside the Acropolis of Athens.

In the classic tradition, the Ottomans responded with horrors of their own. In Constantinople, Gregorius V, the Greek Orthodox patriarch, was seized in the middle of solemn pre-Easter services, taken outside and summarily hanged. After dangling five days at the end of a rope, his body was mutilated, dragged through the streets, and thrown into the Bosphorus. This state-sanctioned murder, done in retaliation for the role of Orthodox priests in the Greek rebellion, forever poisoned relations between the Ottomans and the twenty-five percent of their subjects who were Greek Orthodox. The more famous Turkish massacres soon followed, first in Chios (immortalized by Delacroix) and then in the nearby island of Psara. "For a long time afterwards," wrote David Howarth, "the slave markets of the empire, from Algiers to the Caspian Sea, were glutted with the merchandise of Chios."

The Greek war led to further disasters for Mahmud II. In 1825, after repeated frustration at the hands of the rebels, he was forced to call on Egypt for help. Led by Mohammed Ali's son, Ibrahim Pasha, Egyptian troops sailed to Greece to assist the Ottomans. Once again the sultan's armies began to win against the Greeks, a fact which eventually led the European powers to intervene. When the Egyptian and Ottoman fleets were destroyed at Navarino in 1827, ending the war, Mohammed Ali demanded compensation. He had helped the sultan and received nothing in return but the destruction of his ships. Now he wanted control of Palestine and Syria. When Mahmud II refused, Ibrahim Pasha's armies sailed up the coast in 1831 and took the provinces anyway. After another Egyptian victory at Konya in 1832, Constantinople was saved only by the intervention of the Russians, who coveted the city for themselves. By 1839, after spending seven years building his regular army, Mahmud at last felt ready to move south into Syria.

All this Grant must have known as he traveled on the steamer from Trebizond to Constantinople. Thomas Laurie does not give this background, possibly because he thought that his readers, educated New Englanders, would remember the decade's upheavals and put them into context, or because he had no interest in such political turmoil. Grant himself, in the travel memoir which forms the first half of his book *The Nestorians*, is even more sparing with details. This, even though the Ottoman Empire in 1839 faced one of the greatest crises of the 19th century, one which even contemporaries recognized as a turning point.

In the capital, after dutifully traveling all the way from Persia, Asahel Grant found frustration anew. Rev. Homes, he was told, could not travel with him to Mesopotamia. The mission authorities ordered the doctor to return to the east and wait for Homes in the southeastern city of Diyarbakir. There were, says Thomas Laurie, "persecutions" underway in Constantinople: Homes could not be spared. Thomas Laurie does not identify these persecutions; he leaves the reader to assume that, for some unnamed reason, the Christians of Istanbul were being persecuted by the Muslims. In fact, the American Protestants and their evangelical Armenian converts were being violently opposed by the Armenian patriarch of Constantinople and his fellow clerics, who did not want to see their place in the Ottoman system threatened by foreign interlopers. In the Armenian quarters of Stamboul, people who associated with the Americans were being denounced, beaten, and shunned. Faced with this turmoil, Grant set out, once again alone, for Mesopotamia, aboard the Black Sea steamer.

"From Trebizond," writes Grant, "I rode in less than three days to Erzeroom, a distance by the winter route of at least 220 miles, and over a very mountainous road." From Erzurum he struck south for the city of Diyarbakir. Of this epic ride, from the Black Sea to the edge of the Syrian plain, Grant says little; yet simply by making this journey across the breadth of Asia Minor, he has to be counted a traveler of the first rank. His route threaded a maze of peaks and valleys, for indeed little else lies between the Black Sea and the Syrian desert. In several places, he notes, avalanches had bridged the mountain torrents with snow and ice, allowing him to cross. When a bridge over the Euphrates at Palu was carried away by flooding, he crossed the river on a *kelek,* a raft supported by inflated goatskins. Beyond these facts, he says nothing. His journal, left in Mosul for safe-keeping when he departed for Kurdistan, has been lost.

On May 30, 1839, Dr. Grant arrived in the city of Diyarbakir, the northernmost navigable spot on the Tigris, where he settled in to wait until Homes could be released from Constantinople. Called Amida by the Romans, who built its massive basalt walls, and taken by the Turks in 1515, Diyarbakir has long been the great fortress city of the southeast. Now it is predominantly Kurdish, a focal point for Turkey's endless problems with that minority; but in 1839 its streets contained a multi-ethnic stew of Arabs, Jews, Armenians, Syrian Christians, Kurds, Yezidis, and Turks. Then it was called Kara Amid: "Black Amid," after the great basalt walls that enclosed the city, walls whose forbidding aspect contributed to its grim reputation. "Black the walls," the saying ran, "and black the dogs, and black the hearts of Black Amid." Then, as now, Diyarbakir was considered the gateway to the East. "After Diyarbakir," a bus driver told me in 1973, "it's all Kurd."

Grant found the city in a fever of anticipation. One hundred fifty miles to the southwest, by the banks of the Euphrates, the governor of Diyarbakir, Hafiz Pasha, had assembled an army of 34,000 men, both regular troops and Kurdish tribal irregulars. In the weeks since Mahmud II ordered Hafiz to move south into Syria, it had become obvious that the main battle would be fought near the town of Nizib, where the army of Ibrahim Pasha had advanced to meet him. All of Diyarbakir—indeed, all of Turkey—awaited the results of this combat.

At Nizib, on the west bank of the river, an odd group attended the Ottoman general. Hafiz Pasha's chief military adviser, Baron Helmuth von Moltke, was serving on loan from the Prussian Army. At that time a 38-year-old captain, Moltke later became chief of the Prussian General Staff and achieved fame for his victory at Sedan in the Franco-Prussian War of 1870. With Moltke came another Prussian officer, an engineer named Heinrich von Mühlbach, who brought with him a draughtsman, or field-artist, with the decidedly un-Teutonic name of Corporal O'Flaherty. (Before the advent of photography, European armies made regular use of artists to sketch the fields of battle. In military academies, officer candidates were required to take art courses for that purpose.) In addition to these advisers, Hafiz Pasha employed others whose knowledge extended in quite a different direction. These were the mullahs and soothsayers, steeped in astrology, prophecy, and Islamic lore, whom the pasha loved to consult. Hafiz Pasha, by birth a Circassian, had earned a reputation for energy and courage; yet here, obviously, we are dealing with a deeply divided mind.

Lastly, we see two truly strange observers: an Englishman and a Chaldean Catholic. At that time there was scarcely a corner of the world where an Englishman could not be expected to show up, and the Battle of Nizib was no exception. William Francis Ainsworth, a surgeon and geologist, was traveling in the east under the joint sponsorship of the Royal Geographic Society and the Society for Promoting Christian Knowledge. The geographers wanted to know about mountains, rivers, and resources; the Christians wanted to find places where they could send missionaries. Ainsworth was well-connected. His cousin William Harrison Ainsworth, the author of the novel *Rookwood,* was as famous as any writer in England (with the exception of his friend Charles Dickens). At Edinburgh University, while studying medicine, W.F. Ainsworth befriended the young Charles Darwin, who in his *Autobiography* referred to him as a man who "knew a little about many subjects." He had first come to the Near East in 1836, when he served with the Euphrates Expedition, an attempt by the British government to shorten the route to India by introducing steamboats into the Tigris and Euphrates. Now Ainsworth had come to Nizib at the express invitation of Hafiz Pasha, whom he had met previously in his travels, and who desired that the Englishman should see his new European-trained troops in action.

Traveling with Ainsworth was Christian Rassam, a Chaldean from Mosul. The two had met during the Euphrates Expedition and had traveled together after that endeavor failed. Rassam, though nominally, like all Chaldeans, subject to the pope, had become a zealous adherent of High Church Anglicanism since a visit to Oxford the year before. Rassam's life now revolved around the English. In 1835, while living in Malta, he had married an Englishwoman, Matilda Badger, whose brother, the Anglican missionary George Percy Badger, would play a major role in the last year of Dr. Grant's life. In 1840 Rassam became British Vice-Consul in Mosul.

On June 21, 1839, Ainsworth and Rassam arrived at the camp of Hafiz Pasha. As they settled into their guest quarters, a lavish tent complete with carpets, cushions, and silks, the battle seemed imminent. Ten miles behind them lay the Euphrates River; immediately in front waited the Egyptian army commanded by Ibrahim Pasha and his French chief of staff, O.J.A. Sève. The Ottoman army outnumbered the Egyptians, but Ibrahim Pasha's troops were better trained and equipped; above all, they were better led. Helmuth von Moltke, eventually recognized as one of the great commanders of the century, advised Hafiz Pasha to dig in and wait for the enemy in secure trenches. The pasha's mullahs and Koranic experts contradicted this. They told Hafiz that since the Egyptian Ibrahim was a rebel, Islamic tradition demanded that he be confronted and destroyed on open ground. Hafiz Pasha chose to follow the mullahs' advice.

That night, the Egyptians began a slow flanking movement toward undefended ground at the rear of the Ottoman army. By the morning of June 22, Moltke could see what was happening. He urged Hafiz Pasha to attack immediately and hit the Egyptians while they were on the move, or fall back to a stronger defensive position near the Euphrates. Hafiz dithered, consulted the mullahs, then dithered further. Oneiromancy—divination through dreams—seems to have been another hobby of Hafiz Pasha, and these, in addition to the Koran and the Hadith, he discussed with the soothsayers. On the afternoon of the 22nd, Moltke and his staff, using Rassam as an interpreter, confronted Hafiz and demanded that he pull back or risk losing his entire army. After more dithering, during which Hafiz seemed for a while to be leaning toward the Prussians, the pasha finally was persuaded by the mullahs to stay at Nizib and fight.

The next morning, Hafiz Pasha was cheered by the arrival of a large contingent of Kurdish horsemen led by Bedr Khan Bey, the emir of Bohtan, a territory just west of Hakkari. The Ottomans, who had outnumbered the enemy before, now enjoyed an even greater numerical advantage. Bedr Khan, by far the most powerful and ambitious Kurdish leader in the east (and considerably superior to Nurullah of Hakkari), would also play a large part in the life of Asahel Grant. Their spirits lifted by the new arrivals, the Ottoman troops made ready. Ainsworth and Rassam, carrying expensive scientific and surveying instruments paid for by the Royal Geographical Society, packed their bags. Helmuth von Moltke and his Prussians, by now sick at heart, did their best to prepare for battle.

In Diyarbakir, Dr. Grant waited. He had been in the city for twenty-five days; Rev. Homes had still not shown up, and the weather was getting hotter. No one knew anything about Nizib:

without telegraph, decent roads, or anything resembling modern communications, the 150 miles that separated them may as well have been a thousand. In Constantinople Mahmud II, racked by tuberculosis, was sinking fast. When the news came, it came in battalions: thousands of Ottoman soldiers, chiefly Kurdish draftees, were fleeing for their lives, stripped of their uniforms and equipment by Kurdish tribesmen-turned-robbers, who had taken over the roads. The chaos outside the Diyarbakir city walls soon spread within. The mob, says Grant, blamed Europeans and foreigners, since the sultan's conscripted, European-trained army had proved such a failure. By the end of June, Diyarbakir was falling into anarchy.

At Nizib, the catastrophe could not have been more complete. The battle, on June 24, 1839, was over in two hours. The Prussians' final attempts to deploy some kind of rational strategy proved a failure. The Kurdish irregulars, undisciplined, untrained, and unable to stand up to concentrated artillery fire, simply broke and ran, then lingered in the aftermath to rob their fellow soldiers. In the ensuing chaos, Moltke and his staff were lucky to escape alive. Ainsworth and Rassam became separated; their pack animals, laden with stores and precious scientific equipment, were lost. After a harrowing retreat, during which they were constantly threatened by Kurdish bandits, they managed to escape to Malatya. The Egyptians took some 10,000 prisoners (as well as, no doubt, some very fine English surveying instruments). The disgraced Hafiz Pasha lived to dither another day. Bedr Khan Bey, after witnessing the total collapse of Ottoman authority, returned to his domains with dreams of autonomy and expansion dancing in his head. In the palace of Topkapi, Mahmud II was spared at least one final indignity. He died six days after the Battle of Nizib, just hours before news of the disaster could reach him.

With mixed fear and scorn, Asahel Grant now watched as Diyarbakir erupted. All residents, and especially Europeans, became the target of looters, thieves, and murderers. "Scarcely a man dared leave the walls of the city," Grant writes, "without a large party to accompany him. Each man robbed the man he met, and the arm of the strongest was the only law." The authorities, employing the usual methods to discourage lawbreakers, decorated the bazaar with the heads of five Kurds and the ears of forty more.

It was the beginning of a very bad summer.

5

MOSUL AND MESOPOTAMIA

"The western love of travel for travel's sake is a perpetual enigma to the eastern peasant . . . A man who confesses to travelling without a definite aim, or in search of knowledge, is either a madman or a very clever person disguised as a madman."
—F.W. Hasluck, *Christianity and Islam Under the Sultans*

ON JULY 3, IN THE MIDST of this turmoil, Henry Augustus Homes arrived from Constantinople. His journey, like Grant's, had been arduous in the extreme, involving multiple threats from disease, bandits, and river crossings. For Asahel Grant, alone and restless as he was, the arrival must have been a welcome relief. On July 10, released from his purgatory, Grant set out with Homes for the city of Mardin, some sixty miles to the southeast, accompanied by thirty armed horsemen. They had two goals: to get away from the heat of the Tigris valley (Mardin is some 1300' higher than Diyarbakir), and to extend their survey of the Christians—and especially old-church Nestorians, if they existed—living in the area. In Mardin, however, the situation was, if anything, worse than in Diyarbakir. Here, too, the disaster at Nizib had brought anarchy in its wake. Within days of their arrival, says Grant, they were threatened openly with death by Muslims of the town. The Turkish governor confessed that he had lost control of the situation, and offered to post a guard outside the missionaries' house. Grant and Homes, deciding that the guard would be more a provocation than a help, declined the offer, but kept to themselves as much as possible.

Mardin is a beautiful place, an Arabesque marvel of cobbled streets and limestone perched on a rocky escarpment above the plains of Syria. No one who has been there can forget it, especially the view from the citadel looking south across 2000 miles of emptiness toward the tip of Arabia. It is a testament to the troubles afflicting Grant that he mentions nothing of this view during the two months that he spent there. Frustrated in his attempts to reach the mountains of Kurdistan, he surely wanted to be elsewhere. For the first few weeks, there was no question of leaving: it was dangerous even to step outside their house. Gradually that threat seemed to fade, and soon, says Grant, they had gained the confidence of the governor as well as the religious officials of the town. But violence continued to rule the roads, and, since it was now obvious that no Nestorians independent of Rome existed west of the mountains, the two missionaries considered retreating toward Aleppo.

Then an old enemy came calling. Dr. Grant, as we have seen, had enjoyed relatively good health since leaving Urmia, but now, says Thomas Laurie, a severe "inflammation of the bowels" struck him down. Although we can never be quite sure of the labels placed upon illnesses at that time, it seems likely that Grant was afflicted with acute dysentery: once again, a disease borne by bad water. Whatever its true name, the disease itself was horrible. Neither Grant nor Laurie gives an estimate of the time involved, but it seems to have occupied the greater part of August. Dr. Grant, in unrelieved misery—and threatened, no doubt, by dehydration—came very close to death. Only by the beginning of September had he started to regain his strength.

On September 6, 1839, Grant had recovered enough to join Homes on a horseback ride outside the city. No ride, it turned out, ever did more for a man's health, for it was on that day that the Kurds of Mardin rose in revolt and took over the town. The Turkish governor, the man who had offered protection to the missionaries, was murdered in the courtyard of his residence. Other high officials, too, were slain. The mob then moved on to the house where Grant and Homes were staying, intending to kill the infidels as well. To prevent a relief force from arriving, the rebels had locked the city gates. Returning from their ride, the two Americans were barred from entry, and when they heard the rioting within they retreated at once to Deir Zaferan, the "Saffron" monastery of the Syrian Orthodox Church, several miles outside of Mardin. There, sheltered by the Syrian patriarch and his monks, they waited for the trouble to subside.

Some days later—Grant does not say how many—troops of Mohammed Pasha, the governor of Mosul province, arrived. The pasha, also known as *Injé Bairaktar,* or the Little Ensign, was generally acknowledged to be a man of boundless greed, the greatest cruelty, and a seemingly limitless lust for power. He would later play a large part in our story. Once they reached Mardin, the pasha's troops immediately set to work harvesting heads, severing ears, and generally putting the place in order. Dr. Grant, disguised as a native in a turban and robes, had ridden into town and was moving unmolested through the streets when he heard a cannon announce to the people that, like it or not, the rebellion was over.

It is difficult to count the times that Asahel Grant cheated death, whether from disease, drowning, or storm; yet surely this has to rank among the most frightening. To see death all around; to have been targeted directly for murder and to have escaped through the merest accident of fate: these were not easy experiences to assimilate, even for the most religious of men. Rev. Henry Augustus Homes, a mild and unassuming scholar from a wealthy New England family, seems to have had enough. No doubt he longed to get back to his Istanbul printing press and the writing of religious tracts, work that he had been doing before the whims of the Prudential Committee sent him off to the wild southeast. The two missionaries had found no Nestorians of the independent church; according to their inquiries, there were none to be found west of the mountains. "In view of these considerations," Grant writes, "which left so little hope of doing good, while so much peril was involved, my associate resolved to leave this field, and return to his station at Constantinople." He remarks that "with a full view of the trials which might lie before me in my solitary journey onward, I yielded a cordial and cheerful acquiescence."

If there is a hint of resentment in this remark, surely Grant cannot be blamed for it. What, after all, had been his original goal? The mountain Nestorians that he sought were far more easily contacted from Urmia, where his children and fellow missionaries remained. All he had desired from the Prudential Committee was permission to enter the Kurdish mountains, which lay mere hours from Urmia, and contact the independent Nestorian tribes who lived in Hakkari. He had even gone so far as to obtain an edict from the Persian Governor-General of Azerbaijan, in Tabriz, granting him permission and instructing the governor of Salmas to appoint escorts to guarantee his safety. Instead, on the instructions of the Committee, he had been drawn into a journey of over a thousand miles through some of the roughest terrain on earth. He had almost frozen in the snows of Dahar and drowned in the Araxes, escaped murder in Diyarbakir and Mardin, and all but succumbed to dysentery. And for what? So that the companion assigned to him by the Prudential Committee could now leave and slip back to the capital in disguise.

In the ruins of a church the two men embraced and said their good-byes, ending a brief, futile association in which they had traveled only one day and covered sixty miles together. Grant takes pains to emphasize the gratitude he feels to Homes, yet "while the voice of Providence called [Homes] to return to his station in the metropolis of Turkey, to me it seemed to cry, Onward." Thomas Laurie notes, "Dr. Grant may be deemed an enthusiast." But anyone who has felt the fascination of high mountains will recognize the force that drove him on, as will those who remember the bare landscape of Central Asia, its high peaks patched with snow, its ruined cities looking out at nothingness, its villages in the river valleys cloaked with green. To go back was nearly as dangerous as pressing on, and the doctor had not come all this distance merely to abandon his dream. During one of Grant's visits to Erzurum, a British colonel remarked of him, "The army lost a good soldier when that man became a missionary."

The reassertion of Turkish power over the town of Mardin secured the caravan routes to Mosul, freeing Grant at last to ride south into the heart of Mesopotamia, and with an interesting companion. "On this part of my route," he notes, "I was favoured with the agreeable society and kind attentions of Captain Conolly, an intelligent English officer, who had, through many dangers, reached Mardin, on his way to India with despatches." It is hard to see how the doctor could have met up with a companion more compatible to his nature. While Grant was a missionary with the best qualities of a soldier, Arthur Conolly was the bravest of soldiers guided by missionary ideals. Both were devout Christians; both detested slavery; both believed in the civilizing mission of European culture. Although the two men were together only three or four days, Grant was impressed enough by Conolly to take note of a man he would never see again.

In the previous decade, traveling in disguise as a secret agent in Central Asia, Conolly had already experienced danger in some of the remotest places on earth. In India he had fallen in love with the daughter of an aristocrat and had followed her to England in the hopes of arranging a marriage. It was, however, as a disappointed man that he now returned to India with the despatches Grant refers to. Later this gallant, idealistic officer wrote to a friend that, in his missions into Central Asia, he felt as as if he were taking part in a "great game." With these two words Conolly supplied the label for an era, the century-long struggle between Russian and Britain for the domination of inner Asia. Now remembered as the quintessential player of The Great Game, and especially for his tragic end (with Col. William Stoddart) in Bokhara, Arthur Conolly in September 1839 had less than three years to live.

Grant and Conolly encountered danger only once on their journey south, and this incident, a brush with Kurdish bandits, they dealt with quickly by riding to a nearby knoll and making a show of force with the rest of their small caravan. On September 20 the two men entered Mosul, on the west bank of the river Tigris, the largest city in northern Mesopotamia. As in Mardin and Diyarbakir, its population contained the usual mixture of Ottoman nationalities: Kurds, Armenians, Syrian Jacobites, Turks, Arabs, Jews, and Chaldeans. Its principal language, however, was Arabic. Grant says little about the town— he has, after all, loftier goals in mind—but in the travel literature of the time it is difficult to find anyone with a good word for the place. Sir Mark Sykes, English traveler and diplomat, requires two full pages in his 1915 book *The Caliphs' Last Heritage,* to express his detestation.

"Mosul," he begins, "I found the same foul nest of corruption, vice, disorder, and disease as I have always known it"— and from there the assessment gets worse. In summer Mosul is hellishly hot: on that all are in agreement. Many houses contained a *serdab,* a subterranean room, for refuge from the heat. The city stank of tanneries that, since they were located upstream from it, also polluted its water. Numerous kilns, used for burning marble into lime, blanketed the town in whitish dust. The buildings, fashioned of a soft local marble, were crumbling. Muslin, the cotton cloth named after the city, was nowhere in evidence. Not a tree could be seen. The people were rebellious and violent. "There is not a respectable man here," wrote Austen Henry Layard to his mother in 1845, "whose

father was not murdered." The governor, Mohammed Pasha—
the Little Ensign—was a thug. The streets were filthy; rats and
vermin infested the *serdabs;* centipedes and black scorpions were
in every household. Residents were likely to be afflicted with
the "button," a painless boil transmitted by flies, which lasted
about a year and left permanent scars. In general, witnesses
testified, those visitors who did not succumb to the heat would
be gnawed by rats, fall victim to disease, or suffocate in heaps
of offal. The Rev. W.A. Wigram, an Anglican missionary, observed in 1914 in his book *The Cradle of Mankind*, "There are
more pleasant places in the world than the city of Mosul."

However, Mosul was unavoidable for 19th-century travelers to Kurdistan. It was important for trade, populous (30,000
souls), and close to the mountains. Both French and British consuls were stationed there, an obvious indication of its commercial status. Much of its considerable trade lay in the hands of
Christian minorities—Syrians, Armenians, or Chaldean Catholics. In addition to camel caravans, the city benefited from river
traffic. Mosul sits on the west bank of the Tigris, a river now
almost choked with hydroelectric dams, but then navigable from
Diyarbakir south to the Persian Gulf by *keleks,* rafts constructed
of fresh-cut poplar logs lashed to inflated goat skins. These rafts
were made and operated by the *kelekjis,* a caste of men who
specialized in the trade. The largest raft, says Thomas Laurie,
used some 300 skins, the smallest thirty-two. Before railroads
and motor trucks, these rafts delivered grain, hides, wool, gallnuts, dried fruits and nuts. Each raft was made to order and
used only once. At Baghdad or Basra, the rafts were dismantled
and the timber sold, and the deflated goatskins, heaped on the
backs of camels, transported north to be used again.

Eight years after Grant's visit, Austen Henry Layard, the
pioneer Assyrian archaeologist, used massive specimens of these
same rafts to transport his finds—including the giant twenty-
ton limestone bulls now at the British Museum—to Basra, at

the head of the Persian Gulf. In *Nineveh and its Remains* (1849), Layard describes their construction.

> The skins of full-grown sheep and goats are used. They are taken off with as few incisions as possible, and then dried and prepared. The air is forced in by the lungs through an aperture which is afterwards tied up with string. A square framework, formed of poplar beams, branches of trees, and reeds, having been constructed of the size of the intended raft, the inflated skins are tied to it by osier and other twigs, the whole being firmly bound together . . . Care is taken to place the skins with their mouths upwards, that, in case any should burst or require filling, they can be easily opened by the raftmen. Upon the framework of wood are piled bales of goods, and property belonging to merchants and travellers. When any person of rank, or wealth, descends the river in this fashion, small huts are constructed on the raft by covering a common woooden *takht* or bedstead of the country, with a hood formed of reeds and lined with felt. In these huts the travellers live and sleep during the journey . . . The only real danger to be apprehended on the river is from the Arabs; who, when the country is in a disturbed state, invariably attack and pillage the rafts.

Asahel Grant spent seventeen days in Mosul, living next to the Syrian Orthodox Church of Mar Toma (St. Thomas), a place he would visit again. There he made ready for the challenge ahead. He exchanged his pack horses for mules, the better to negotiate mountain paths. He engaged a small party of helpers: two Nestorians from Urmia, a Kurdish muleteer, and a *kawass*, a police officer supplied by Mohammed Pasha of Mosul, the Little Ensign. Since his travel journals were likely to arouse suspicion, they were left behind in the city. He kept his money closely secreted on his person, and for extra security hid several gold coins in a roll of blister salve among his medicines. To lend dignity to his presence he had let his beard grow thick, as befitted a priest or a mullah. Though Grant never pretended to be anything but a foreigner, he was determined to present the smallest possible target for thieves.

In those seventeen days he wrote letters tinged with foreboding. To the Rev. Justin Perkins and his wife Charlotte, whose favorite son, named after his father, had recently died, Grant wrote his condolences. "You and I," he says, "are called to drink often of the cup of affliction. Would that I could have been with you." (Eventually six of the Perkinses' seven children would die in Persia, and Charlotte Perkins would retreat to America suffering from epilepsy.) He ruminates on the danger ahead: "Since I left you, I have more than once feared I should never rejoin your peaceful circle, and even now the prospect looks uncertain." He acknowledges the duty of a missionary to preserve his own life so that he can serve others; but "I also believe that a readiness to face danger, and even death, is implied in the command to take up the cross."

The day before he left Mosul, Dr. Grant wrote to James Lyman Merrick, the missionary who had accompanied the Grants on their journey from America in 1835. Here he talks about his perplexities at both the danger ahead and the difficulty of accomplishing anything useful. "Why then," he asks, "am I still prosecuting further plans and labors in this region, while my path cannot be free from danger, and so many of my brethren have advised me to leave the field?" Grant retains the hope that this great project will prove useful for their missionary endeavors and for the Nestorian Church. Of the political situation in the mountains he says nothing. But then he gives the real reason for the journey, in what might be his epitaph: "I cannot leave the field till I have reasons which I can plead at the judgment-seat, where I expect soon to stand."

Here speaks the 19th-century conscience. Death is imminent, the world is a vale of tears: better to die young on the field battling for good—which his cause embodies—than to live a long life in comfort. This echoes Grant's statement in 1834, when he accepted the call for missionary work ("I cannot, I dare not go up to judgment . . . "). A contemporary, Richard Francis Burton, far up a stinking river in equatorial Africa, wrote "Who knows?" about the "why" of his journeys, "The devil drives." Asahel Grant had no doubts. Like Farragut at Mobile Bay, it was "full speed ahead" for the cause, and his words in their tenacity echo those of another Grant twenty-five years later who wrote, "I purpose to fight it out on this line, if it takes all summer." But unlike that famous general, the life the doctor risked was his own.

6

INTO KURDISTAN

"This hunger for enemies is what gets me down."
—Freya Stark, *Riding to the Tigris*

FOUR BRIDGES NOW SPAN the Tigris at Mosul; in 1839 there was one. This was the bridge of twenty-one boats, shackled together and surfaced with planking, over which Asahel Grant and an army of peasants, pack animals, and wagons passed on Monday morning, October 7.

> The bridge of boats [wrote Grant] was thronged with a motley crowd of Koords, Arabs, Turks, Christians, and Jews, clad in their various and grotesque costumes; and in their confused jargon of dissonant voices, bearing unequivocal testimony to the curse of Babel. Their camels, mules, horses, bullocks, and donkeys were laden with the various produce of the country, with which the markets are crowded at an early hour in the morning, especially at this season of the year, when grain, fruits, melons, and vegetables are cheap and abundant. Some of the loads had fallen upon the bridge, increasing the confusion, which already threatened to precipitate man and beast in the deep and rapid current of the Tigris.

In a telling aside, Grant reports that on leaving the city he was required to produce his passport, a recent innovation in Turkey, utterly unknown in Persia. Here we see the beginnings of the Ottoman reform process: the attempts to exert official control over the distant provinces. The passport checks were especially important for Mohammed Pasha, the Little Ensign, to catch young Muslim men who might be leaving the city to avoid conscription into his army. Christians and Jews were exempt. On the plains of the east bank (now sprawling with suburbs), Grant rode past Koyunjik, the vast mound which covered the ruins of Nineveh, where Austen Henry Layard would be excavating only six years hence. A few miles beyond Nineveh the ground rose to meet the hills, and on the first night the doctor encamped amidst olive groves in Bashiqa, a village of the Yezidis, those mysterious Kurds whose religion, with elements of Zoroastrianism and pagan practices, antedates both Christianity and Islam. With this arrival Grant's journey in Mesopotamia ended, and his trek through Kurdistan began.

It is difficult even to begin to explain that geographical abstraction known as Kurdistan. It is hard enough just to decently define the word. "Kurdistan" does not denote an independent nation, nor does it mean a place with any recognized boundaries. To call it "the land of the Kurds" glosses over the other nationalities that live—or have lived—there, and it ignores the fact that substantial numbers of Kurds live elsewhere, including Armenia and Syria. In general, Kurdistan could be said to encompass those mountainous areas of southeast Turkey, northern Iraq, and northwest Iran where Kurdish-speaking peoples form a substantial majority of the population. Yet here again, "Kurdish-speaking" can mean different things. The Kurds that Dr. Grant encountered spoke Kermanji (or Behdini), the language of most Kurds in Turkey and northern Iraq. Farther south other dialects, such as Sorani and Gorani, predominate. In the northwest, in the Turkish province of Dersim the people speak Zaza, a language unintelligible

to other Kurds. These dialects belong to the Indo-European language group, related to Persian, and the people who speak them
have traditionally been regarded as Kurds. Even this mosaic, however, is splintering, as some Zaza have begun to think of themselves as a separate group entirely, neither Kurd nor Turk.

Then there is religion. Most Kurds are Sunnis, the majority
branch of Islam, though many of the Zaza-speakers of Dersim
are Alevi, a version of Islam closer to Shi'ism but utterly different
from both. Within these divisions exist more groups, including
dervish orders whose members follow the teachings of particular
sheikhs. In Grant's time, the religious mosaic of Kurdistan was
richer than today, not only because of the Christians but because
of Kurdish Jews, all of whom have now emigrated to Israel. The
Jews were scattered widely, in agricultural villages and in towns,
where they worked as merchants and craftsmen. In one startling
passage of *Discoveries in the Ruins of Nineveh and Babylon,*
Austen Henry Layard tells of his encounter with a tribe of Jewish
nomads in the mountains south of Lake Van, probably the last
Jews known to have lived this way since their beginnings in Sinai.
The Jews, like the Nestorians, spoke Syriac, a variation of the
Aramaic spoken by Jesus.

The Yezidis, long slandered as "devil-worshippers"—though
in reality they hold no such belief—were concentrated in Sinjar,
west of Mosul, and in the hills northeast of Mosul near the
shrine of their prophet, Sheikh Adi. Farther south the members
of another heterodox non-Islamic sect, the Kakai (or Ahl-e-
Haqq), clustered along the border with Persia. Of the Christians, four groups—Armenian, Syrian Orthodox (Jacobite),
Chaldean Catholic, and Old Church Nestorian—made up virtually all the population, and all of these were the objects of
missionary activity, whether by French and Italian priests, German Lutherans, Russian Orthodox, Anglicans, American Episcopalians, or other American Protestants.

After noting linguistic and religious divisions, we get down
to the really basic ones, those of tribe and clan. Here the mind

boggles at the complexity of it all—a complexity that matches the terrain. In Hakkari, the heart of Kurdistan, mountain is packed against mountain like vertical cordwood, as if two great invisible hands, one in the north at Lake Van, the other at Mosul, have taken between them a patch of earth and pressed it into a tight, wrinkled heap. In this crack one clan may live; in this fold another tribe, and through this crazing the rivers rush, separating each from the other. Ferzende Kaya, writing in the *Turkish Daily News* of September 23, 2002, analyzed the voting patterns of no fewer than eighty-nine Kurdish tribes in twenty-two provinces of eastern and southeastern Turkey—and this, remember, is only Turkey. "The tribe," she writes, "is an unchangeable fact in Turkey. Their power, especially in the eastern and southeastern regions, is at a level which cannot be underestimated." If that is true now, it was doubly true in 1839. And of course the divisions reach deeper, as the tribes split into branches, the branches into clans, the clans into families. Given four elements: (a) the harshness of mountain life, (b) the tendency of the human race to quarrel, (c) the extreme importance of personal and family honor, and (d) an unsurpassed love of firearms—and a situation exists where the potential for violence was as high as any in the world.

The societal patterns of the Kurds were mirrored by those of the mountain Nestorians. An English-speaking middle-class Christian, one habitually biased toward the underdog, might tend to assume that the Nestorians were somehow "better behaved" than the Kurds. This—at least at first—was the assumption of the missionaries, but it was an assumption with no basis in fact. "Blood for blood" was the code by which the mountain Nestorians lived, a code no different from that of Nurullah Bey or any of his tribesmen. Frederick Coan, an American missionary in Urmia during the last decades of the 19th century, had no sympathy for the Kurds, but in his memoirs (*Yesterdays in Persia and Kurdistan*, 1939) he gives ample evidence of the willingness of both Kurds and Nestorians to engage in robbery,

murder, and subterfuge. His missionary father, Rev. George
Coan, wrote in 1851: "The Nestorians are continually embroiled
in quarrels . . . My very soul was made sick by their endless
strifes." Other travelers were often just as wary of the Christians as they were of the Kurds. (As we shall see, the Muslims of
surrounding areas were petrified at the thought of entering
Christian domains.) Thomas Laurie tells us that Asheetha, the
district where Asahel Grant planned to settle, was notorious
for its plunderers and thieves. The Anglican missionary W.A.
Wigram, relates that one tradition among the mountain
Nestorians involved raiding Jewish villages every year on Good
Friday, in retribution for the death of Our Lord. This tradition
he considers evidence of the mountaineers' boyish energy and
high spirits; he does not tell us the reaction of the Jews.

The Christians of Hakkari even acquired a certain fame in
19th-century America as confidence men. According to Wigram
and Coan, they travelled from church to church in rural areas
of Europe and the United States, making speeches and collecting money to pay ransom for their church's patriarch, who they
claimed was being imprisoned unjustly by the Turks. This claim,
of course, was false. These men would take the money and run—
back to Hakkari, where they lived like kings for a few years
before returning to America to repeat the swindle. The
Nestorians' districts—Jelu, Baz, Tkhoma, Diz, Tal, Ishtazin,
Oramar, to name a few—yielded their own tribal structure, their
own pattern of blood feud and theft. Often one Christian clan
might enlist the help of a Kurdish tribe in a feud, and the Kurds,
on another occasion, might ask for help against their own enemies. All was fluid in this Hobbesian world, where nothing
remained constant but conflict.

On their first night after leaving Mosul, Asahel Grant and
his party spread their carpets on the street of Bashiqa and slept
under the stars. The villagers, unfriendly at first when they
thought he was a Muslim, changed their attitude on learning

that he was a Christian. A slight drizzle fell before daybreak, and Grant woke to hear his horse neighing. Immediately he got up and found that thieves had loosened the animal's halter, but had been frightened off by the neighing. Grant makes little of this incident, but it is worth noting that on his first night in Kurdistan he was confronted by an attempted theft.

The next day Grant crossed a broad plain watered by the Khazir, another stream flowing to the Tigris, and found desolation in what should have been a prosperous agricultural area. Attack, counterattack, and general lawlessness had swept the region for the past six years as armies lived off the land. The Mir of Rowanduz, Blind Mohammed—so called because he had only one eye—had taken advantage of Ottoman weakness in the 1820s and '30s to build a sizeable domain in the mountains east and northeast of Mosul. The Mir, legendary for his cruelty, had begun his reign by killing off all possible rivals for power, then going on to plunder and conquer his neighbors. At the height of his power, Blind Mohammed of Rowanduz fielded as many as 20,000 warriors. Like so many Kurdish lords, he resented the Ottoman government's efforts at "reform," which meant paying taxes for the first time ever and getting nothing in return. Eventually the Mir was subdued, and in 1836 he was persuaded to travel to Constantinople to receive honors, including the governorship of the border regions with Persia. On the return trip, which began with an ocean voyage to Samsun, Blind Mohammed mysteriously died. Some said that he was lost at sea, others that he had been poisoned in Amasya, ancient home of Mithidrates the Great, another despot forever associated with toxic ingestion.

Despite the ravaged villages, Grant could at least report a rich array of vegetation as he penetrated the mountains. By the end of the second day's ride they had reached the town of Aqra, "imbosomed in gardens and fruit orchards":

> For a mile before reaching the town, our path was imbowered
> in arbours of pomegranates, blending their golden and crim-

son hues, contrasted with the rich green olive and the more
luscious but humble fig, and interspersed with the peach, apri-
cot, plum, and cherry; while the unpretending blackberry lined
our avenue, and held out its fruit for me to gather while seated
upon my saddle.

Instead of taking the direct route to the Tiyari country, Grant
had detoured to Aqra, to seek the protection of the local chief, a
Kurd who, after the recent wars, had been installed as a puppet
ruler by the Turks and given nominal authority over the country
up to the borders of the Nestorians' domains. The document the
doctor sought was a *buyurultu*, from the Turkish verb *buyurulmak*,
meaning "to be ordered," and it treated him, as Grant noted, like
a bundle of goods, to be handed safely from one person to another
in his journey north. This the Kurd agreed to without any demur,
telling Grant that he regarded his visit as a gift from God, because
he had been ill for a long time. After taking the man's pulse and
listening to his complaints, Dr. Grant engaged him in a long conversation on "a variety of subjects." But when the Kurd started to
recount his family's many grievances against the Turks, Grant, looking through the open window at the vale of Aqra, began praising
the town's beautiful scenery. Politics, as we shall see, was a topic he
could not afford to broach.

The doctor stayed two nights in Aqra at the Kurd chief's request, and on the second night he was invited to attend the local
Turkish governor, or *mutesellim*, who, having been appointed by
the pasha of Mosul, held the real reins of power. This man was
also sick, but in a different way. He had grown ill from the water,
he told Grant, and in order to counteract its effects had begun
drinking large quantities of brandy. Of course it was only for
medicinal purposes, but the governor had taken so much, Grant
notes, that he was "fast verging on delirium tremens." In order
to calm his nerves the *mutesellim* had summoned a group of
twenty local citizens and a musician who played on a harp with
seventy-two strings, eight of which were broken. Grant found

this serenade "altogether harmonious and agreeable." For the *mutesellim* he prescribed complete abstinence.

On October 10 Grant set out from Aqra on a northwesterly course toward the town of Amadiyah. His mount was now a mule, as he had sold his last horse before leaving Aqra. That night he stayed in a Kurdish village where the residents were locked in a blood feud with a nearby village. The cause of this feud Grant does not say, but in the village he stayed in, three men had been killed, while their neighbors had lost only two. So they were plotting to even the score, which meant killing the first man they came upon from the neighboring village, whoever he was. When this was accomplished, the feud would end.

After two more days of mountain travel, Grant entered Amadiyah, a fortified town atop a rock mesa some 100 miles northeast of Mosul. He was, according to Thomas Laurie, the first European to set foot within its walls. Here by the river Supna, in a valley known for its excellent grapes and wheat, a decade of wars had left the usual devastation. George Fowler, an English traveler in Persia in the 1820s, described the soldiery of the time as "complete destructives, having full licence to help themselves wherever they come; which they do without mercy, having no regular pay." The town's hereditary ruler, Ismael Pasha, had first been driven from power by Blind Mohammed of Rowanduz and then kept out by Mohammed Pasha, the governor of Mosul. Ismael, who had met Dr. Grant in Urmia, was still rallying support among the Kurds and Nestorians for a return to his ancestral home. Out of a thousand houses in the town, Grant estimated that three-quarters lay in ruins. The fortress was garrisoned by Ottoman soldiers, most of whom—Albanian irregulars, according to Layard, who visited seven years later—were laid low with malaria and stomach complaints.

Besides the Kurds and Christians of the town, the doctor noted its population of Jews, all of whom spoke the same Syriac as the Nestorians—a fact he would later emphasize in his book about the Lost Tribes. Amadiyah was, in fact, the home of David

Alroy, the only Kurdish Jew to have entered recorded history. In the year 1147, claiming to be the Messiah, this scholar and magician initiated a revolt against the Seljuk Caliph that gained adherents as far away as Urmia and Tabriz. This Messiah did not last long, as Alroy's head, detached from his body, was presented to the Caliph at the end of that year. Grant spent a quiet Sabbath in Amadiyah and followed it with a hectic Monday, treating a horde of patients from the town and nearby villages. This included dispensing medicine for some fifty Albanian soldiers of the fortress, a favor for which the commander thanked him profusely.

Beyond Amadiyah, the Kurdish mountains, rising in waves, build toward their climax in the domains of the Nestorian *ashirets*. So far Dr. Grant had encountered many Christians, yet all of these people were *rayahs*, subject to Kurdish overlords, and the vast majority, he noted bitterly, had become "Chaldean" and "gone over to the pope." For Grant, described by Thomas Laurie as "an unyielding foe of popery," this was dreadful news. In Amadiyah, for example, he encountered a *qasha*, a Nestorian priest, named Mendo:

> The Nestorian priest lamented the low state to which their Church had been reduced, and said he feared that the people, in their gross ignorance, would fall a sacrifice to the wiles of the papists; who he had been told, were about to make more vigorous efforts than ever to convert the whole of his people to Romanism. He told a sad tale of their past efforts and success, stating that his own father was bastinadoed to compel him to become a Roman Catholic!

Catholic missionaries in Mosul, most of whom were French, had assured Grant that they would not rest until all the Nestorians had turned Catholic, a prospect that this Oneida County Presbyterian was determined to thwart. Here, we get a

glimpse of other forces, apart from the doctor's innate kindness, restless ambition, and plain human curiosity, that were
driving him. Grant writes:

> There must be a final struggle with "the man of sin," and it
> must be boldly and promptly met. With God and truth on our
> side, we have nothing to fear, if the Church will come up to
> her duty. The Nestorians have nobly stood their ground, and
> they are still upon the watch-tower . . . Hitherto they have
> prevented the emissaries of Rome from entering upon their
> mountains. But the latter are looking with eagerness to this
> interesting field; and, while they are extending their labours
> in the East, no effort will be spared to spread their influence
> among the mountain tribes. Will Protestant Christians, to
> whom the Nestorians are stretching out their hands for help,
> suffer the golden harvest to fall into the garner of the pope?

Grant is exhorting Protestants to support the American
Board (himself) in its (his) crusade: he does not aim to convert
the Nestorians to Protestantism; he wants to help them resist
the blandishments of the Catholics. Here is the Puritan abhorrence of "popery" at its most strident: the late-Byzantine cry of
"Better the turban than the tiara" in 19th-century evangelical
dress. "God and truth" are on his side. The pontiff is equated
with the Devil, the mountains with a battleground of creeds.
When he speaks of "the Church," Grant means the God-fearing folk of New England, not the "false edifice" of "the man of
sin." The Nestorians, he says, are "stretching out their hands
for help."

Unfortunately for him, this was not true. In 1839 and the
decades after, the Nestorians of Hakkari, newly discovered by
Europeans and as "trendy" as an ancient religion could get,
were not really "reaching" for any particular church. On the
contrary, many hands were thrust in their direction, and they
did not know whose—if anyone's—to grasp. The Kurds

Nurullah, Ismael Pasha, and Bedr Khan, as we shall see, wanted the mountaineers' aid (or acquiescence) in maintaining the region's independence from the Turks. Russian influence in Persia was growing every year, and their Orthodox missionaries, already active among the Armenians, saw the Nestorians as natural allies. The Catholics had long courted them, and within a year the Anglicans would arrive. Now came the Americans.

There were, in fact, practical reasons why the mountain Nestorians might have gone over to Rome. For one thing, the French Lazarist missionaries offered them union with a larger, stronger church. And there was the implied (ultimately useless) protection of France, which, after becoming, in the 17th century, the first nation to establish trading relations with the Ottomans had arrogated to itself a special protectorate over the Empire's Catholic population. But for Grant, this was a journey that had to be made, a battle that had to be won by him, and not by any Catholic.

Manna and Its Heaven

"This is a great moment, when you see, however distant, the goal of your wandering. The thing which has been living in your imagination suddenly becomes a part of the tangible world. It matters not how many ranges, rivers or parching dusty ways may lie between you; it is yours now forever."
—Freya Stark, *The Valleys of the Assassins*

SYRIAC VOICES, DEEP AND guttural, booming in anger, told Grant that a line had been crossed. He heard them on the afternoon of October 15, and they were, he admits, "not a little startling." At that point his party had been on the march some seven hours from Amadiyah, a "toilsome" ride over rough mountains. They were in a canyon descending toward the village of Duree when knots of men appeared above. "Who are you?" the voices called out, "What do you want?" The volume and number of the cries rose, says Grant, until their echoes seemed to spring from the rocks overhead. They threatened robbery; they demanded to know if Grant was a "Catoleek." The party's lone police escort, a Kurd, turned pale with fright. Grant recalled an earlier warning.

"To the borders of their country," said the vigorous pasha of Mosul, "I will be responsible for your safety; you may put gold upon your head and you will have nothing to fear; but I warn you that I can protect you no farther. Those mountain infidels (Christians) acknowledge neither pashas nor kings, but from time immemorial every man has been his own king!"

Such was the Nestorians' reputation for ferocity. In Amadiyah, visiting mountaineers were not allowed in town after dark, for fear they would storm the citadel and capture it. "They are regarded as almost invincible," Grant says, "and are represented as having the power of vanquishing their enemies by some magical spell in their looks."

Even in Duree, the first real Nestorian village he had reached, Grant was not yet where he wanted to be. Duree lay in Berwar, a district still nominally subservient to the Turks and to a Kurdish chief. One more range, higher than the last, separated him from Tiyari, the first true district of the independent Nestorians. Still, even here in Berwar, the change in the people was obvious. The belligerence and swagger of these Christians, loyal to the church of Mar Shimun, had been quite intimidating. This changed when they learned that Grant was not only a Christian but a Syriac-speaking *hakim*. He stayed for two days in Duree, dispensing medicines, talking to the people, visiting the village church and watching red squirrels, the first he had seen in the East, skip about in the black walnut trees. The doctor's Turkish boots, the villagers told him, would no longer do for the terrain ahead; instead, he received, as a gift from the local bishop, goatskin sandals, their hair side out for traction on the rocks, Thus equipped, on Friday morning, October 18, Grant set out for the district of Tiyari.

He could have detoured around the range ahead, but chose instead the steepest and most direct route to his goal. In this Thomas Laurie sees the hand of God at work. Nothing else, no other approach, he says, could have appealed so deeply to the romantic adventurer in Asahel Grant. By now, besides his goat-hair sandals, the American had adopted full native dress. His beard grew as thick as that of any imam or priest. He wore a turban, flowing robes, and the *shalvar*, the wide pantaloons of the peasants, essential for climbing the mountainsides. After a steep ascent of an hour and a half, he reached the summit of the pass.

There on October 18, 1839, Asahel Grant stumbled upon the great moment of his life. In his text there is no preparation for the event. He climbs and arrives, and in one breathless second everything has changed. A "sequestered pinnacle of rock" beckoned, and he withdrew there to stare and to dream. We can only imagine the silence of that moment, and the wonder that informed his life. Judith had died in delirium only ten months before, and through snows, deserts, and disease—over a thousand miles of earth and ocean—he had struggled on. Now the heart of autumn had arrived, and the sun, late-risen and low, must have lain upon him like a warming hand. To the north, he says, lay "a scene indescribably grand."

> The country of the independent Nestorians opened before my enraptured vision like a vast amphitheatre of wild, precipitous mountains, broken with deep, dark-looking defiles and narrow glens, into few of which the eye could penetrate so far as to gain a distinct view of the cheerful, smiling villages which have long been the secure abodes of the main body of the Nestorian Church. Here was the home of a hundred thousand Christians, around whom the arm of Omnipotence had reared the adamantine ramparts whose lofty, snow-capped summits seemed to blend with the skies in the distant horizon. Here, in their munition of rocks, has God preserved . . . a chosen remnant of his ancient Church, secure from the beast and the false prophet, safe from the flames of persecution and the clangour of war.

This was Moses on Pisgah; Brigham Young at Salt Lake. We can feel the happiness, resolve, and hope welling within him, as the fevered world spun on that pole of solitude. To the north, Russia's war raged on against the Chechens and the tribes of Daghestan. Across the Atlantic, the cargo of the *Amistad* languished in chains. But for Asahel Grant, sitting in thralldom on his rock, this was the future, spread before him like a map.

> I had been brought at length, through many perils, to behold a country from which emanated the brightest beams of hope for the long-benighted empire of Mohammedan delusion . . . My thoughts went back to the days when their missionaries were spread abroad throughout the East, and for more than a thousand years continued to plant and sustain the standard of the cross through the remote and barbarous countries of Central Asia, Tartary, Mongolia, and China . . . I looked at them in their present state, sunk down into the ignorance of semi-barbarism, and the light of vital piety almost extinguished upon their altars, and my heart bled for their condition. But hope pointed her radiant wand to brighter scenes, when all these glens, and rocks, and vales shall echo and re-echo to the glad praises of our God; and, like a morning star, these Nestorians shall arise to usher in a glorious and resplendent day. But, ere that bright period shall arrive, there is a mighty work to be done—a conflict with the powers of darkness before the shout of victory. Let us arm this brave band for the contest.

In this exhortation, Grant is writing for an evangelical audience, one whose pennies and shillings are important to the survival of missionary work. Like so many Victorians, he lived in a world of infinite material and spiritual possibility, where the New Jerusalem lay within sight, if not immediate reach. Still, the modern reader wonders: could Grant really have thought it possible to transform Hakkari, this cockpit of Kurdistan, into a version of Presbyterian New England? Very few, after all, of the "happy, smiling villages" remained secure from blood feuds and strife. And how could he "arm this brave band for the contest" and yet remain free from political entanglement?

It is not easy to relate to this level of idealism. It makes the modern reader—cosseted in his ergonomic chair, annoyed at the slowness of his Internet connection—feel petty and uncharitable. One thinks of the young Judith, donating her woollen mittens to tropical Hawaii, praising God for having taken only one of her eyes, then dying in fevered madness at age twenty-five. Perhaps in the end it doesn't really matter that Dr. Grant's "map" of the future was an illusion, that in less than four years the Nestorians' aura of invincibility would vanish in a bloody mist, that seventy-five years later their world would be irretrievably lost, and that, as the 21st century dawned, the rock where Dr. Grant rested would mark the mined and monitored border between Turkey and Iraq. To this place, one of the most remote and dangerous on earth, a man had come, alone and unarmed, to try to alleviate suffering. For Grant, that was good enough. And for those who admire him, it will have to suffice.

For six weeks and two days Asahel Grant climbed passes, forded rivers, and passed long hours in villages, meeting people and giving out medicines to the sick. For the doctor from Oneida County, this autumn tour was the fulfillment of a dream. Grant was the first "European" to enter Hakkari successfully, but he was hardly the last. By the end of the 19th century, the Nestorians of Kurdistan had become England's pet minority in the Middle Eastern mosaic, visited by missionaries, explorers, travel writers, and even a member of the House of Lords.

With this tour in October 1839, Asahel Grant became the first writer to describe the Christian mountaineers of Hakkari. But for the best descriptions of their world, we must rely upon a woman. In our time the name of Isabella Bird (1831–1904) has become synonymous with "Victorian Lady Traveler," a phrase which belittles her accomplishments. She was only eight

years old when Dr. Grant first penetrated Hakkari. In 1890,
when she endured the trip described in her two-volume *Journeys in Persia and Kurdistan*, she was nearing sixty. Her entire
journey, which began with a terrible mid-winter crossing of the
Zagros Mountains, took a year to complete. During that time
she spent scarcely a fortnight in Hakkari, and yet she managed
to paint the finest word-pictures of mountain life that we have.

No one, for example, described the Nestorians' mode of
dress better than Isabella Bird. In November 1890 she spent a
week at the home of Mar Shimun in Kochanes. During that
time they were visited by men of Tiyari, where Grant made his
first contact with the mountaineers.

> Mirza tells me that there are 115 guests today! Among them
> are a number of Tiyari men, whose wild looks, combined with
> the splendour of their dress and arms, are a great interest . . .
> Their jackets are one mass of gold embroidery (worked by
> Jews), their shirts, with hanging sleeves, are striped satin; their
> trousers, of sailor cut, are silk, made from the cocoons of their
> own silkworms, woven with broad crimson stripes on a white
> ground, on which is a zigzag pattern; and their handsome jack-
> boots are of crimson leather. With their white or red peaked
> felt hats and twisted silk *pagris* [head-cloths], their rich girdles,
> jewelled daggers, and inlaid pistols, they are very imposing.

The only things she leaves out are the shaven heads and
twin top-knot pigtails worn by the men of Jelu, the roughest
district in Hakkari. The best of her portraits shows Marbishu,
a Nestorian village close to Urmia but deep in the mountains
that separate Persia and Turkey. After a long sojourn among
the Bakhtiari nomads of the Zagros, Isabella Bird made her
way up the length of that mountain chain to Lake Urmia. There
she visited the mission—by then greatly expanded—that Justin
Perkins and Dr. Grant had established in 1835. From Urmia

she rode directly into the mountains and soon was approaching Marbishu, just across the border into Turkish territory. Like Dr. Grant's journey of fifty-one years before, this took place in October. Marbishu was exactly the kind of place—with the same dangers—that Grant would have known.

> [W]e spent nine hours in a grand defile, much wooded, where a difficult path is shut in with the Marbishu torrent. The Kurds left us at Bani, when two fine fellows became our protectors as far as a small stream, crossing which we entered Turkey. At a Kurdish semi-subterranean village, over which one might ride without knowing it, a splendidly-dressed young Khan emerged from one of the burrows, and said he would give us guards, but they would not go farther than a certain village, where two of his men had been killed three days before. "There is blood between us and them," he said. After that, for five hours up to Marbishu, the scenery is glorious. The valley narrows into a picturesque gorge between precipitous mountains, from 2000 to 4000 feet above the river, on the sides of which a narrow and occasionally scaffolded path is carried, not always passable for laden mules. Many grand ravines came down upon this gorge, their dwarf trees, orange, tawny, and canary-yellow, mingled with rose-red leafage. The rose bushes are covered with masses of large carnation-red hips, the bramble trailers are crimson and gold, the tamarisk is lemon-yellow.

In this sublime place, with a "blue gloom" in the defile and new snow glittering on the peaks, brute reality intervened. A Kurdish chief, whose men had just robbed another group of travelers, now barred Isabella Bird's passage as well. A confrontation ensued. The robbers took a horse but then returned it, presumably after extorting money. At last the party moved on, but the terrified muleteers declared that they would go no further than Marbishu. The day's march ended there.

In the wildest part of the gorge, where two ravines meet, there is fine stoneless soil, tilled like a garden; the mountains fall a little apart—there are walnuts, fruit trees, and poplars; again the valley narrows, the path just hangs on the hillside, and I was riding over the roofs of village houses for some time before I knew it. The hills again opened, and there were flourishing breadths of turnips, and people digging potatoes, an article of food and export which was introduced by the missionaries forty years ago. The glen narrowed again, and we came upon the principal part of Marbishu—rude stone houses in tiers, burrowing deeply into the hills, with rock above and rock below on the precipitous sides of a noisy torrent, crossed by two picturesque log bridges, one of the wildest situations I have ever seen, and with a wintry chill about it, for the sun at this season deserts it at three. Rude, primitive, colourless, its dwellings like the poorest cowsheds, its church like a Canadian ice-house, clinging to mountain sides and spires of rock, so long as I remember anything I shall remember Marbishu.

Marbishu was famous for its church, a place of pilgrimage for Nestorians. After a tour of the church, Isabella Bird ended up at the home of the *qasha*, or priest.

Many a strange house I have seen, but never anything so striking as the dwelling of Qasha Ishai. Passing through the rude verandah, and through a lofty room nearly dark, with a rough stone dais, on which were some mattresses, and berths one above another, I stumbled in total darkness into a room seventy feet by forty, and twenty feet or more high in its highest part. It has no particular shape, and wanders away from this lofty centre into low irregular caverns and recesses excavated in the mountain side. Parts of the floor are of naked rock, parts of damp earth. In one rocky recess is a powerful spring of pure water. The roofs are supported on barked stems of trees, black, like the walls, wherever it was possible to see them, with the smoke of two centuries. Ancient oil lamps on posts or in recesses rendered darkness visible. Goat-skins, with the legs sticking out, containing butter, hanging from the blackened crossbeams, and wheat, apples, potatoes, and onions in heaps and sacks, piles of wool, spinning-wheels, great wooden cradles here and there, huge oil and water jars, wooden stools, piles of bedding, ploughs, threshing instruments, long guns, swords, spears, and gear encumbered the floor, while much more was stowed away in the dim caverns of the rock. I asked the number of families under the roof. "Seven ovens," was the reply.

There is a dream-like quality to this scene, the aura of ancient romance. One expects hooded figures to emerge from the shadows, the firelight flickering on their bronzed cheekbones, and stride off in search of the Holy Grail. The reality, of course, was one of poverty and danger. Marbishu, which Asahel Grant knew from his time in Urmia, contained all the elements that the doctor would have recognized: the intensive agriculture, the beleaguered self-sufficiency, the ability to improvise a dwelling in the unlikeliest place. In 1890 this world was twenty-five years away from extinction.

The word "self-sufficiency" occurs often in descriptions of Hakkari life. "On the whole," says Dr. Grant, "they are the most independent people I ever saw, in every respect." Those few items which the mountaineers did not make, they traded for. Indeed, it is hard to imagine how it could be otherwise, given the fastnesses in which they lived. In Turkey, a land untouched by the Industrial Revolution, virtually all village-dwellers (especially the mountain Kurds) lived lives of extraordinary self-sufficiency, yet in the independent *ashiret* districts of Hakkari this was raised to an even higher standard. Their agriculture we have glimpsed in Marbishu. In other villages—including Kurdish villages, we should add—it was even more remarkable, with extensive, highly complex systems of terracing and irrigation that amazed all who saw them. At the village of Asheetha, which Grant reached on October 21, its gardens, interspersed with houses, stretched for five miles along a lateral valley west of the river Zab.

In other districts the "valleys" were mere slits in the rock, and the torrents, crashing down the mountainsides, were difficult to tame. In this near-vertical landscape the people fought a constant battle to hold the soil, while avalanches and rainstorms played havoc with the terracing systems. But the true basis of the Nestorians' agricultural self-sufficiency would always be their flocks of sheep and goats, providing milk for cheese and yoghurt, wool for clothing, felt-making, and trade, leather for sandals, and meat for the times when they could afford it. These animals were their real wealth, the things they fought hard to retain and which they stole when they had to.

Once again we come to the subject of fighting and theft. Especially useful, in this land of perpetual strife, was the mountaineers' ability to make their own gunpowder, weapons, and bullets. All the ingredients for black powder—charcoal, sulphur, and niter—were available to those who knew where to look. Charcoal, of course, could not have been easier to find. The hot springs and steam vents which produced orpiment, that yellow compound which had cost Schultz his life, also yielded sulphur. Saltpeter, or niter, a naturally-occurring form of potassium nitrate, was found in caves. The mountaineers also mined their lead for bullets, usually in shallow pits from which they extracted galena, a mineral that is primarily lead sulphide. In the village of Duree, before he entered Hakkari, Dr. Grant noted the presence of lead mines owned by the local Kurdish chief, and he found other mines as he penetrated further into the mountains. As for weapons, W.A. Wigram notes that the finest gunsmith in Hakkari lived in the district of Jelu, in the heart of the mountains. He was, fittingly enough, a priest of the Nestorian Church.

But no people can be wholly self-sufficient: all need goods to trade for the things they cannot make themselves. Besides wool and hides, the greatest part of their exports, the mountains of Kurdistan provided two unique products, each of which relied on insects and oak trees.

In North America we think of mountains as wooded: the Appalachians clad in hardwoods, the vast coniferous forests of the Pacific Northwest. The high peaks of the Rockies and the Cascades display a distinct timberline, above which trees cannot grow. But there is no obvious line in the mountains of Kurdistan, because they have no timber. Three millenia of human habitation have finished off the forests, just as they have finished off the magnificent Caspian tiger (deliberately exterminated by the Russians around 1900) and the lions that roamed Iraq until the 1920s. Now trees grow primarily in the river valleys and in the cultivated rows of poplars that provide wood for village life. A few stands of forest survive in the remote mountain recesses, and most of those are oaks.

Of these oak species, the first is not really a tree at all. The Aleppo oak (*quercus infectoria*), also known as dyer's oak or gall oak, was the world's principal source of high-quality gallnuts. Many oaks form galls, which are also formed on sumacs in East Asia; but Aleppo oaks have long yielded the best and most abundant supply. This oak is a shrub, at most five to six feet tall, which ranges from the mountains of northern Syria and Turkey across the Taurus range into Iraqi and Iranian Kurdistan. About gallnuts (also called nutgalls) we should make one thing clear: no one will ever *think* of eating one. They are not nuts at all but foul insect-filled sores that form on the twigs of the plant and grow to about the size of an acorn. In the spring, after the snow has receded in the mountains, a tiny species of wasp begins to breed. This is the *cynips,* or gall-wasp, which bores a microscopic hole in the twigs of the Aleppo oak and lays its eggs inside. The twig then swells in response to the infection (this is, after all, *quercus infectoria).* The natural tannin contained in oaks begins to collect in the sore and eventually attains high concentrations. By July the insects inside have gone through their larval and pupal stages and are approaching the time when they can emerge. This is the critical moment for harvesting, before the nascent wasps inside have consumed the tannin-rich substance of the gall. The best, highest-priced galls are thus gathered before the wasps have perforated the gall and taken wing, because it is then that the highest concentrations of tannin can be obtained. In notes of a mountain journey from Urmia to Mosul in 1849, Rev. Justin Perkins observed:

> The quantity of gall-nuts yielded annually by each bush, or tree, varies from half a dozen to many pounds, according to the size and thriftiness. The labor of gathering them, scattered as the trees and bushes are, over the Koordish mountains, scores and hundreds of miles in different directions, must be immense, furnishing employment to multitudes of men, women and children, for a considerable period every year.

This, in other words, was big business. Blind Mohammed, the Kurdish bey of Rowanduz, established a monopoly on the trade in his domains. Gall merchants made regular forays into the mountains from the larger trading towns of the region, and the galls they purchased were shipped in great quantities to Europe, North America, and around the world. As late as 1890, when synthetic dyes had begun to make inroads into the demand for oak galls, Isabella Bird reported that Baghdad's trade in gallnuts amounted to some £35,000 per annum. This may not seem like much, but Baghdad was only one of many towns, throughout Persia and Turkey, that dealt in this commodity. And of course, the pound sterling was worth far more then than it is today.

So what did they make with these foul nodules? Many things—drugs, tannic acid for the tanning of leather—but, most of all, dyes and ink. Iron-gall ink, which produces its intense blackness through the chemical reaction between the tannin and dissolved crystals of ferrous sulphate, was first made in the 12th century, though it wasn't used commonly until the Renaissance. From the very beginning oak galls, and specifically Aleppo galls, formed the most potent source of tannin in the ink. By the time Asahel Grant arrived in the East, no one wrote anything without iron gallotannate ink, whether it was the novels of Dickens and Trollope, Dr. Grant's letters home, or the speeches of Daniel Webster in the U.S. Congress. Those words, now tinted reddish-brown by the rusted iron in the ink, owed their substance to a tiny wasp and a scrubby oak bush in Kurdistan. Virtually the same compound found its way into the ubiquitous black dyes of Victorian clothing. Here again, it is oxidation that gives the game away. At the end of Trollope's *The Way We Live Now*, the wastrel baronet Sir Felix Carbury, penniless and out of credit at his tailor's, finds his waistcoat gone "rusty" with age.

Besides gallnuts, the region's oaks yielded another product, one not nearly as important in commerce, yet equally mysterious and actually edible. For this, the Kurds and Nestorians used not only the Aleppo oak, but other species as well, including the valonia (*quercus aegilops*), the belut (*q. balluta),* and *quercus mannifera,* or "manna-producing" oak. Unlike the shrubby Aleppo, these were proper trees, though not of the stature we normally associate with oaks. They were at most twenty feet tall, and they ranged throughout the Kurdish mountains and Hakkari especially. Of the three, the valonia was the more important. Besides its acorns, eaten by both humans and animals, the primary product of this oak was, as its name denotes, valonia, an extract made from the acorn cups. As with oak galls, valonia provided tannin—albeit of a lower grade and less concentrated—for use in dyes and leather. But another substance entirely derived from this tree and its cousins, a confection the Arabs called *man-es-sima,* or "manna from heaven."

The English phrase comes of course from the Old Testament, where the Hebrews, wandering in the Sinai, found upon "the face of the wilderness" food ("a small round thing, as small as the hoarfrost") that had seemingly fallen from the sky. This Biblical manna, like other mannas found in the Middle East, probably derived from the honeydew secretions of various insects, chiefly aphids. The most famous manna, however, was that of Kurdistan, because of the large quantities gathered and the culinary imagination that transformed it into a delicacy. Some sources call it *gez*: Isabella Bird refers to it as *gaz*, and George Fowler, declaring it "the most indigestible of all food," called it *guzanjibin*. In an appendix to his *Nineveh and Babylon*, Layard calls it "*Ghiok-hel-vahsee.*" This in modern Turkish would be *gök helvası*, or "halvah from the sky," halvah being the sweet cakes made of sesame flour, butter, and sugar commonly found in Middle Eastern groceries.

The image of "sky" or "heaven" is important, for the villagers who gathered the manna believed that it had dropped from the sky. And why not? It appeared suddenly at dawn; but only on certain mornings in the year; and some years it didn't appear at all. Usually it showed up on the oaks in June, after a night of clear skies and cold temperatures. But if it rained or was too warm, there was little or no manna to be had. Entomologists tell us that millions of aphids, gathering on the undersides of the oak leaves in the pre-dawn cold, secrete a sweet, sticky residue that either drips onto the earth or collects on the tops of the leaves below. To the mountain peoples, however, those who gathered the globules and masses from the oak leaves, its appearance was a mystery. Even under perfect conditions, if the manna-pickers came too long after dawn, the manna would not be there. The reason: the ants that "herded" the aphids during the daylight hours, living off their secretions, would quickly return to take up the task, and the previous night's manna would become their breakfast.

But if conditions were right and the villagers found what they were looking for, the harvest was on. The solidified manna, packed in a mass with leaf and twig fragments, was carried from the mountains and sold to confectioners in the market towns of the area. There the transformation began. The manna was first dissolved in water, and any floating impurities were skimmed off. Then it was strained twice through cloth. Last, it was boiled down, amended with rosewater and almonds, and allowed to cool and solidify into a pure-white cake. These highly esteemed confections, cut into squares and sold in the bazaars, were considered a gift of heaven.

Asahel Grant mentions little of all this flora, fauna, and economic activity in *The Nestorians,* unlike Ainsworth, Layard, and Bird, who serve up pages loaded with botanical and ethnographic information. At first glance, this omission might be thought to betray a lack of observation and acuity. But Dr Grant was not aiming to provide an encyclopedic account of mountain life. He, as we have seen, assiduously avoided any overt note-taking or gathering of information. He traveled alone and unarmed and certainly remembered the murder of Schultz. As the first European to traverse the high mountains of the Hakkari country, Grant wanted also to be the first to come out alive. William F. Ainsworth, hurrying through Hakkari with Christian Rassam in 1840, made no attempt to conceal his researches, and in doing so he aroused suspicions that would have profound consequences. There is another important distinction: Dr. Grant had not come to gather material for a book. While Ainsworth the scientist traveled through the mountains cataloguing mineral samples, rock strata, and the Latin names of plant specimens, Grant the physician had come as a healer, and everywhere he went villagers lined up by the hundreds to receive treatment.

Lezan, the first village visited by Asahel Grant in the Tiyari district, lay on the right bank of the Zab, just north of what is now the Turkish-Iraqi border. On that October afternoon joy mingled with trepidation as Grant made his scrambling descent to the river. But as the first villagers came forth to greet him, all uncertainty evaporated.

> The only person I had ever seen from this remote tribe was a young Nestorian, who came to me about a year before, entirely blind. He said he had never expected to see the light of day, till my name had reached his country, and he had been told that I could restore his sight. With wonderful perseverance, he had gone from village to village seeking some one to lead him by the hand, till, in the course of five or six weeks, he had reached my residence in Ooroomiyah, where I removed the cataract from his eyes, and he returned to his mountains seeing.

Remarkaby, this same young man now emerged with "a smiling countenance, bearing a gift of honey." Grant was, in other words, already known in this village. His fame as a great *hakim* had preceded him, and his welcome could not have been more cordial.

Lezan, a feast of greenery, flourished amid the crags. He stayed in the village three nights and everywhere found intense cultivation—grape vines, vegetables, millet, orchards of pomegranate, apple, and fig, with rice ("to the detriment of health") growing in the terraced fields. Gall-oaks carpeted the hills. Water was plentiful: springs gushed from the mountainside, and the Izani, a powerful stream flowing from the northwest, joined the Zab just above the village. It was the "peaceful, smiling village" that the doctor had dreamed of.

At dawn on the Sabbath, October 20, the people of Lezan were summoned to worship by the sound of a mallet beating rapidly on the *nakoosha,* a thick perforated board. Every person who entered, says Grant, took off his shoes and kissed the church's doorpost or threshold, then proceeded to the altar to kiss the Gospels, the cross, and finally the hand of the priest.

All stood; there were no pews in the mountaineers' churches. The prayers and psalms were chanted in the ancient Syriac, a language which none of the villagers, and almost none of the priests, could understand. A priest then read part of the Gospels, also in the ancient language, which he translated, if he could, into the Syriac of the people. This, says Grant, was the extent of their preaching, though sometimes legends and stories were told. The Eucharist could not have been simpler. The bread and wine were consecrated, then brought forward, and each worshipper went forward in turn to partake. To Grant's relief, there was none of the "idolatrous adoration" practiced by the "Romanists" and the other Eastern churches.

The building at Lezan, he noted, resembled every other Nestorian church he saw in the mountains. These structures, spare and simple, bore little resemblance to churches elsewhere. Several features stood out. First was their strength. Some, according to their records, had stood for over fourteen centuries when Grant saw them. Heavy stones, mortared with lime cement, were the only materials used. Yet these alone would have done little to ensure their longevity had not their roofs and portals employed the catenary arch, a building technique unknown to many mountain Kurds and a testament to the Nestorians' origins in Mesopotamia. In May 1977 I saw such a church in the village of Kespiyanish, near Beytüşşebap, in Hakkari. It was utterly bare, yet intact, a structure no doubt centuries old and likely to last for centuries more. The Kurds of Kespiyanish marveled at the church's construction: "These people were rich!" they declared, and it was useless to argue with them.

The oddest feature of a Nestorian church was its entry, and in this the Kespiyanish church matched the pattern described by 19th-century visitors to Hakkari. According to Thomas Laurie, the mountain tribes quoted Matthew 7:14 ("strait is the gate and narrow is the way") to explain it. Imagine a bare stone structure, some twenty feet on a side, surmounted by a vaulted roof. No windows were visible; the walls were a foot thick.

Piercing the facade was an arched portal, perhaps three feet high, more like the entrance to a cave than to a house of worship. The threshold barrier reached to knee-height, and to enter, the visitor had to step over it with one leg and bend almost double to avoid hitting his head. Inside was a tiny vestibule, then two stone columns and another arch leading to the sanctuary. There, in a bare grotto the size of an average suburban living room, two square openings high up on the ceiling pierced the blackness of the dome. Such was the typical church of the mountain Nestorians: monuments to insecurity, masonry vaults that could not be attacked, defended, or modified, and that in the end served only two purposes: worship services and the preservation of sacred texts. In these churches Christianity survived from late Roman times until 1915.

The rest of the Sabbath passed quietly, and at dawn on Monday morning crowds of people, many from surrounding villages, came to Grant for medical help. Soon he was overwhelmed, and the throng had to be kept back so that three or four patients could come forward at a time to receive the medicines, folded into separate packets for ease in handling. "There were many," he writes, "suffering from bilious affections, intermittent fever, etc., the consequence of the rice-fields and extensive irrigation of the gardens in the village, together with the great heat of the summer, which must become oppressive from the concentration of the sun's rays in these narrow vales."

By "intermittent fever" he meant malaria. Grant could see that fevers were more prevalent near rice paddies and their stagnant water, but not until the end of the century was the connection made between that water and the mosquito larvae that bred in it. In Grant's time it was thought that malaria rose mainly from the decay of vegetable matter. "Bilious affections," could mean a dozen things, including dysentery, hepatitis, and general diarrheal misery. The word "bilious" obviously derives from "bile," and both yellow and black bile were two of the "humours" which affected bodily health in traditional theory. Here the questions must be confronted. How much did Grant and his fellow physicians really know about diseases and their treatment? What were these medicines that he doled out? How did they work, if they worked at all? The probable answers, if we hope for scientific plausibility, are not comforting.

We first met Asahel Grant, lancet in hand, performing an act of torture upon himself as a remedy for facial swelling. It was a practice—phlebotomy, or bleeding—familiar to most people with any knowledge of early medicine. Doctors knew that people bled to death, that blood is necessary for life. But that was serious, uncontrolled bleeding. They thought that a measured amount for medicinal purposes was a good thing. "A bleeding in spring/ Is physick for a king," ran an old saying. This prophylactic measure, it was assumed, worked like a tonic: it upset the patient and therefore had to be good for him. Bleeding, doctors believed, gave the body a jolt and provided a stimulus for health, much like the pruning of a rose before the growing season.

Of course, medical remedies weren't always so pleasant as a nice cup of blood in the springtime. When people got really sick, doctors responded with tougher treatment. Desperate diseases demanded it, and by the 19th century the amount of blood drawn by doctors became truly startling. John S. Haller, Jr., tells us that bleeding became the treatment of choice for virtually every illness known to man. There were "patients bled of nearly two and a half gallons within a few days." Indeed, Haller says, many physicians advocated bleeding patients until they fainted. Haller gives an example of an English doctor who, despite his name, is not a character out of Dickens. This was Sir William Blizard, of the London Hospital Medical School, who in 1833 treated a man with several broken ribs suffered when he was run down by a carriage in the street.

Dr. Blizard got down to work by purging the patient (i.e., making him throw up and empty his bowels, a strenuous exercise for the ribcage) and then taking fifteen ounces of blood. The next day he took twenty ounces more. On the third day Blizard attached twenty leeches to the side with the broken ribs, and three days after that he drained an additional thirty ounces of blood. (For those keeping track, we have now exceeded one half U.S. gallon, not counting the leeches' lunch.) On the following day he took twenty ounces more, and he followed this in twenty-four hours with—you guessed it—more leeches. In the midst of all this, Haller tells us, Blizard used blisters, emetics, and purgatives, and "when last heard of, the victim was in poor health."

The Blizard of '33 was hardly alone in his blood-letting—or his leeches. Applied almost anywhere on the body, from the arm or neck to inflamed gums, or even (God help us) the male and female genitalia, leeches were used by the millions to bleed patients, and across Europe were gathered by peasants who brought them to apothecaries for sale. All this hunting and sucking took its toll on the species. Wordsworth, in his 1802 poem "Resolution and Independence" mentions meeting such a hunter, a man who found the leeches getting scarcer every year.

These creatures were so valued that by the end of the century medicinal leeches had become extinct in Britain. France was no better off, and by 1833 imports reached 41.6 million per annum. Rev. Justin Perkins, traveling in northern Persia in 1852, met two "French leech merchants" on their way to Tabriz, presumably to begin harvesting there as well. The Anglican missionaries James Fletcher and George Percy Badger, enroute to Mosul in 1842, told of encountering a young Swiss named Krug at Amasya, on the river Iris in central Anatolia. Krug, the only foreigner living in the town, hired the local Turks, who donned thick, knee-length felt socks, waded into the rivers, and allowed the leeches to attach themselves to the wool. These were then plucked off by the thousands, packaged in jars, and shipped off to his employer, a pharmaceutical company in Trieste.

Dr. Grant could not carry leeches with him into the mountains; nor does he mention using them in Urmia. However, he did, as we know, carry a lancet, and he was certainly familiar with phlebotomy. Writing to his mother in October, 1836, he told of treating a serious illness of his own:

> The Lord has been visiting us by sickness for some months past. I have had two or three attacks of fever, and on the 16th ult. [of the month past] was brought to the confines of eternity by a sudden and violent attack of the cholera. I vomited and passed off gallons of rice-colored water; had severe spasms in every part of the system; extremities, face and tongue quite cold; features sunken and livid, and great restlessness and thirst; difficulty of breathing, almost entire loss of voice. My eyes have been so much inflamed as to render it necessary to take a large quantity of blood—to mercurialize and blister freely. Of blisters I had ten upon my neck and arms.

Mrs. Grant's anxieties could hardly have been soothed by this letter. But her son survived and went on to bleed others. (The blisters, produced by caustic agents or boiling water, were another method of "drawing out the poison." Grant had hidden his gold coins in a roll of "blister salve.") He believed that it was this attack of cholera that brought about the spasms of vomiting which continued to plague him. He may have been wrong about this: cholera may not have been the cause. We see the word "mercurialize" and note that Grant used mercury as "freely" as he bled himself. "Mercurialize" refers to the drug calomel, or mercurous chloride, a common household potion used as a remedy for nearly everything, from stomachache to syphillis. Young Leo Tolstoy, serving in the Russian army against the Chechens in 1851, dosed himself with calomel for a venereal infection contracted from a Cossack girl.

Mercury is toxic, and over time causes terrible damage to the body, especially the nervous system. It left Tolstoy's tongue and the inside of his mouth covered with sores. If Grant's cholera caused him to throw up, if the illness then prevented him from eating, and if he proceeded to fill his empty stomach with large doses of calomel, he could very well have done permanent damage to his digestive system. The chances are very good, in other words, that Asahel Grant poisoned himself with his own medicine.

In the pharmacopeia of 1839, calomel was anything but unusual. The ideology of unpleasantness guaranteed its position and that of many other loathsome potions. If a substance tasted vile and immediately caused the patient to (a) throw up, (b) sweat, or (c) expel everything from his bowels, it was virtually guaranteed to be in a physician's medicine chest. In theory, nothing else mattered. The human body, it was felt, was governed by the action of various "humours," or fluids, and disease resulted from their imbalance or congestion. These harsh medicines jolted the body, "broke up" the congestion, and, like bleeding, provided a stimulus for the system to right itself. Medical men believed this because they had always believed it. The doctors, having no clue to the real causes of disease, relied upon humoral theories reaching back to the ancient Greeks. Instead of observing and drawing conclusions from phenomena, physicians of the time clung to established ideas and interpreted reality according to those principles. Only in a few cases—quinine, opium, smallpox vaccine—did they happen upon real medical relief.

Another stalwart of the medicine chest was tartar emetic (antimony and potassium tartrate), which Dr. Grant mentions several times in his memoir. It, too, was toxic, and produced one drastic effect: the patient immediately violently threw up everything in his stomach. No self-respecting physician, especially in the 1830s, would have done without it. Even amateurs dispensed tartar emetic. In the summer of 1846, when Austen Henry Layard was excavating the ruins of Nineveh near Mosul, he took a break from the killing heat of the plains and set out for Kurdistan, to explore and follow in the footsteps of Asahel Grant and W.F. Ainsworth. Though not a doctor, Layard carried medicines, knowing that the people would demand them. In Amadiyah, the ruined fortress town just south of the Nestorians' territory, he found the Albanians of the garrison stricken with malaria, just as they had been when Grant rode through in 1839. As if this weren't bad enough given the heat and the long summer days, they were also in the middle of Ramadan, and no Muslim could ingest anything, even water, from dawn until nightfall.

> It was the hour of afternoon prayer before Selim Agha, the Mutesellim or governor, emerged from his harem; which, however, as far as the fair sex were concerned, was empty . . . The old gentleman, who was hungry, half asleep, and in the third stage of the ague [malarial chills], hurried through the ordinary salutations, and asked at once for quinine. His attendants exhibited illustrations of every variety of the fever; some shivered, others glowed, and the rest sweated. He entreated me to go with him into the harem; his two sons were buried beneath piles of cloaks, carpets, and grain sacks, but the whole mass trembled with the violence of their shaking. I dealt out emetics and quinine with a liberal hand.

After hearing the governor's tale of woe ("a most doleful history of fever, diminished revenues, arrears of pay, and rebellious Kurds"), Layard left him waiting anxiously for sunset, so "that he might console himself with a dose of tartar emetic." Thus we see Layard dispensing two drugs for malaria, one a valuable substance discovered in South America, the other a potion designed by Europeans to make men vomit. To those of us who grew up with an heroic vision of the great age of travel, it is indeed distressing to think of these explorers trekking through the wilds, leaving a trail of purged and exhausted natives. Yet such were the realities of 19th-century medicine.

But beyond this grim reality lay another, which at first seems hard to accept. The fact is, these poisons often worked—that is, they made people feel distinctly better. Tartar emetic so exhausted its victims that they tended to fall into a dreamless, and healing, sleep. Obviously, bleeding would have had the same effect. In December, 1839, some six weeks after Grant's entry into Nestorian territory, a dose of tartar emetic administered to a patient may have saved the doctor's life. This is not so outlandish as it may seem, for, as so often happens with physicians, what Grant was offering was not so much efficacious treatment as the halo of medical infallibility. To the villagers, after all, he was a creature fallen from the sky, a great *hakim* from the land of the *Ferenghis,* the Franks, where steamboats plied the waters, iron horses rode the rails, and the Dark Satanic Mills spewed calico by the mile. Grant brought, for better or worse, the latest and most wonderful medicines of the *Ferenghis.* Even if he was an infidel, he was the nearest thing to a divine being that they would ever see.

Above all, Grant had come from far away to comfort and to heal. More than medicine, he brought kindness. Contrast this, for example, with native diagnostics, as encountered by the traveler Alexander Kinglake in 1834. His companion, another Englishman named Methley, had fallen gravely ill in Adrianople (now Edirne), a city west of Constantinople. Plague was spreading in the town, and the British consul, fearing contagion, had refused Kinglake and Methley sanctuary in his home. Kinglake wrote in his 1844 *Eothen:* "We called to aid a solemn Armenian (I think he was), half soothsayer, half *hakim* or doctor, who, all the while counting his beads, fixed his eyes steadily upon the patient, and then suddenly dealt him a violent blow upon the chest. Methley bravely dissembled his pain, for he fancied that the blow was meant to try whether or not the plague was upon him." And it was not only natives who lacked a bedside manner. Any *Ferenghi* was assumed to be a medical expert, and was soon dragooned into action. In 1829, besieged in the town of Malazgirt by Kurdish bandits, the English traveler George Fowler was called upon to treat a wounded man. All his medical knowledge, he confessed wryly, consisted of bleeding and drenching (with warm water drunk in huge quantities). In the absence of medical instruments to effect the former, he resorted to the Fowler Method: "'Knock him on the nose,' said I; this done, it spared me the trouble of bleeding him.'"

Dr. Grant's medicines may have been harsh, but there is little evidence that he hit men in the nose or chest in order to treat them. He did not, as one traveler testified of a native physican, propose to cure a case of trachoma by piercing the patient's skull with a rod in order to relieve the pressure. Nor did he follow the practice of Persian quacks, who typically wrote a verse from the Koran on a scrap of paper, gave it to the patient to swallow, and held out their hands for payment. Grant's patients—villagers, soldiers, or pashas; Christians, Jews, and Muslims—were filled with joy at his coming and sorrow at his departure. He was both gentle and energetic. Even with the techno-obsessions of our own century, we have come—again—to appreciate the power of selflessness and empathy in human healing. Amid the brutalities of mountain life, this was something new.

8

THE PATRIARCH AND THE KURD

"Lead, kindly light, amid th' encircling gloom,
I am alone, and far from home: lead thou me on!"
—John Henry Newman (1801–1890), "The Pillar of Cloud"

AFTER THREE DAYS IN LEZAN, which included a restful Sabbath and a Monday morning dispensing medicines to an army of patients, Grant moved upstream. At each village along his route more patients came to him pleading for medicines. As he left the Zab and rode along its tributary, the Arzani, Lezan village gave way to Minyanish, Minyanish to Zawitha, and these to others along the path to Asheetha. Zawitha, a village of some 1000 people, boasted no fewer than forty men who were capable of reading verses from the liturgy, though Grant did not believe that many of them could actually understand the ancient Syriac words. For miles a continuous village stretched along the creek, with fields and terraces spilling down the mountainside and detached houses dispersed among the orchards. Grant had never seen detached houses in the East, where villagers normally massed their dwellings together for safety and to conserve arable land. Here the extensive terraces demanded that their caretakers live close by, and the Nestorians' well-earned reputation for truculence kept enemies away.

In Asheetha, a word meaning "avalanche" in Syriac, Grant found a nexus of Nestorian life and a focal point for his goals. The valley was both secure and inviting. Water was abundant, and snow remained year-round among the surrounding cliffs. This village was the center of life in Tiyari, the most populous and most abundantly cultivated district. Grant estimated its population at 3000 people. The most learned priest in the Nestorian domains lived there, Qasha Auraham, who had spent twenty years studying and copying the Scriptures in a perfect Syriac hand. Even he, however, did not own a complete copy of the Bible—only the patriarch had one of those, in his home at Kochanes near Julamerk. Grant stayed overnight at the qasha's home, and told this aging scribe about the wonders of the modern printing press. One of these, he knew, was waiting in Trebizond for transport to the mission station in Urmia, where Justin Perkins and a team of Nestorian priests were laboring over a translation of the New Testament into modern Syriac. Auraham, amazed by this news, immediately requested a copy as soon as the book became available. Most importantly, the priest expressed a strong interest in schools. He told Grant that if the doctor were to open a school in Asheetha, "multitudes" would attend. Grant, who had had a good deal of experience superintending the mission's highly popular schools in and around Urmia, had no reason to doubt this.

The romantic dreams of Asahel Grant grew ever stronger as he marched on. He arrived in Chumba, his next stop, after an eight-hour trek over two steep ranges, during which his mule fell into a torrent—with, thankfully, no damage to the mule or his medicines—and he ended up riding the last miles through a lightning storm. When the rain finally struck, it fell for thirty hours straight. Yet here again, sheltered with Malek Ismael, the village chief, he found the work that he loved, meeting people and spending time among the sick. "Though the village was small," Laurie writes, "yet from that and the hamlets round about multitudes flocked to see the stranger, whose benevolence surpassed all they had ever known before." Once again Grant was overjoyed at the people's interest in the outside world and their desire for schools to be opened.

The headman of Chumba, Malek Ismael, was one of the mountaineers' most highly regarded leaders and was close to the family of the patriarch Mar Shimun. Ismael's late wife had been Mar Shimun's sister. The word *malek* (or *melek*) means "king," and only three men in Hakkari held that title. These "kings" wielded great power, but it was the patriarch Mar Shimun who held the final authority, both civil and ecclesiastical, over the tribes. Mar Shimun held the power of anathema, or excommunication. This was a severe punishment, indeed: to be anathemized was tantamount to execution, for in that environment the life of an outcast was no life at all.

Malek Ismael's late wife, fondly remembered by the people, had been one of the few women who could read and write. Grant delighted in hearing of this affectionate respect for the lady and her literacy, because the education of girls was a high priority for his mission. In this the New England Protestants were far ahead of their time. Education and literacy for both sexes, they felt, led directly to the Bible, which in turn promoted piety in the home and in society. This was why they eagerly awaited their new printing press, and why Justin Perkins was working hard on his translation.

Learning and piety, however, did not always bring happiness. Thomas Laurie tells the tale of a girl named Nazee, who was living in Chumba when Grant first visited there. After the events of 1843, Nazee escaped from Chumba and made her way across the border to Persia, where she was taken in by the missionaries. There she stayed, became a convert and learned to read and write. When Nazee returned to her native village, however, all was not well. The new attitudes inculcated by the evangelical Americans did not mesh with the old ways. Her new-found piety was resented, and she was dogged by envy and bitterness. By that time Mar Shimun had turned against the

Americans, and his servants treated her cruelly. Even her mother scorned her. When Nazee received a new dress as a present from her friends in Urmia, it was torn apart before her eyes. The young missionary George W. Coan, touring the mountain villages in 1851, found Nazee living in misery among people who despised her. The girl followed him about, hanging on his every word, hoping for a rescue. Eventually Coan had to leave her, with only a small copy of the Gospels as a present and the cold comfort of religious platitudes. Before he left, they knelt together by a roaring torrent—probably the same torrent near which Grant had slept upon his *arzaleh*—and Coan prayed, "Come unto me, all ye who labor and are heavy-laden . . . " Nazee was sobbing the whole time.

This should not be surprising. By being "born again," Nazee may have gained salvation in the eyes of the missionaries, but to the rest of her tribe she had become a renegade. These tribes, both Kurd and Nestorian, had hacked from their rocks a world of amazing richness, but all their achievement and the beauty of their surroundings could not obliterate the fact that they were living lives that were nasty, brutish, and short. Religion for them had little to do with goodness and piety. If they were Christian (or Muslim, or Jewish) it was not out of conviction or desire for moral betterment but because they had been born into that tribal unit. If they prayed, it was because that was the law of their people. This was the reality throughout the Middle East, and Americans were naïve to think otherwise. Rev. William Goodell, of the American Board's mission in Constantinople, stated the case starkly in a memoir of 1853.

> There is an abundance of religion in the East, but it is all ceremonial. The Jews, Greeks, Armenians, Catholics, and others, are . . . most superabundantly religious. But this religion of theirs has little or nothing to do either with the heart or with the life; that is, it is not necessarily supposed to exert any influence on a man's moral character . . . The fact is, nobody

in those countries ever expects to find a man more honest, more hospitable, more benevolent, more heavenly-minded, because he prays. . . . Nobody there ever feels that his life and property are in any degree the more secure, because he has fallen into the hands of those who pray.

"With us," Goodell says, "there can be no religion without morality." In the Middle East, it was quite otherwise. Did Asahel Grant understand this? Of course. He had already spent four years in Persia, about which Judith had written, "I am every day more and more convinced that this is a most *dreadfully wicked* country." His writing contains much the same sentiment, especially as to the "low" state of the Nestorians' religion and the "corruption" of its clergy. But did he have any idea of the profound difficulties involved in moving from tribal religiosity to the kind of evangelical faith that he professed? Did he realize the inevitable political implications of such a change? This seems less likely. Even if he had only an inkling of these issues, the transports of joy he felt on that first tour of Hakkari probably allowed him to ignore them. It was the old story of 19th-century idealism and enthusiasm in conflict with the real world. Eventually that world's evil would fall in upon this kind, well-meaning man, and there is good reason to believe that the knowledge of it helped to lead Asahel Grant to an early grave.

When he left Chumba on the morning of October 24, Grant for the first time was forced to deal with the Zab, his only major river crossing since the bridge of boats at Mosul. This task, seldom easy even in the best of times, was especially terrifying when it involved the use of a so-called "bridge." There was only a tenuous link between real, working bridges and the Hakkari contraptions. In fact, in all his mountain travels, Grant never found a decent bridge. The best were of wicker, and could sometimes be used by mules, but they were always on the verge of collapse at any moment. At Chumba he found the old structure swept away and two "long, bare poles"—probably the trunks of poplars—put down in its place. It took a total of three such contraptions to span the entire river. "The bridge at Chumba is one hundred fifty feet long and three in width," Thomas Laurie declares, with ominous exactitude. Malek Ismael had assigned a trusted servant to accompany the doctor, who was urged to climb on this man's back to make the crossing. Grant decided to trust his own feet. The results were satisfactory, if terrifying: Laurie calls the bridge's vibrations "appalling."

On the left bank of the Zab, the terrain grew steeper and more difficult. Grant's mules could not cross the river, nor could they negotiate the narrow catwalks that served as paths alongside it. Grant had no choice but to walk, and he retained two of the Nestorians from Chumba to help carry his medicines and baggage. This, Thomas Laurie says, was the correct decision: some years later, when he himself and a colleague took mules along this same stretch of pathway, the animals were more hindrance than help. They could not be ridden three-fourths of the time, and at others were prone to catch their feet in the crevices of rocks. On one occasion one of the poor creatures turned two complete somersaults before landing in the river with the missionaries' baggage. In all the tales of Hakkari travel, one is constantly confronted by the suffering of these unfortunate animals.

So, muleless, Grant trekked on afoot. He was, as usual, wearing hair sandals, and intermittent rain showers chilled his wet feet. But, he says, "We were six in all; and a cheerful, happy party as ever traversed such wild goat-paths as led us along the base of these rocky heights."

On either side the prospect was bounded by wild, rocky mountains, whose summits were fringed with the lowering clouds, above which the loftier snow-clad pinnacles raised their hoary heads, and sparkled in the rays of an Oriental sun. Here and there their sides were studded with clusters of trees, which aspire to the name of forests in these Eastern lands, where often, for days together, the traveller's eye is not greeted by a single tree. Below me the swollen river roared and dashed along over its rocky bed, which is often confined between the opposing faces of almost perpendicular rocks, that rise like gigantic battlements, and invite the passing stranger to stop and gaze upon the bold and varying scene.

Grant had arrived in his earthly heaven. To stride on, breathlessly, in clear pursuit of a goal; to discover beauty anew at every corner: no one, least of all Asahel Grant, could have asked for more than this. He traveled, he says, with a "buoyant heart." Occasionally the mountains would recede a bit from the river, and in these pockets they would find villages nestled amid orchards, vineyards, and greenery. One night his party reached a Nestorian village called Bemeriga, where he purchased, with medicines, a new pair of hair sandals. These wore out very quickly, and as part of their equipment the mountaineers carried needles with which to mend them. On the next day, October 25, Grant walked ten hours over some of the roughest terrain in the Middle East. At the village of Kerme, their stopping place for the night, the doctor found yet another of his Urmia patients, a sick, destitute man to whom he had given medicine and money two years earlier. Again, Grant rejoiced. He had cast his bread upon the waters, and it returned to him as unbounded hospitality.

On October 26, 1839, Asahel Grant made history. News traveled fast in the Nestorian domains, and Mar Shimun, patriarch of the Nestorian Church of the East, soon heard of the doctor's approach, and sent a horse to Kerme village. This was the first horse that Grant had seen in the mountains, and he set out astride it at eight in the morning to ride the final miles to Kochanes. The Zab, some sixty yards wide and only waist-deep, was easily fordable at Kerme, and after that the road, the regular caravan track from Salmas in Persia to Julamerk, made traveling easier than it had been in weeks. There the river cuts a deep canyon between craggy peaks on the north, amidst which sits the town of Julamerk (now Hakkari), and on the south bank the beetling, 12,000-foot mass of Sümbül Dagh. Grant bypassed Julamerk, which along with Başkale was one of the Kurd Nurullah Bey's twin capitals. At Diz, a slit of a canyon joining the Zab on the south bank, Grant passed beneath the summer castle of Suleiman, nephew and second-in-command to Nurullah. From this post the Kurds inspected him closely as his horse climbed the last miles, and Mar Shimun himself, in his home just beyond Suleiman's castle, could be seen peering at the American through a spyglass. Isabella Bird describes the track as she rode it in 1890:

> From the Zab we ascended the gorge of the Kochanes water by a wild mountain path, at times cut into steps or scaffolded, and at other times merely a glistening track over shelving rock, terminating in a steep and difficult ascent to the fair green alp on which Kochanes stands at the foot of three imposing peaks of naked rock.

The village was simplicity amidst grandeur, a stone church and scattered houses perched on the edge of a precipice, where three torrents met and plunged toward the Zab. There, at half-past twelve on October 26, Asahel Grant shook the hand of Auraham, Mar Shimun XVII, Patriarch of the East.

The meeting, says Grant, could not have been more cordial, and his welcome was "without that flow of heartless compliment and extravagant expression of pleasure which is so common in the mouth of a Persian." Mar Shimun had long awaited a visit from the Urmia mission, and he had begun to think, he said, that they would never come. Now it was a "happy day" for them both. Grant notes:

The patriarch is thirty-eight years of age, above the middle stature, well proportioned, with a pleasant, expresssive, and rather intelligent countenance; while his large flowing robes, his Koordish turban, and his long gray beard give him a patri-archal and venerable aspect, which is heightened by a uni-formly dignified demeanour. Were it not for the youthful fire in his eye, and his vigour and activity, I should have thought him nearer fifty than thirty-eight. But his friends assured me that the hoariness of his beard and locks was that of care and not of age.

This "care" was real, and it was incessant. No president or prime minister endured more than was daily visited upon Mar Shimun. Consider his geographical position. Only half a mile from Kochanes sat the castle we have just mentioned, the sum-mer residence of Nurullah's deputy ruler. The town of Julamerk, Nurullah's second headquarters, lay, Layard says, only "three caravan hours" away. Thus Mar Shimun, the temporal and spiri-tual leader of the Nestorian tribes, lived in such close proximity to the Kurdish rulers of Hakkari that he could have been taken at any time. Then there was the job to which heredity had con-demned him, a job which would have taxed the powers of even the strongest personality.

His own people quarreled amongst themselves, and he was constantly called upon to adjudicate their disputes. Sheep-steal-ing, murder, highway robbery, marital contracts—anything which custom or the local maleks could not resolve was brought to the patriarch. Moreover, the Christians did not exist in a vacuum, sealed off from the Kurds. In most places they could not graze their flocks without coming into contact with each other, and the possibilities for conflict were endless. Technically, Mar Shimun was a vassal of Nurullah, but his Nestorian tribes-men considered themselves totally independent. This delicate balance was difficult to maintain. When Dr. Grant was staying with Mar Shimun, the patriarch was called upon to decide the fate of two Kurds, who came from a tribe that had killed two Nestorians in the Jelu district. These captives had not done the actual killing; their guilt lay in being part of the tribe that had done it. "Blood for blood" was the law, and the tribes knew that each of their members would be held accountable for the deeds of others. Mar Shimun felt inclined to mercy, says Dr. Grant, but his people demanded justice. Eventually the patriarch finessed the situation by finding that, since the two captives were, in a sense, residing with his people, they had become to a degree the Nestorians' guests. So they could be spared if they paid blood money for the two men who had been killed. Thus Mar Shimun, treading the narrow bridge between vengeance and discretion, managed to settle the dispute.

From the first words of their conversation, Grant could have seen troubles ahead. In the town of Aqra he had managed to avoid discussing the political grievances of the local Kurdish leader. Here among fellow Christians it would be more difficult.

> [Mar Shimun's] first inquiries related to [his people's] political prospects, the movements in Turkey, the designs of the European powers with regard to these countries; and why they did not come and break the arm of Mohammedan power, by which many of his people had been so long oppressed.

Grant does not tell us how he responded to these concerns. No doubt he tried, as in Aqra, to keep clear of entanglement. He had come to heal and do good, and despite his millenial fantasies, for the present he had nothing more in mind. Yet native observers saw another reality. They saw that the Russians, who only eleven years before had occupied Urmia, were positioned in Azerbaijan and Armenia, as well as in the Balkans and the Caucasus. They knew that the Europeans possessed great power, that they had forced the sultan to grant independence to the Greeks and kept the Egyptians from taking over Constantinople. Now this Frank had appeared, a foreigner from

the powerful lands of the West, a great *hakim* who had jour-
neyed many miles over land and sea to meet a man whose status was, to the Kurds, simply that of another tribal leader. In his
own mind, Dr. Grant had come not to pick sides in a quarrel
but to make personal friendships and advance the cause of his
mission. He apparently did not realize that for the residents of
Hakkari, political neutrality was like Beluga caviar: even if they'd
known what it was, they still could not have afforded it. In a
country where strife was endemic and only "my enemy's enemy" a friend, Grant's very arrival, whether he liked it or not,
made a powerful political statement.

Asahel Grant stayed five weeks with the patriarch Mar
Shimun in Kochanes. Besides the usual hours seeing patients,
both Kurds and Nestorians, he spent this time in study. Little
was known then about the Church of the East, and by talking
to people, visiting nearby villages, and making notes, Grant tried
to gather as much information as he could. Here Thomas Laurie, paraphrasing Grant, makes a curious point about the
Nestorians' organization.

> Their form of church government is hierarchical; and yet, there
> being no word in Syriac for *bishop*, they had to borrow
> *episcopos*, as well as *patriarch, catholicos*, &c., from the Greek.
> This is more worthy of note, as their language was spoken in
> Palestine in the time of our Saviour, and their Scriptures trans-
> lated in the beginning of the second century everywhere ren-
> der e*piscopos* (translated *bishop* in English) by the word *pres-
> byter*, or *priest*.

To a modern reader this digression might seem irrelevant,
but such theological disputes were important to *presbyterians*
like Laurie and Grant; they were disputes that would bear
directly on missionary troubles to come. In this aside Laurie
is talking about the doctrine of apostolic succession, the idea
that the divine grace of Jesus Christ was bequeathed to his

apostles, and that these apostles, in turn, passed on that power to the bishops of the church. Thus, according to this principle, it is the bishops (and the pope, remember, is the Bishop of Rome) who rightfully speak with the authority of Jesus Christ, not the presbyteries and congregations of the "Dissenters." Thomas Laurie is taking the opportunity to dispute this. He is saying, "Look, among these people who speak the language of Jesus, there is not even a word for bishop." Thus, he implies, how can these bishops arrogate to themselves *alone* the authority of Jesus Christ? Dr. Grant, in *The Nestorians,* makes the same argument, and he points out that with the exception of the Jelu tribe, there were no bishops among the independent mountain Nestorians. There were, however, many bishops among the Nestorians of the Urmia basin, and the Church of the East had ordained bishops from its earliest beginnings. It is a small point of linguistics and doctrine, about which many disputatious volumes have been written, but one which would have profound consequences in the next four years.

Kochanes was "Rome" for the Church of the East, yet no place could have differed more from the Vatican and its splendors. Mar Shimun's robes, as he have seen, were far from papal. Instead of a scepter, the patriarch carried a rifle when he went out, a precaution not against human enemies, but against the bears and wolves in the hills. Each Mar Shimun, having inherited the title from an uncle, was expected to remain celibate, and he in turn would pass the patriarchate to a nephew when he died. Thus he lived a life shorn of luxuries, with the eternal worry of politics as his preordained fate. Grant writes: "[Mar Shimun's] income is moderate, and he lives in a plain, patriarchal style. Two brothers, and a younger sister about twenty-two years of age, with five or six servants, male and female, comprise his household. As the patriarchs never marry, his domestic affairs were managed by his favourite sister, who supplied our table in the best and neatest style."

After the patriarch's sisters had married, one of these would become the mother of the new patriarch. A priest in Syria describes the tradition.

> As soon as the sister of the actual patriarach realizes she is pregnant, she dedicates herself to God. This means that she stops drinking wine or other alcoholic beverages. In addition, as on a conventional fast, she never eats meat or fat. When the child is born, assuming it is a male, he is dedicated to God, and he abstains from eating meat and fat. When he becomes twenty years old, he is consecrated as Bishop, and as soon as the patriarch is dead he is nominated in his place.

The friendship between Grant and the Nestorians prospered during those five exhilarating weeks. The doctor's warmth and energy, his zeal and kindness—the sheer novelty of his presence—no doubt had their effect. As with Judith in Urmia, it seems unlikely that the people of Kochanes had ever seen anyone like him. His plans must have seemed a revelation: schools, learning, medical care, a revival of the Nestorians' ancient glory. Something new in their world! Both parties looked forward to great things. The mountaineers, Grant later reported to his superiors in America, "eagerly drank of the encouragements I presented." And no wonder. One can imagine the American, his eyes shining in the firelight, weaving a spell with his tale of the future, which he saw as a march toward spiritual rebirth: a renewal of the Nestorian church along evangelical lines, an explosion of piety amidst the crags. Raised in the abundance of North America, suffused with Protestant righteousness, he scorned earthly goods and dreamt of the same mountain-rimmed Jerusalem that he had espied from the pass above Lezan.

But these mountain villagers could not afford such spiritual sweetmeats. If they welcomed this kindly man, with his effusive talk of schools and medical care, they did so for sensible reasons. In Urmia the missionaries hired teachers and assistants, as well as artisans to build their homes and schools. These people were paid with real money, and except for the post-1837 cutbacks, their number had grown steadily since 1835. The residents of Hakkari no doubt hoped for similar opportunities. Moreover, the doctor came from an unknown country, a great "English" land to the West which could someday swing the balance of power in their favor. For the patriarch this hope exceeded all others. But in a land where avalanches thundered down in winter, and summer brought a constant need for vigilance, spiritual regeneration was surely not high on the list of priorities. As for religion, the Nestorians took it as it came. They saw no reason to question their church and its traditions. Indeed, had they read the missionaries' letters home, with their scandalized disapproval of the Nestorian church and its "corruption," they would surely have been baffled at best. The church's rituals annotated their days; its words defined who they were. For well over a millennium it had served them adequately. If their priests chanted the liturgy in a language that no one understood, as they had always done, what possible difference could that make? After all, did the Kurds understand their Arabic prayers ? Of course the Nestorians grew grapes and made wine out of them—or rather, at God's command, the grape juice made itself into wine. And if the priests got drunk occasionally, what of it? What did God make the wine for, if not to drink? What these people craved was life, not moral censure. Thus, in this classic confrontation, foreigner and native each saw in the other the reflection of his own desires.

Yet if any knowledge of this dissonance marred his sojourn in Kochanes, Grant does not say. All thoughts of Judith, his children, and his illnesses seem banished. Soon November had passed away, and winter was enrobing the peaks. One way or other, he had to leave. Grant considered retracing his steps to Mosul; this might have appeared the most prudent course but it would have been arduous, as well as cowardly. And Dr. Grant wanted to return to Urmia as quickly as possible. He had come to clear the way for schools and stations, to lay a foundation for missionaries unborn. To build that future he had to deal with reality; and reality meant the Kurd Nurullah, emir of Hakkari.

Such a meeting was inevitable: Grant could not avoid consorting with killers, no matter where he turned. Nurullah is always labeled "the murderer of Schultz," both in Grant and Laurie's accounts as well as those of English travelers, and there is no doubt that as the lord of Hakkari he bore the ultimate responsibility. Yet strangely enough, the person consistently named as the Macbeth who actually planned the deed, enlisted the roadside assassins, and rode with them to carry it out, was none other than Mar Shimun's closest friend among the Kurds, Nurullah's deputy ruler or *mutesellim,* Suleiman Bey. Already Grant had spent five weeks within sight of this man's summer castle. Normally Suleiman lived at Julamerk, probably because it had been the home of his father, the late emir, while his uncle Nurullah dwelt in another castle at Başkale, further northeast along the Zab. It is odd that Nurullah is branded a murderer, while Suleiman's culpability is mentioned only in passing.

Witness the encounter described by Austen Henry Layard during his visit to Hakkari in the summer of 1846. We have already seen him giving out quinine and tartar emetic for the malaria-stricken garrison at Amadiyah. Later, amid rumors of war and after finding evidence of unspeakable horrors in Lezan, Layard had reached the towering mountains of Jelu and was approaching Julamerk. There in a high, desolate canyon he records the following incident.

> All signs of cultivation now ceased. Mountains rose on all sides, barren and treeless. Huge rocks hung over the road, or towered above us. . . . The savage nature of the place was heightened by its solitude.

Soon Layard and his party met a shepherd boy, who was dragging a sheep that had been killed by bears, and beyond that they found the stinking carcass of a bullock that had also fallen victim to bears.

We were steadily making our way over the loose stones and slippery rocks, when a party of horsemen were seen coming towards us. They were Kurds, and I ordered my party to keep close together, that we might be ready to meet them in case of necessity. As they were picking their way over the rough ground like ourselves, to the evident risk of their horses' necks as well as their own, I had time to examine them fully as they drew near. In front, on a small, lean, and jaded horse, rode a tall gaunt figure, dressed in all the tawdry garments sanctioned by Kurdish taste. A turban of wonderful capacity, and almost taking within its dimensions horse and rider, buried his head, which seemed to escape by a miracle being driven in between his shoulders by the enormous pressure. From the centre of this mass of many-colored rags rose a high conical cap of white felt. This load appeared to give an unsteady rolling gait to the thin carcase below, which could with difficulty support it. A most capacious pair of claret-coloured trowsers bulged out from the sides of the horse, and well nigh stretched from side to side of the ravine. Every shade of red and yellow was displayed in his embroidered jacket and cloak; and in his girdle were weapons of extraordinary size, and most fanciful workmanship. His eyes were dark and piercing, and overshadowed by shaggy eyebrows; his nose aquiline, his cheeks hollow, his face long, and his beard black and bushy. Notwithstanding the ferocity of his countenance, and its unmistakeable expression of villainy, it would have been difficult to repress a smile at the absurdity of the figure, and the disparity between it and the miserable animal concealed beneath . . . .This was a Kurdish dignitary of the first rank; a man well-known for deeds of oppression and blood; the Mutesellim, or Lieutenant-Governor under Nur-Ullah Bey, the Chief of Hakkiari.

This mountain chieftain was Nurullah's nephew and deputy ruler, Suleiman Bey. If in 1839, Suleiman had been kindly disposed to non-Kurds, by 1846, he seems to have felt that way no longer. The *mutesellim* greeted Layard with barely a nod and a grunt, as the two parties brushed past each other in the narrow canyon. The Englishman's party rode on, and had gone only a short distance when one of the Kurds came back and called three of Layard's companions to parley. When the three men returned, they were terrified, especially a man from Asheetha named Yakoub.

> The Mutesellim, he said, had used violent threats; declaring that as Nur-Ullah Bey had served one infidel who had come to spy out the country, and teach the Turks its mines, alluding to Schultz, so he would serve me; and had sent off a man to the Hakkiari chief to apprise him of my presence in the mountains.

Thus, seventeen years after Schultz's death, Suleiman was still boasting about Shultz's murder and its cause, the danger to its mineral mines. It should be noted that to this day no exploitable minerals of any importance have been found in Hakkari, and, despite its spectacular scenery, it continues to be the poorest of all Turkish provinces. In this drama Suleiman Bey seems to fill perfectly the role of Evil Henchman. Layard took his threats seriously, and after a clever act of deception left at dawn the next day for Mosul. That was in 1846, but in December 1839, Asahel Grant could not turn back.

The doctor does not tell us the exact day on which he left Kochanes; but as December 1, 1839, fell on the Sabbath, he must have left on or about Monday, the next day. Mar Shimun's sister packed food for his journey and gave him a pair of goat-hair mittens she had knitted. From the patriarch he received a pair of silk-trimmed *shalvar,* the voluminous pantaloons worn by everyone in the mountains. Last, and most wondrous of the gifts, Grant received from Mar Shimun a copy of the Gospels some 740 years old, hand-copied on parchment in antique Syriac characters. "A thousand blessings were invoked upon my head," Grant says, "and ardent wishes were expressed that I might return with associates." It was the high-water mark of their friendship.

Grant was well aware of the dangers that lay ahead, and he would gladly have avoided Nurullah had that been possible. But he knew that making a favorable impression on the emir would go a long way toward securing a place for the missionaries. And he had come prepared, bearing letters of introduction from Turkish and Persian officials. Grant emphasizes the precautions he had taken. He traveled light, with gold coins secreted in a roll of blister salve. He visited no mines, made no measurements, and gathered no specimens. Whenever he took a compass bearing, he did it unobserved. "Learning that Schultz had fallen a victim to the jealousy and cupidity of the Kurds," he writes, "I took special care not to awaken these dominant passions of a semi-barbarous people."

Grant tells us that Başkale was almost two days distant from Kochanes, but he seems to have made the trip in less time than that. There were alarming rumors of bandits on the road as the doctor made his way along the banks of the Zab. At length he spied the "strongly-fortified castle" of Nurullah Bey, high above the village of Başkale. Nurullah was not well.

> Most unexpectedly I found the chief upon a sickbed. He had taken a violent cold about three days before my arrival, which had brought on inflammation and fever. I gave him medicine, and bled him, and then retired to my lodgings in the town, at the foot of the mountain on which the castle was built.

It's not always possible to guess the exact nature of 19th-century diseases, but in this case it seems likely that Nurullah was suffering from flu or a really bad cold virus. No matter: the doctor's lancet was at hand, as was his medicine chest. How much blood did the emir of Hakkari give to cure his cold? No more, we can assume, than a bowl or two. And the medicine dispensed by Dr. Grant? Perhaps a remedy like Dover's powder—ipecac and opium—or calomel. One can only guess.

By evening Nurullah was no better, and word came down from the castle that the emir demanded relief immediately. Grant sent back a message telling him to have patience and let the medicine do its work. Then for hours he heard nothing, but just before midnight Nurullah's messenger came again. The emir's sickness raged on, and he wanted the doctor now.

What happened next was a signal event in the saga of Asahel Grant. He faced a situation pregnant with drama and peril and with far-reaching implications. He had no choice but to obey the call, so with the emir's messenger leading the way, he immediately set out on the long ascent to the castle. The fear in his heart must have been great; but, he says, though he lay at the mercy of Nurullah Bey, he felt "under the guardian care of One who had the hearts of kings in his keeping." Religious faith had brought him to this far corner of the earth, and there was no reason why it should fail him now. Still, he was alone and friendless in a stony land. The only protection he carried was quackery incarnate, alchemy in modern garb, potions with the power of myth.

Grant does not exaggerate when he describes a "long winding pathway" leading up to Nurullah's castle. No place in Başkale stands on level ground. It covers a bare mountainside overlooking the broad valley of the Zab, and today when southbound travelers enter the town they are descending from an 8000-foot pass. Onward roll the trucks and buses, past the dusty hovels and rocky creekbeds posing as streets, and when they leave, the river still lies 4000 feet below. At the dawn of the 21st century its population, swollen with refugees, exceeds 12,000. In 1839 it may have reached 500, and the town was, like Amadiyah, a center for Jewish merchants and artisans. It was just north of here that Layard, in 1849, encountered his tribe of Jewish nomads.

Başkale, according to Freya Stark, boasts of being the highest sub-province in Turkey, with an elevation over 7000 feet.

At that altitude, on a December midnight, a bitter chill had surely taken hold. Perhaps, too, the pariah dogs of Başkale were howling. Grant does not say whether the Kurd lit their way with a torch, but it is certain that otherwise the town would have lain in total darkness, black shapes on a black mountain over a lightless abyss. Even if somewhere a candle glowed, Grant would not have seen it, for the dwellings of Kurdistan were windowless. We can assume that a few dung fires smoldered, and a whiff of their smoke no doubt came to him along with the smell of raw goat hair from his new mittens. As Grant approached the castle,

> The sentinels upon the ramparts were sounding the watch-cry in the rough tones of their native Koordish. We entered the outer court through wide, iron-cased folding doors. A second iron door opened into a long dark alley, which conducted to the room where the chief was lying. It was evident that he was becoming impatient; and, as I looked upon the swords, pistols, guns, spears, and daggers—the ordinary furniture of a Kurdish castle—which hung around the walls of the room, I could not but think of the fate of the unfortunate Shultz, who had fallen, as it is said, by the orders of this sanguinary chief.

With a "fervent aspiration" for God's guidance and blessing, Grant began his task. The fact that the doctor was dressed in Kurdish style, with a thick beard as befitted a *hakim* no doubt helped, as did the fact that he could speak to the emir in Turkish, the *lingua franca* of the country. After examining Nurullah, Grant told him that the medicine was producing "a good effect," and he could, if the emir desired, administer more palliatives. However, in his judgment the patient needed a more powerful medicine, one which in the short run would make him feel a lot worse before he got better. It's hard to think of a

bedside strategy more common than this. People have always
expected to be tortured by doctors "for their own good," and
this Kurd was certainly no different. Grant's advice, his decision to prescribe a stronger potion, brings us squarely into the
mainstream of 19th-century medicine. That morning Grant had
taken blood from Nurullah Bey, then tried a gentler medicine,
probably one which contained opium, like Dover's powder or
laudanum. It now became obvious that the emir's body needed
a greater, more brutal jolt. For a bad cold, Grant reached into
his medical bag and resorted to the ultimate in modern therapy:
he made the patient throw up.

Nurullah assented to the doctor's advice. Grant gave him
"an emetic," no doubt the same tartar emetic so universally
popular among his colleagues. Nurullah, ever vigilant, first told
his aides to taste the nauseating drug before he drank it. The
doctor stayed with his patient through the night, and in the
morning Nurullah felt, *mirabile dictu,* considerably better. And
no wonder. With his system purged and spirit drained by con-
vulsive vomiting, the man had no doubt fallen into the deepest
of sleeps. Nothing, of course, could have been better for him.
Macbeth, another troubled ruler given to bloody deeds, might
have told him about the benefits of slumber, as could any mother
with an ounce of common sense. Nurullah pronounced himself
cured, and thanked the doctor profusely.

> He rapidly recovered, and said he owed his life to my care. I
> became his greatest favourite. I must sit by his side, and dip
> my hand in the same dish with himself. I must remain with
> him, or speedily return and take up my abode in his country,
> where he assured me I should have everything as I pleased.

After a harrowing climb and an anxious night, the doctor's
prospects had changed utterly. The Murderer of Schultz had
emerged from the shadows, and in the light of day he seemed

almost human. Now, having "cured" this all-important patient, Grant could contemplate a future of school-building, healing, and "everything as I pleased." The revival of piety and missionary spirit in the mountains had taken a giant step forward.

Grant stayed an extra day with the emir, no doubt taking the opportunity to treat the sick of Başkale. Nurullah, he says, was greatly amused by his tale of a Kurdish woman, blinded by trachoma, whose scar tissue Grant had removed during his stay in Kochanes. The woman, removing her bandages too soon, had so frightened herself with her newly-regained eyesight that she resolved ever after to obey the doctor's orders. Nurullah enjoyed a good laugh at the woman's expense. He repeated this tale endlessly to his courtiers, says Grant, and to the American's medical skill he paid lavish compliments that were "too Oriental to repeat."

By the end of his stay the now affable emir and his doctor were on such friendly terms that before he left Grant received a horse as a token of Nurullah's esteem. Nurullah, in his thirties, was "a man of noble bearing," Grant declares, with a "fine, open countenance." Thomas Laurie repeats his friend's description, but with a caution. "The emir," he writes, "is a man of noble mien. His figure is commanding, and his countenance manly, when not darkened by suspicion and jealousy."

In the end, the new friendship of Nurullah Bey and Dr. Grant seems as evanescent as manna on the leaf. Having effected a "cure," Asahel Grant now found himself bound in friendship with a man whose rival, Mar Shimun, had welcomed him in his home for five weeks before this. The potential for conflict is obvious, and this rivalry doesn't come close to completing the picture of intrigue. In Mosul, to the south, and Erzurum, to the north, the Ottoman pashas were under standing orders to extend Turkish power into the mountains. The Kurdish emir of Amadiyah, having lost his home to the Turks, was plotting to regain that stronghold. Bedr Khan Bey, already the lord of Bohtan to the west of Hakkari, was taking every advantage of the Turks' weakness after the Battle of Nizib to expand his territory. And, as always, it is impossible to overemphasize the specter of Russia, looming in Azerbaijan and Trans-Caucasia. Asahel Grant, walking untouched through this volcanic landscape, had found a friend, a man of "noble mien," keeping watch over his own personal caldera. For good or ill, the friendship was a fact.

9

THE ARMS OF URMIA

Clouds hang in bunches
Over the heads of the snowy mountains.
Would you let down your hair for me?
Would you weep tears for me?

— Yunus Emre (1238–1320?)

ON DECEMBER 7, 1839, after an absence of eight months, Asahel Grant returned to Urmia. "For half a year," writes Thomas Laurie, "he had not seen a chair, and had long dispensed with knives and forks." More importantly, he could once again speak English. So changed was he in appearance, Laurie declares, especially in his Kurdish clothes, that the *hakim sahib* was not at first recognized by the mission servants. The final miles had passed easily on horseback. From Başkale he had joined a small caravan that crossed the headwaters of the Zab enroute to the plain of Salmas in Persia, and from there rode south to Urmia. The journey from Başkale took two days, over the same route that he would have taken into Hakkari had not the Prudential Committee commanded the long detour through Constantinople. Still, through blizzard, murder, and riot, he had triumphed. "In all the perils through which I had passed," he wrote, "the angel of the Lord had encamped round about me for my deliverance." Only the presence of Judith, his "dearest earthly friend," could have made the homecoming sweeter.

Letters now began to pour from him, first to his superiors in Constantinople and Boston, then to his close relatives in New York. To the American Board he continued to press the cause of the Mountain Nestorians. Their patriarch Mar Shimun, he told them, had welcomed him with open arms. The people were uniformly hospitable and receptive to his plans. Even Nurullah Bey had promised full cooperation. Everywhere Grant saw opportunities: schools to be built, medical work to be done, souls aching for Jesus. To the Prudential Committee he pleaded for more missionaries to aid him in the task.

His mother, brother, and sons received even better news. While he was traveling in Mesopotamia, Grant had received permission from the Board to return to America with his motherless children, to find homes for them there and provide for their future. He could not stay long: God's work still played the most important part in his future, and for now his children would have to be left behind in the care of others. But as soon as winter had passed from the mountains, Grant, his son Henry Martyn, aged four, and the twin baby girls, Mary Electa and Judith Sabrina Grant, would enter upon the long journey to Trebizond, Constantinople, Smyrna, and Boston.

Of the twin girls we hear little. They were then some sixteen months old, having been born on August 24 of the previous year. Judith Grant had almost died giving birth to them, and, as Dr. Grant wrote to his brother Ira, "My dear wife lay for many days on the borders of the grave." That delivery and the long recovery which it entailed, combined with subsequent illnesses, led to her death five months later. When Grant returned, the twins and young Henry were healthy and thriving. Dr. Grant promised his sons in New York that they would soon be introduced to the "cheerful prattle" of their baby sisters.

For Grant, as we have noted, the year 1839 was overflow-ing with peril and bracketed with death. Now as 1840 began, the Urmia plain stretched out its feverish arms and claimed two more victims. No one with the least knowledge of the 19th cen-tury and its rate of childhood mortality will be surprised at what happened. Terrible diseases ran riot: scarlet fever, whooping cough, diphtheria, influenza, to name a few. The death of any child is poignant, but the loss of the twin daughters of Asahel and Judith Grant evoke a special sorrow; they died so far away from their New England home, at the age of seventeen months. Within two weeks, on January 13 and 25, 1840, first Mary Electa and then Judith Sabrina went to her tiny grave, Mary dying from influenza and Judith from measles.

Asahel Grant was far from alone in his sorrow. Indeed, no one can look upon those thirteen months in Urmia, from Judith's death in January, 1839, through February of 1840, without some feeling of shock at the steady onslaught of grief. After the birth of her twin girls in August, 1838, her subsequent illness and loss of sight in one eye, Judith Grant, writes Justin Perkins, seemed to prepare herself for death. When the final fever at-tacked, she knew immediately that it would be the end. Her loss, so devastating to the mission, was only the beginning. By then the population in the mission compound had grown. After the Grants and the Perkinses, other couples had taken the cara-van route from Trebizond to Urmia. New names—Rev. and Mrs. Albert Holladay, Rev. and Mrs. W.R. Stocking—appear on the mission rolls; and more would soon follow. In their black clothes and fervent piety, these people might seem old to us, as if they had leapt from childhood directly into middle age. Yet all—especially the women—were very young, and all newlyweds, and they immediately began to have children. Just as quickly, those children began to die.

The American mission cemetery on Mt. Seir, near Urumiyeh, Iran, contains fifty-nine gravesites, the last of which was dug in

1931. In these are forty-one children, most of whom did not live past the age of three. All families suffered in some measure, yet for stark, unrelenting desolation, Justin and Charlotte Perkins stand alone. They had come first, utterly friendless, with Charlotte traveling the rough caravan routes in the late stages of pregnancy. Of the first families, they stayed longer than anyone, and their losses seem beyond endurance. Charlotte's first baby, Charlotte Nisbet, had already been buried in Tabriz when, with the Grants, the Perkinses made the move to Urmia. Their second child, William Riach, named after the Scottish doctor in Tabriz, was born in Urmia on April 14, 1836. Another son, Justin, came just before the Grant twins in August, 1838. Eleven months later, Asahel Grant was in Mardin hiding from the mob when he heard that the Perkinses had been forced to drink again from "the cup of affliction." Justin died a few days short of his first birthday, on July 23, 1839. Charlotte had now buried two of her three children. By January 25, Mary Electa and Judith Sabrina Grant were gone. Charles Stocking, eighteen months old, the son of William and Jerusha Stocking, expired six days after Judith Sabrina. Catharine Holladay, nineteen months, departed on February 2. Charlotte Perkins had become pregnant with a fourth child when, only five days after little Catharine, the death of little William, aged three years and ten months, left her childless again.

In six and a half months, six children of the Urmia mission had died, five of them within the span of a month. "Our houses," wrote Justin Perkins, "are now left to us desolate." Only Henry Martyn Grant and one baby, Harriet Stocking, aged one month, remained alive, and by March 1842, Harriet too had gone to her grave. For a time Charlotte Perkins had better luck. The daughter born on August 8 she named Judith Grant, after both her mother and the woman so beloved in Urmia. In December of the following year, Charlotte delivered another son, Henry Martyn, named like Dr. Grant's son after the famous pioneer missionary. Both of these babies survived the critical period of infancy, and when their parents returned to the United States on home leave in 1842, they were in good health. From 1846 to 1849, the curse of the Urmia plain descended again. Two more babies were born; two more died, neither lived past eleven months. As the 1850s began, Charlotte Perkins, age thirty-eight, had borne seven children. Only two were left alive.

Grant does not mention the twins' death in *The Nestorians*, and refers to Judith's death only in passing. That is understandable. He had written his book, after all, for posterity and the missionary cause, not to reveal his personal tragedies. Even in his letters home, the doctor allows only a spasm of sorrow to escape before he wraps his feelings in words of faith. "No language can express," he tells his brother Ira, "the agony of soul that comes over me at times." But never once does he waver. God's will was done; the dead have "fallen asleep in Jesus" or "gone to a better place." They have, in the words of Judith's brother, the Rev. A.C. Lathrop, "suffered the great and last change in the dissolution of the clay tenement." By January of 1840 Grant had lost his first wife Electa; his father, who died while Asahel and Judith were enroute to Urmia; three sisters, two brothers; his second wife Judith, and his children Mary Electa and Judith Sabrina.

Now Grant seems to have realized that he must bring his youngest son home to save the boy's life. Death, he knew, could strike in an instant. To his son Seth Hastings, he wrote, "Yes, if God spares us all another year I hope we shall meet face to face, and spend many happy hours together." To his mother, in February, after telling her of his impending visit: "Should I not live to see you accept my cordial, my warmest thanks for your kindness . . . May kind Heaven reward you for all you have done and suffered on my account." If ever a person lived as if each day might be his last, Asahel Grant would be that person.

In Urmia, meanwhile, despite death and the continuing U.S. economic depression, Yankee energy remained unabated. Justin

Perkins, with the help of Nestorian assistants, had immersed himself in the study of Syriac and was working late into the night on his translation of the Bible into the vernacular. More schools were opening, more teachers employed, more buildings erected. Asahel Grant's replacement, Rev. Austin H. Wright, M.D., was already enroute to Persia. In America a printing press, specially cast in small pieces for delivery by horses, had been purchased for the mission. Its arrival was expected later in the year.

That winter two of Mar Shimun's brothers visited Urmia and, says Grant, "urged the extension of our labours through all parts of their country." For Asahel Grant, words like these could only stir the fire within. Despite his personal losses, he was working at a peak of emotion. "We must," he wrote the American Board, "without fear enter their mountain fastnesses, pour the light of life around their pathways, arouse and direct their dormant or perverted energies, and under the Captain of our Salvation lead them forth to conquest and to victory." Here we see the gap between Presbyterian dream and Nestorian reality. The Hakkari Christians, like their Kurdish neighbors, had developed a centuries-old distinctive culture. Could their energies fairly be called "dormant" and "perverted"? But we must remember that we are dealing here with English-speaking people at the very apex of cultural self-confidence, people who believed implicitly in their civilizing mission and its Godly power. And when they strove to heal the sick and to open schools, for girls as well as boys—how can they be faulted? In 1840 Asahel Grant knew absolutely that he was on the road to Glory.

Besides sending his brothers to visit Urmia, Mar Shimun himself wrote a cordial letter filled with flattering phrases: "My heart went with you, O *hakim*, in the day you went from me," and "You and I are one; and there is no change touching the things you heard from me." Grant had no intention of letting this friendship lapse, and "I therefore resolved to pass through the regions of Central Koordistan and revisit the patriarch, and proceed thence on my route towards my native land." Even with the imperative need to deliver his youngest son to safety, Dr. Grant could not resist a detour through the mountains. He would set out for America late in the spring.

In Constantinople, meanwhile, a new sultan and a moribund polity were fighting to stay alive. The Ottoman Empire had fallen among thieves—Mohammed Ali of Egypt and his son Ibrahim Pasha had conquered all of Syria and in every battle smashed the sultan's incompetent, European-style army. The calamity at Nizib the previous June had been bad enough, but when the commander of the sultan's navy stole the entire Ottoman fleet and sailed off to Alexandria, Ottoman fortunes could not have sunk lower. This fleet had been Sultan Mahmud's pride and joy. During the 1830s, at the Ottoman shipyard on the Golden Horn, two American naval architects, Henry Eckford and Foster Rhodes, had built it from scratch using American shipwrights and Greek, Italian, and Turkish workers—with loads of timber from the New World. After these twin calamities and Mahmud's death in July 1839, it seemed almost that the Empire could have been taken over by a company of Cossacks.

The Russians, massed on Turkey's borders, waited cheerfully for the Ottoman government to implode. In Trans-Caucasia and Central Asia the tsarist juggernaut rolled on. The Kingdom of Georgia had been absorbed, as had the Khanate of Erivan— now the Republic of Armenia. In 1828 Russian armies had held Gümüşhane and Urmia, each a day away from Trebizond and Hakkari, respectively. In that year, in the Treaty of Turkmenchai that ended the war with Persia, the shah ceded to the Russians all of Azerbaijan north of the Araxes River, which remains to this day the northern border of Iran. Only in the Caucasus, where the Muslim leader Shamyl continued to elude them, were the Russians temporarily stymied.

Luckily for the Turks, the British held India and could be counted upon as an adversary of the Russians. The tsar's forces had to be kept away from India, and would on no account be allowed to take over Constantinople and the Straits. It became official British policy to preserve and strengthen the Ottoman Empire as a counterweight to the Russians. Mohammed Ali's Egyptian armies in Syria had to be stopped from further aggressive moves by the prompt assertion of European power. After the Nizib catastrophe, Britain, France, Russia, and Austria threatened the Egyptian ruler with immediate action if his forces were to move further north into Anatolia. Mohammed Ali had no choice but to comply. At that point the diplomats of Europe took over, and a year of bargaining began. In the spring of 1840, the parties were nowhere near a settlement.

For the preservation of the empire, the consensus among the European powers was that reforms had to continue. The new sultan, Mahmud's son Abdul Mejid, might have been expected to cave in to reactionaries and declare the reform process dead. He was saved, however, by the timely arrival of Mohammed Reshid Pasha, a leading reformer, who returned from a diplomatic post in Europe and helped Abdul Mejid to prevail against the enemies of progress. Reshid now became Ottoman Foreign Minister. On November 3, 1839, while Asahel Grant was staying in Kochanes with Mar Shimun, Reshid Pasha, speaking in the name of his sultan, stepped before a crowd of assembled dignitaries, including the entire diplomatic corps of Constantinople, and read out what has come to be regarded as one of the defining documents of the Tanzimat, or reform period, in Ottoman Turkish history. This took place outside the Topkapi Palace in Gülhane Square; thus, the document which Reshid Pasha read has come to be known as *Gülhane Hatt-i Sherifi*; or, the Noble Edict of the Rose Garden.

For those who believed in progress and centralization, the Edict made good reading. The sultan's subjects received guarantees of their lives, property, and honor. Instead of the old system of "tax-farming," where the right to collect taxes was sold to local lords, a new regime of centralized, uniform taxation was to be imposed. These taxes would support the expansion of the army, for which a new empire-wide system of conscription would be enacted. Last, the document proclaimed the principle of equality before the law for all Ottoman citizens, no matter what their religion.

In the main, these words were meant for Lord Ponsonby, the British ambassador. The Turks desperately needed Britain's support against Mohammed Ali, and Britain needed some sign of reform as their price for that support. Of course, no document, especially one so reluctantly pried from its promulgators, ever delivers as much as its audience hopes. The liberal ideals of equality and personal liberty couldn't have meant much in a government where for centuries the sultan's bureaucrats and officials had been slaves. But the Noble Edict of the Rose Garden was, at least, a start. More important than vague liberal promises were the new systems of taxation and conscription. These demonstrated the continuation and expansion of Mahmud II's efforts to gain control of his empire. The inspection of internal passports, which had surprised Asahel Grant when he left Mosul the previous October, would become far more common in the future; the Ottoman bureaucracy was about to explode in size; and the centralizers' push into the far reaches of the empire would have profound consequences, especially for Hakkari.

It is not surprising that Asahel Grant gives little indication that he heard about the Noble Edict. Current information did not flash beacon-like across the Ottoman lands. Not only were there no railroads, there were no *wagon* roads, and the telegraph did not arrive until 1855. The empire's first newspaper, a weekly sheet of government notices written in Ottoman Turkish, a flowery court language few could read, had begun publication only nine years before. The first private Turkish newspaper, founded by an Englishman, William Churchill, came out later in 1840. Yet despite obstacles, the news eventually reached Urmia. The missionaries maintained a voluminous correspondence, which included regular advisories from their brethren in Constantinople.

If Grant gives little account of current events, perhaps it was because they seemed of small importance at the time. Or maybe he ignored them. In his travel memoir of 1839, for example, the battle of Nizib seems no more significant than a skirmish in Afghanistan. It is an offstage distraction, a violent event that made the roads too dangerous for travel but otherwise had no impact on his life. Through this turmoil Grant walked unconcerned, focused upon other-worldly goals, although not unaware of the brewing storms. "Wars and rumours of wars;" he wrote to colleagues in May 1840, "but *be not troubled,—* GOD *reigns."* Yet he could only be dismissive for so long. The battle of Nizib, the weakness which it exposed, and the efforts to keep the empire intact would have profound consequences for the doctor and the people he had come to serve.

Grant's journey homeward began on May 7, 1840, with little Henry riding in the saddle beside him. From Salmas, two of Mar Shimun's brothers and a group of Hakkari Nestorians joined the party as they turned west toward Turkish territory. Even in May, freezing temperatures came upon them as they climbed the pass leading from the plain of Salmas into Turkish territory. Nightfall caught the travelers on the mountainside, and on that first night out of Salmas they were forced to camp in the open under heaps of carpeting provided by Mar Shimun's brothers. These mountains, still wild and dangerous, have in our own time claimed the lives of Afghan and Iranian refugees, among others. The route has become a favorite for people-smugglers and those seeking asylum in the West.

Though the road along the Zab was blocked in many places by the remains of avalanches, on the evening of May 10, Grant reached Julamerk, where Mar Shimun was staying with Suleiman Bey. Thomas Laurie, concluding with the inevitable Bunyanesque metaphor, describes the scene:

The ascent from the river to Julamerk is truly grand. The road climbs in a zig-zag line up the face of the mountain, till the traveler looks down almost perpendicularly one thousand feet. The roar of the waters rises from below, re'choed by the snow-capped mountains round about; while the castle, from its lower eminence, looks sternly down the ravine, reminding the way-farer how much the violence of man adds to the natural diffi-culties of his rugged path.

At the castle of Julamerk, Grant's reception could not have been more cordial. According to Laurie, Suleiman Bey, having headed the party that murdered Schultz, "now seemed, by spe-cial kindness to him, endeavoring to blot out the memory of that deed of blood." In truth, as a friend Grant received typical Kurdish hospitality, no doubt aided by the presence of his young son, Henry Martyn, who by then could speak Turkish and Syriac, in addition to English. The boy became a "great favorite" of the mothers of both Suleiman Bey and the patriarch Mar Shimun. They were struck too at Grant's appearance: he had abandoned the turban and flowing robes that he had worn on his first visit. His beard he retained, but the "Frank clothes" he now wore made him look considerably diminished in stature. They did the same for Suleiman, who borrowed them to wear before the highly amused ladies of his harem. In all it was a most success-ful visit, with both Mar Shimun and Suleiman the Kurdish *mutesellim* urging Dr. Grant to return quickly and begin his work among them.

Only Nurullah, the emir of Hakkari, was missing from this happy group, and his conspicuous absence points to signs of Ottoman encroachment. We have called Nurullah a murderer, but we cannot call him a fool. He knew what was happening around him, and he acted accordingly. Up to this time he had ruled as an independent chief, paying tribute to no one and constrained only by his unruly tribesmen. He disliked the Otto-man government, but he knew that the world was changing. A census of the empire's population, the first ever attempted, had been completed in 1838. The previous year, four English steamboats carrying mail and freight had begun plying the rivers of Mesopotamia, and everywhere else startling novelties—railroads, foreign merchants and missionaries, European machines and ideas, manufactured goods and armaments—were thrusting themselves upon the Ottoman consciousness. The Turks may have been beaten at Nizib and Konya, but they were far from dead. In the 1830s they had reasserted their authority in Baghdad and Mosul, and to the south the holy cities of Mecca and Medina were once again ruled by Ottoman governors. Closer to Nurullah's home, the Turks had soundly defeated Blind Mohammed, the bey of Rowanduz, and they had taken Amadiyah from the sheikh of Berwar. Now, in a development more important than any of these, the English were taking their side against the Russians.

Hakkari had to be next, and Nurullah knew it. That is why in the spring of 1840 the emir made the long trip north to Erzurum to meet with its governor, Hafiz Pasha—the same Circassian ditherer who had commanded the Ottoman forces at Nizib. To Hafiz Pasha the emir made a proposition: he would forfeit his independence and acknowledge the authority of the Ottoman government if they in turn would appoint him governor of Hakkari. Instead of fighting the inevitable, he was trying to control its uncertainties through an alliance with the Turks. The real losers, if the Turks chose not to accommodate him, would be Mar Shimun and his Nestorian tribesmen. Hafiz Pasha had accepted this bargain, and Nurullah, flush with his new powers, was now returning from Erzurum.

Asahel Grant had left Mar Shimun and Suleiman Bey on May 25, and after a rough journey via Başkale, during which he was shown the site of Schultz's murder, reached Van on June 1, 1840. This was his first visit to that city, famous for its great castle, large Armenian population, and extensive gardens, as well as for the lake which bears its name. Lake Van, though not quite as large in surface area as Lake Urmia, is much deeper, and far more beautiful in its mountainous setting than Urmia. In the town where Friedrich Schultz, suspended in a basket, copied the castle's cuneiform inscriptions, Grant met Nurullah Bey, who was enroute to Hakkari, and stayed with him for ten days of rest and interviews.

In Van, Grant concentrated on Nurullah, whom he calls "my old friend," and his moods—as they related to his mission. The Kurd's cordiality, he found, had not waned. "It was gratifying to find him still cherishing the friendly feelings with which he welcomed me," the doctor notes. Then comes a caveat: "but it remains to be seen how valuable his friendship may yet prove." Despite this reservation, Grant viewed Nurullah's new political arrangments positively.

> Changes have occurred which have modified his power, and hereafter the traveller through his heretofore lawless country will have less to fear. It is now placed under Turkish jurisdiction. The chief has bartered his independence for an appointment from the Pasha of Erzeroom; and he was returning, an officer of the Porte, to govern his spirited clans, whom he had found too restless to control by his single arm. He also foresaw that the extension of European influence, and the consequent changes occurring in the East, might at no distant day wrest his independence and his country from him. He therefore deemed it wise to make such voluntary overtures as would enable him to retain his station as the immediate head of the Hakary tribes.

Nurullah appeared to be a benign despot. But the question remained: was he a villain or merely a politician? Or both? Grant does not seem to know what to make of him. At this point in *The Nestorians; or, The Lost Tribes,* Asahel Grant is less than a page from the end of his travel memoir, those 128 pages which form the first half of the book. The last half is a long discourse on the Lost Tribes of Israel and their possible connection with the Nestorians. It is a curious conclusion, this ambiguous meeting with the emir. Dr. Grant summarizes other events in his last page: the overland journey to the Black Sea; the cordial welcome given him by the English residents of Erzurum, and by Lord Ponsonby, the British ambassador in Constantinople; the steamer to Izmir; and the seventy-day voyage to Boston aboard an American merchant ship. But Nurullah remains the great question. Six months' leave in America would not make the answer any easier to come by.

10

COMPETITION

> "The Mother of Abominations and her Puseyite daughter did the Nestorians and their beloved missionary teachers much evil."
> —Rev. A.C. Lathrop, *Memoir of Asahel Grant, M.D.*

IN A DIARY ENTRY FOR December 29, 1842, a 22-year-old New Yorker named George Templeton Strong reported that he had gone that day to "have myself Daguerreotyped." He doesn't say where he went for this primitive photograph, but it shouldn't have been difficult to find a place. By then New York, and indeed the entire East Coast, was well supplied with daguerreotypists, all using the technique which had arrived from France only three years before. The session was "a great bore," Strong reported: "One doesn't know till he has tried how hard it is to sit without moving a muscle for two minutes." To help in this task the daguerreotypist typically used a clamp to hold the subject's head from the rear. Still, Strong wrote, "The portrait of a man staring intently into vacancy and trying desperately to keep still must be unlike his usual appearance."

Strong spoke the truth. Anyone who views these early images tends to see people with the very life sucked out of them. A case in point is the engraving of Asahel Grant, made from a daguerreotype, which forms the frontispiece of Thomas Laurie's biography. In this picture, probably taken toward the end of his stay in America, we see a beardless face, stunned and rigid, an erect military bearing, and a touch of weariness. There is no hint of the charm, energy and vitality for which he was known, nor of the courage and dedication which had impelled him to ride alone into the heart of Kurdistan.

But Grant had good reason to be weary. His health, though improved, still troubled him, and instead of rest and relaxation he found as much work to do in his homeland as in Persia. During his brief stay in America, from October 2, 1840, to April 1, 1841, virtually every letter that the doctor wrote to Rufus Anderson, Secretary of the American Board, was dashed off "in haste." The phrase, in closing, becomes almost a mantra; his words, impeccably spelled yet often illegible, seem to race across the page. Demands upon his time came flying at him. He had to visit his mother and attend to his sons. He was preparing his book for publication at Harper and Brothers, in New York City. There were lectures to give, hands to shake, and meetings with missionary colleagues. On January 18, 1841, he was in Boston as two more couples, Rev. and Mrs. Abel K. Hinsdale and Rev. and Mrs. Colby Mitchell, embarked for the Middle East, enroute to the mountain Nestorians. And all this had to be done during a North American winter, in a country where railroads had only begun to shrink the distances.

Again and again, throughout the short, intense life of Asahel Grant, we see a man over-stretched and over-obligated, a man trying too hard to pay too many debts to too many people. Never was this more obvious than in the first months of 1841. "Concentrated effort is effective effort," Rufus Anderson had written in his Instructions to Justin and Charlotte Perkins in 1833: "There is such a thing as attempting too much." Grant's romantic nature and extreme sense of duty prevented him from accepting this. Most people would agree that his clearest duty was to his sons, and the modern reader finds it painful to consider their predicament. Grant, of course, loved them dearly, and he did everything he could for Henry, Hastings, and Edwin within the limits of his missionary ambition. But the fact is, the three boys needed a father, and it was entirely their father's choice that they did not have one.

Evidence of trouble appeared almost immediately. After arriving in Boston on October 3, 1840, Grant hurried to his home in central New York. In a letter written at Waterville on October 9, Grant summarized for Rufus Anderson the situation as he found it. He had left his sons in the care of a guardian, an older man who had subsequently moved with them to Illinois. There the man had died, and when Grant's younger brother in New York also died, the two boys were left without a home. As Grant's older brother could not take them, Hastings and Edwin ended up with his widowed mother.

For a few months, young Hastings Grant now emerges from the background of his father's life. He was, by his father's account, a "bright and docile" lad, one who wrote "a good hand" and with his younger brother had made "commendable" progress in school. But he was unhappy, and with good reason. Hastings had barely known his mother when she died; he was brought back to Utica very soon thereafter. Then, when he was six, a little boy scarcely old enough for school, he was told that his father had taken a new wife and was leaving home for a foreign country, leaving him and his brother behind. How could he possibly have understood such an action, especially in an era when an ocean voyage meant great peril and almost permanent exile? No doubt Dr. Grant tried to instruct and comfort him; yet all the piety and preaching in New England could not have assuaged the boy's feelings of abandonment, nor could his elderly guardian begin to make up for the loss of a father.

In his letter from Waterville of October 9, Grant gives the embarrassing details. For almost three months, since the 18th of July, Hastings had been missing from his grandmother's farm on Grant Hill. Dr. Grant's brother had followed the boy as far as Buffalo, but after that he had lost all trace of him. Eventually a letter arrived from Illinois, written by the father of Grant's sister's husband. After a journey of six weeks, through what hardships we can only imagine, young Hastings had arrived at the man's home near Peoria. There he was staying until Dr. Grant could make new arrangements for him.

In the letter Grant's chagrin is painfully obvious. "I can not enter into an explanation of this singular & unexpected movement till I see you;" he wrote to Anderson, "but it is quite obvious that he should be brought under my personal influence as soon as possible." Dr. Grant had hoped to be in Boston to prepare the Mitchells and Hindsdales for their coming journey to Mosul, but the discovery of his son's "escape" to Illinois completely upset his plans. "What shall I do?" he asks. He feels an obligation to these missionary couples; he has to be back to "devote the necessary attention to matter [i.e., his book] which I may prepare for the press," but he had parental duties to fulfill.

There are no published letters detailing Dr. Grant's trip to Illinois; and both Thomas Laurie and A.C. Lathrop ignore this episode. Happily, the facts of his son's life lead us to believe that things turned out well enough. S. Hastings Grant married, had children, and grew up to become head of the New York Mercantile Library Association. After a long and productive life, he died in 1910 at the age of 82. But the fact remains that the boy's early years were not his father's finest hour. As late as March 19, less than two weeks before Grant's scheduled return to the East, he had not yet found a permanent home for his eldest son. As subsequent events would show, Hastings was far from resigned to his father's departure. Edwin—and certainly little Henry Martyn—could not have been pleased either. Asahel Grant never failed to provide materially for his sons, and to the end he maintained a correspondence filled with ardent professions of love and admonitions to be good and love Jesus. Yet there can be no doubt that for these three children, the price of one man's altruism was abandonment and heartache.

Writing from New York City on New Year's Day, 1841, Dr. Grant takes note of a new presence in the Hakkari mountains. He begins the letter with a familiar topic, his hopes that he can meet the Hinsdales and Mitchells in Syria and travel with them to Mosul before the "poisonous" winds of summer strike the Syrian desert. To this end, he is working mightily to get his book through the press so that he can leave by March 1 and get to the mountains as soon as possible. If things work out as they should, he says with obvious eagerness, "we might gain nearly a whole year in the occupancy of the field." He continues:

> The importance of such a course must be too obvious to re-
> quire a formal proof. I will only remind you of the late intel-
> ligence from Bagdad and Ooroomia evincing the increasing
> zeal of the Romanists, intrinsic importance of the field, & the
> danger of preoccupancy of the ground by others. I have just
> learned that a notice of Mr. Ainsworth's visit to the patriarch
> has reached this country through the English journals, & that
> he dwells particularly upon friendly disposition of the
> Nestorians towards the English Episcopal Church. Now I have
> no idea that the patriarch comprehends the difference between
> English & Americans, or Independents & Episcopalians, but
> I allude to this feature in Mr. A's report as an index of the
> interest which will be felt in England upon the subject.

With these words, the doctor acknowledges a new reality, a hint of forces that would produce discord and disaster. Until then, both in Europe and America, the mountain Nestorians had been only a rumor. Now with Ainsworth's article, and especially with the approaching publication of Grant's book, this obscurity would yield to "discovery." To Dr. Grant this was personal. An Englishman had visited his friend, Mar Shimun, and the patriarch was, reportedly, well-disposed toward the Anglican Church. The reader can almost feel the quickening of Grant's pulse as he writes of this encroachment upon his territory. For this missionary, within whose breast competitive zeal forever vied with Christian charity, time was now of the essence.

Ainsworth, to whom Grant refers here, was the English surgeon/geologist who, with his translator Christian Rassam, lost his money and equipment at the Battle of Nizib. The two had hoped to penetrate the Hakkari mountains later in the summer of 1839, but in the aftermath of Hafiz Pasha's defeat, they retreated to Stamboul, where they counted up their losses and pleaded with the Royal Geographical Society for more funds. The officers of the RGS, understandably, did not respond with enthusiasm. Eventually, after much correspondence, Ainsworth convinced the RGS to fund his researches in partnership with an Anglican missionary organization, the Society for Promoting Christian Knowledge (SPCK). In January of 1840 Ainsworth and Rassam traveled south to Mosul, to await the melting of the snows and the arrival of replacement instruments from England.

In his *Travels and Researches in Asia Minor, Armenia, and Chaldea* (1842), William Ainsworth tells of their journey, the Expedition to Explore Kurdistan. The RGS got little in the way of data (partly because Ainsworth was forced to leave Mosul before his scientific instruments arrived), and the SPCK received only the most cursory introduction to the Eastern churches. Asahel Grant, for example, had stayed three weeks with Mar Shimun the previous November, learning all he could about the patriarch's church and its people. Ainsworth took less time than that for his entire journey through Hakkari, and his interview with Mar Shimun lasted only eight hours. Moreover, the religious discord he sowed, albeit inadvertently, certainly helped no one. Still, his work remains a trove of information, as his scientist's eye picked up many things that Grant—who deliberately avoided taking notes—did not. Above all, more clearly than anyone else, Ainsworth foresaw the danger that lay ahead.

After his second visit to the mountains, Asahel Grant had left Mar Shimun on May 25, 1840, and made his way north enroute to America. He must have known about Ainsworth's projected journey, because in May he sent a helpful note to the Englishman in Mosul telling him about conditions in the passes. On June 7, just eleven days after Grant left Mar Shimun, Ainsworth and Rassam, accompanied by guides, muleteers, and a merchant named Da'ud, who dealt in oak galls, crossed the bridge of boats at Mosul and began the ascent into the Kurdish hills.

Almost immediately Ainsworth scored a minor coup, becoming the first European to visit the chief shrine of the Yezidis at Sheikh Adi, two days' journey from Mosul. The practices of these obscure people were then one of the region's more tantalizing mysteries. Ainsworth learned little, for the Yezidis who showed him around their temple refused to answer questions about their religion. Moreover, he couldn't stay long in Sheikh Adi, because Mohammed, the pasha of Mosul, and his army had crossed the Tigris into Kurdistan, threatening Amadiyah and hoping to bring the infidels of Tiyari under Ottoman control. Because of the need to arrive in Amadiyah ahead of Mohammed, Ainsworth had to leave Mosul without his new instruments, which arrived a month later, totally smashed in their packing crates. By June 10 Ainsworth's party entered Amadiyah, finding it in the same ruinous state that Grant had seen the previous autumn. There Ainsworth met the priest, Qasha Mendo, whose father had been bastinadoed for refusing to turn Catholic.

On the heels of the explorers was Mohammed Pasha, who encamped before the fortress and proceeded to make terms with the Kurdish chiefs for an attack on Tiyari. Ainsworth, traveling without official escort, had to leave town quickly, but first he needed a guide, a local man who could negotiate with armed Nestorian tribesmen who were gathering in the passes to oppose the Pasha's army. The search for a guide kept Ainsworth in Amadiyah until June 13, when Qasha Mendo at last volunteered to guide the party. The Expedition to Explore Kurdistan hurried out the back gate of the town and headed north into the mountains.

At first Ainsworth followed closely in Grant's footsteps. In Berwar, the last Kurd-dominated district before Tiyari, he too visited the village of Duree and met the same Nestorian clerics. As was Grant's, his reception was cordial, as it was in Lezan after he had crossed into the independent Nestorian districts. In Amadiyah, reports were circulating that the men of Tiyari had recently descended upon a Kurdish village in Berwar, plundered it and massacred its inhabitants. Because the Nestorians welcomed him warmly, Ainsworth decided not to give much credence to this report, and indeed its truth can never be ascertained; still, the existence of such a rumor reflects the dread and loathing with which the Tiyari tribes were regarded, a reputation which, as it evolved, they richly deserved.

From Duree, Ainsworth followed the Zab north, along the right bank of the river. He described the iron mines of Berwar, as "worked on the surface in beds of oxide of iron, disposed parallel to the strata of a fissile yellow limestone dipping west at an angle of 26°." Such eye-glazing prose was often employed by Ainsworth, determined perhaps to justify himself to his sponsors at the Royal Geographical Society no matter what the cost to his readers. He discusses the baseless native conviction that their mines were coveted by foreigners, pointing out that these mines were important to the villagers, because without the lead, iron, and sulphur they yielded, the people would be unable to maintain their independence. What the Hakkari people failed to realize, however, was that a deposit sufficient for their needs would not necessarily fulfill commercial demands. They feared that the mere discovery of these great treasures would mean an immediate invasion by the Turks, Russians, or whomever. As Ainsworth blandly notes, this was "quite a mistake."

Unlike Grant, Ainsworth did not conceal his note-taking or attempt to hide his curiosity about the country. If his scientific instruments had arrived in time, he would have done much more investigating. In a village called Leihun, close to Julamerk, he encountered a Kurdish chief, a "fine but ferocious-looking old man" who embodied the xenophobia that Asahel Grant had successfully avoided. Without any of the customary greetings, the man walked out onto the roof of his house as Ainsworth's party rode up.

"What do you do here?" he asked them. "Are you not aware that Franks are not allowed in this country?"

This chief's village was subject to Nurullah, emir of Hakkari, and he certainly knew what the emir had done to Schultz. The chief asked who had brought the foreigners to his village, and one of the Nestorian guides boldly replied that he had done so. The Kurd then spoke in a quieter, more menacing tone: "You are the forerunners of those who come to take this country. Therefore it is best that we should take first what you have, as you will afterwards take our property."

This was a direct threat of robbery, and if Ainsworth's party had not been traveling under the protection of the Tiyari tribes, it probably would have been carried out. As it was, Christian Rassam spoke some soothing words to the old man, the rest of the travelers readied their firearms, and in the end nothing happened. But it was a telling incident.

By the third week in June Rassam and Ainsworth approached Julamerk, where the patriarch Mar Shimun was in residence—probably at the home of the *mutesellim*, Suleiman Bey. The patriarch sent word that he would not meet the Englishman in Julamerk, since it was primarily a Kurdish town; he preferred to meet the travelers in a place where they could talk more freely. Ainsworth and Rassam were directed to Pagi, a nearby Armenian village. There, in the vestibule of the village church, they waited through two days of rain, continually pestered by the villagers, who did not leave them alone for a second.

At last, at five o'clock on the morning of June 20, 1840, Mar Shimun made his appearance. The patriarch, Ainsworth wrote, is "in every respect a fine man, thirty-nine years of age, tall, strong, well proportioned, with a good forehead, and pleasant, expressive, and rather intelligent countenance, while his large flowing robes, his Kurdish turban, and his long grey beard, give him a patriarchal and venerable aspect." Ainsworth had brought presents, including calico, soap, snuff, olives, and frankincense. After a cordial welcome, Mar Shimun asked the travelers the purpose of their visit.

The ensuing conversation lasted until one in the afternoon, and through these eight hours the patriarch fasted, seemingly to keep his mind clear. Christian Rassam now took on an important role, both as translator and advocate. He translated his and Ainsworth's thoughts into Arabic, passing them on to Da'ud, the oak-gall merchant who accompanied them. For Mar Shimun, Da'ud then translated them from Arabic into Syriac. As advocate, Rassam played a different role. It is important to realize that the young Chaldean was not there simply as an aide and translator. The Society for Promoting Christian Knowledge had specifically given Rassam the responsibility to make contact with the Church of the East and find out as much as he could about them. They had done this not only because of Rassam's ethnicity but because of his religious convictions.

By this time Rassam had become, in a religious sense, more "English" than most Englishmen. He had already married an Englishwoman, worked for the English in Malta and on the Euphrates Expedition, and had accompanied Ainsworth in his travels thereafter. Yet this was only the beginning. In England in the fall of 1837, Rassam separated from Ainsworth for a time and made his way to Oxford. There he met and came under the influence of William Palmer, a church historian and fellow at Magdalen College. Palmer is now considered to be only a minor figure in the Oxford Movement, or Puseyism, that faction within the Anglican Church, dominated by Edward Pusey

and John Henry Newman, which was reacting against theological liberalism and advocating a return to the church's roots
in Catholic doctrine and ritual. William Palmer detested evangelical Protestantism, especially Methodists, Presbyterians, and
Congregationalists. These were labeled Dissenters, and their
views were anathema to High Church Anglicans such as he. Of
prime importance was the fact that the Dissenters did not accept the doctrine of apostolic succession. They allowed women
to preach. The doctrinal authority of the bishops, those priests
appointed in a line of succession from the original apostles, was
less important to Dissenters than the personal religious experience of each believer. High Church Anglicans had, the Puseyites
hoped, more in common with Rome than with other Protestant
sects. Unlike Rome, however, the Church of England had no
desire to dominate the remaining churches in the Middle East.

With the zealotry of the young and newly converted, Rassam
embraced these Puseyite ideas, which seemed to mesh with the
practices of his native Chaldean church. When Rassam visited
Palmer at Oxford that Christmas of 1837, the two men travelled north to Palmer's home in the village of Mixbury. At a
public house where they were waiting for a coach, Rassam picked
up a Methodist tract lying on a table. Palmer did not note what
the tract said. Probably, as it had been left in a public house, it
inveighed against those who would waste time talking and drinking ale, instead of heeding their preachers and doing good works.
Rassam did not care about idleness and intemperance. What he
objected to was the tract itself. Immediately he began, in broken English, to berate the landlady and her patrons, workmen
from the town. It was disgraceful, he said, that they should display a document that promoted schism in the Christian church.
They should try living for a time among the Turks—that would
keep them in order. The landlady protested that she had no idea
the tract was there. Rassam stuffed the paper into his pocket,
and stalked out. To the undoubtedly bewildered patrons, Palmer
announced that his swarthy young companion was a native of

the Biblical land of Babylon and Nebuchadnezzar, Nineveh and Abraham. "I have no doubt," Palmer wrote, "his words made a deep impression."

The point of the story is obvious: in the space of a few weeks, Rassam had become a dedicated High Church Puseyite. On June 20, 1840, in his eight-hour meeting with Mar Shimun and Ainsworth, he explained the doctrines and structure of the Church of England and its relation to other Protestant churches. Ainsworth described the exhortation:

> We . . . informed the Patriarch that there were among us many zealous Christians who seemed to have read the Bible, rather to invent new doctrines and rebel against the Church than to give them increase of wisdom and holiness, and have preferred following such doctrines rather than that of the bishops who are appointed to teach the nations . . . that these persons have seceded from the Church of England and have corrupted the doctrines of Christianity; but as we do not think these corruptions so bad as to destroy the Christian faith we do not call them heresies.

Mar Shimun seems to have known only that he did not want his people to become Catholic, and he did not want to be subjugated by the Kurds. The patriarch, a man of the mountains who dressed in robes and a turban and carried a rifle against bear attacks, probably didn't know what to make of the Ainsworth-Rassam visit. At that time the peoples of the Middle East lumped Americans and the English together. The English, they knew, were great and powerful. They had great armies, many ships, and consuls in Erzurum, Baghdad, Tabriz, and Tehran. But the Americans—well, nothing was really known about them except that they spoke English. Mar Shimun by this time had met with Dr. Grant twice, and a sincere friendship had formed between them. He knew the good works that the missionaries were performing amongst his flock on the Urmia plain. He knew that they wanted to open schools in the mountains and were willing to give him money to do so. Now came Ainsworth and Rassam, representatives—they said—of the all-powerful English nation and its church. This mountain priest, scarcely able to tell the two nations apart, was expected to discern the political difference between the style of Christianity practiced by Dr. Grant, a man he knew and—so far—trusted, and this newly-introduced Church of England, whose nation possessed the power to wipe his enemies off the face of the earth.

Unfortunately, but not surprisingly, in the midst of this linguistic and doctrinal fogbank, Ainsworth and Rassam chose to denigrate the American missionaries. They did it in the most civilized and condescending manner possible, telling the patriarch that if one of the American missionaries joined the Church of England he would have to be ordained, because the Church considered these missionaries to be outside the tradition of apostolic succession. Ainsworth and Rassam went on to talk about opening schools, aiding Mar Shimun's church, and making translations of the New Testament. They gave, however, not one concrete proposal for the execution of these promises. At length the interview ended, and Mar Shimun departed for the castle of Julamerk.

Ainsworth continued his cursory inspection of the mountains, managing to avoid both the Kurdish emir Nurullah and his nephew Suleiman Bey. He passed through Urmia without meeting the local Nestorians or stopping to call upon the missionaries—a blatant discourtesy which he lamely excused by saying that he lacked the proper clothes and preferred sleeping in the open. By July he had returned to Mosul by the southern route through Rowanduz. There the smashed remnants of his instruments provided a suitable metaphor for his luck as an explorer. But as an observer, Ainsworth should not be written off. Despite his anti-missionary bias, he tried to be fair. And one last nugget of prescience will always be associated with his

name. As he sees more people like himself entering the mountains, and the Nestorians' growing prominence, he sums up their
predicament:

> This sudden interest, so explicitly and so actively shown on
> the part of other Christian nations, towards a tribe of people,
> who have almost solely prolonged their independent exist-
> ence on account of their remote seclusion, and comparative
> insignificance, has called them forth into new importance in
> the eyes of the Mohammedans, and will undoubtedly be the
> first step to their overthrow.

This, in a nutgall, was the problem. No one ever wrote a
wiser or more perceptive word about the Nestorians' situation,
although the alternative he suggests is an unconvincing one.
Disaster would certainly befall them *unless*, he said, "they are
assisted in such an emergency by sound advice, or the friendly
interference of the representatives of brotherly Christian nations at Constantinople." This of course was no remedy at all.
If the attention and interest of Europeans was a prime cause of
the Nestorians' impending troubles, it is hard to see how "sound
advice" and "friendly interference" could lessen the jealousy
and resentment of Muslims. As it happened, they could not and
did not. With this weak suggestion, Ainsworth tries to camou-
flage the reality that the Christians of the Hakkari mountains
were doomed.

II

CRITICS, SNIPERS, AND FRAUDS

"If the prayers of dogs were accepted, bones would rain from the sky."—*Turkish proverb*

ON APRIL 1, 1841, less than six months after his return from Turkey, Asahel Grant sailed from Boston on one of the new Cunard steamships, which had begun transatlantic service only the year before. Despite continuing illness, he had worked long and hard on his book *The Nestorians; or, The Lost Tribes*, and now it was ready for Harper and Brothers to publish in May. Still feeling the obligation to his missionary brethren, the Hinsdales and the Mitchells, the doctor had hoped to leave sooner, and had just missed taking another brand-new steamer, the *President*, which departed New York on March 11. Unlike other missionaries, who typically made the long voyage to Smyrna by sailing across the Atlantic and directly into the Mediterranean, Dr. Grant was traveling back to Turkey via the Continent.

The reason for this detour was contemporary copyright law. Grant had good reason to expect that his book would sell well. First-hand accounts of travel and exploration were very popular, so Grant's unique, dangerous journey had to arouse interest. He had had no problem finding a New York publisher for his manuscript; in fact, he received multiple offers. The big danger was piracy, and with the advent of steamships plying the Atlantic that danger had increased. Without an international copyright treaty— none existed until 1887—it was a simple matter for someone to buy newly published books in New York, Boston, or London, take them aboard a transatlantic steamer, and bring out cheap pirated editons on the other side of the ocean.

Grant was determined to avoid this. Writing from New York on March 14, he told Henry Hill, treasurer of the American Board, that he had sent him an express package containing the printed pages of his new book. Hill was instructed to forward the package by "the next steamer" to John Murray, Esq., in London. By delaying publication in New York and sailing as soon as possible on the Cunard boat for Liverpool, Grant hoped to secure the copyright with simultaneous publication in both Great Britain and the United States. From Liverpool, where he landed on April 15, Grant proceeded to London. There he heard that the *President* , the steamship he had just missed taking, was overdue from New York. By the end of April all hope for the ship was given up. In fact, no trace of the *President* was ever found. In this fateful event, Rev. Thomas Laurie of course saw the hand of God protecting His servant.

In London, as in New York, Grant found no lack of offers for his manuscript. Though Longmans expressed interest, in the end he stayed with John Murray, the venerable firm that had published Byron and Scott and would go on to publish Austen Henry Layard, Isabella Bird, Freya Stark, and many other travel writers. Murray's *Handbook for Travellers in Turkey* was the standard guidebook of the time. In a letter dated April 19, 1841, Grant reports that Murray had already begun to print his book. On May 1, by which time Grant was on his way to Kurdistan, *The Nestorians* was published simultaneously in London and New York.

This, Grant's only published work, is divided into two parts, of which the first, describing his journeys in the mountains, is by far the most interesting. It was also the easiest to write, being little more than an edited compilation of his journals as they had appeared in the *Missionary Herald*. The second half is a 200-page argument that the Nestorians were the "Lost Tribes" of Israel—the ten Hebrew tribes carried off to captivity in Assyria in the 8th century B.C. For a long time this "problem" greatly exercised the thoughts of religious zealots and dreamers. Some argued that the Indians of North America were the remnants of the Lost Tribes; others that they could be found among the tribes of Afghanistan. Grant, characteristically, took up his cause with vigor, arguing that the Nestorians' language (a form of Aramaic, shared with the Jews of Kurdistan), names, traditions, and physiognomy all pointed toward a Hebrew origin.

But he was no scholar, and his thesis found little support among theologians. Over a thousand years had passed between the tribes' abduction to Assyria and the rise of the Nestorian Church of the East; after that another millennium-and-a-half had come and gone. Justin Perkins, Dr. Grant's closest friend among the missionaries, was a skeptic from the first. In May, 1840, the doctor, about to leave Urmia for America, wrote to Dr. Rufus Anderson of the American Board and excitedly informed him that he had completed his essay on the Ten Tribes, and that all the brethren in Urmia had read it, and all were in agreement with his thesis except for one: Justin Perkins.

Perkins, indeed, was too sober and scholarly a man to indulge in this sort of speculation. "Concentrated effort is effective effort," he liked to say, quoting the Instructions given him by Dr. Anderson before he and his wife left for Persia. In contrast to Grant's ardor and romanticism, Perkins was the steady kind of man who could spend years of work on one great achievement: the translation of the Bible into modern Syriac.

Then there was the American scholar Edward Robinson (1794–1863), theologian and Biblical archaeologist, who had by then achieved an international reputation. After graduating from Hamilton College in Clinton, New York, mere miles from

Grant's birthplace, he had studied in Germany, and the Holy Land, and had been a colleague and instructor of Justin Perkins at Andover Theological Seminary. His three-volume *Biblical Researches in Palestine, Sinai and Arabia Petraea* (published by John Murray in 1841) was awarded a gold medal by the Royal Geographical Society—the first ever given to an American. In his *Residence of Eight Years in Persia*, the station's senior missionary noted that Dr. Robinson had rejected Grant's Ten Tribes thesis, pointing out that Grant repeatedly ascribed to the Nestorians as "Jewish," characteristics—Biblical names, Semitic features—shared by many of the peoples in the Near East. To American and British scholars, Robinson's opinion counted far more heavily than Grant's.

Equally scornful—and wonderfully snide in saying so—was William Francis Ainsworth, second in the race to reach the mountain Nestorians. In his *Travels and Researches in Asia Minor*, Ainsworth makes a creditable attempt to be generous to Grant, several times quoting his observations favorably, and acknowledging Grant's helpful letter informing him of conditions in the pass. Sour grapes, however, appear before long. Ainsworth points out that Dr. Grant had managed to get into Hakkari first only because of his and Rassam's misfortune at the battle of Nizib, and that the American missionaries had decided to propose the visit only after his own expedition had appeared at Constantinople. This, of course, was absurd. As early as 1833 Perkins—and later, Grant—had been given specific instructions to contact the patriarch Mar Shimun as soon as they could do so safely; and a mere six months after the Americans' arrival in Urmia, the patriarch had written extending a cordial invitation to them to visit him in Kochanes.

For Dr. Grant's ideas on the Ten Tribes, Ainsworth reserves his most withering comments: "The enthusiasm of the Americans in searching for these lost tribes, even among the Indian races of their own country, is well known." He then, like Edward Robinson, charges Grant with drawing extravagant conclusions from minimal data. The facts, he says, are simple: these very interesting people are "Chaldean, speaking a mixed Chaldean and Syriac dialect." (Why he was qualified to assert this he does not say: Grant, after all, was fluent in both Turkish and Syriac, and Ainsworth spoke neither.) These "Chaldeans," he says, had been living and practicing their religion in Mesopotamia and Kurdistan for a very long time, and there was much to be learned about them. He implies that most people would find them sufficiently fascinating as they are. But, he says, that is not enough to satisfy "that morbid desire for striking novelties and wondrous discoveries which has such a charm for our transatlantic brethren."

Happily for Grant, his three sons, and his publisher, none of this criticism affected the public's response to the book. *The Nestorians* attracted considerable notice, and sold well. (A pirated French version appeared in 1843.) It was, after all, the first book to present the Christian tribes of Hakkari in Britain and America. Earlier travelers in Kurdistan had mentioned rumors of the Nestorians, but this American had done what no Western writer had done: he had penetrated the Hakkari massif, met its people, seen their world—and made it out alive. Grant's book is unclear in many of its political and geographic details, devoid of maps, and wrapped in piety—it is not easy reading today. But within his limitations of time and scholarship, Asahel Grant had written the best book that he could. Most important, royalties from *The Nestorians* paid for the support and education of his three sons Hastings, Edwin, and Henry Martyn.

In London, when he was not working with John Murray, Asahel Grant busied himself preparing for skirmishes to come. Ainsworth's visit to Mar Shimun had unsettled him, and he feared sectarian sniping—that "ruthless verbal in-fighting," as Auden called it, "taught in Protestant rectories upon drizzling Sunday afternoons." He had always known that the "man of

sin" was marshalling his forces, sending out boatloads of Dominicans and Lazarists, their purses packed with gold, to buy
the allegiance of the Nestorians. But now the Church of England also, it seemed, was looking toward Hakkari.

To find out what the Anglicans were planning, Grant went
to see Rev. Josiah Pratt at the Church Missionary Society. Since
Pratt, a friend of Dr. Rufus Anderson and Corresponding Member of the American Board, came from the evangelical (not the
High Church) wing of the Anglican Church, Dr. Grant was received with "a good deal of paternal kindness," and assured
that he and his fellow missionaries had nothing to fear. Rev.
Pratt knew of no Episcopal organizations in England planning
missions to the Nestorians. The Church's only goal, he said,
was the opening of friendly discourse between themselves and
the leaders of the Eastern churches.

In a letter to Rufus Anderson posted from Marseilles on April
30, Grant expanded upon his conversations with "our good Father Pratt." The High Church Anglicans, Pratt told him, regarded
dissenters as "unclean" and "not to be admitted into their Christian fraternity or cooperation." They would not send a mission
to the Nestorians because they did not consideer that church a
proper subject for missionary activity. Their plan, Pratt said, was
"to hold fraternal correspondence with the heads [of the Nestorian
church] and to aid them" by whatever means seemed appropriate. But Grant remained wary. If the High-Church Anglicans sent
representatives to Constantinople calling them "delegates" instead of "missionaries," the difference was only a matter of ter-
minology. These same "delegates" could still set themselves up in
opposition to the American missions and do considerable damage to them. At St. Paul's, Westminster Abbey, and the chapel of
the British Embassy in Paris, Grant looked on with grim disapproval as the allegedly Protestant Anglicans conducted services
that seemed to him dangerously close to those of the hated papists. In the Paris chapel, he listened to "one of the most exclu-
sive sectarian sermons I have ever heard," delivered by a bishop

who solemnly warned his listeners against the heresies of "those schismatics who preached another gospel."

To a young, fervent evangelical like Grant, these words, delivered by fellow English-speaking Christians, would have seemed the deepest sort of insult, even worse than the "wiles" of Roman Catholics. Differences of class, education, and nationality probably worsened the doctor's resentment. Born on an upstate New York farm, educated in country schools, granted an M.D. without having graduated from a college or university, Asahel Grant was righteous to the core. From righteous beginnings he had struggled to a higher level of righteousness, worked hard for it, sacrificed his family and his physical and financial health for it. On his father's farm he had done more dirty, difficult labor in a day than an English vicar would have undertaken in a lifetime.

In his dealings with the English authorities in Turkey and Persia, Grant had been treated with nothing but the utmost kindness and respect. This was the experience of all his missionary brethren. In Persia the British allowed them *gratis* the use of their official couriers for the mission's mail. In Stamboul, Erzurum, Tabriz and Tehran, Her Majesty's ambassadors and consuls invited them to dine, gave immediate attention to their needs, and took their part repeatedly in dealing with the authorities. In 1834, imprisoned on the Araxes River by thuggish Russian officials, Justin and Charlotte Perkins were saved only by the intervention of Dr. Riach, doctor to the British legation, who had ridden a hundred miles to help them. Indeed, in the years to come, three of the Perkinses' seven children would be named after Englishmen, a clear illustration of their high esteem. Yet now, with these sermons from the Episcopal throne denouncing reverent, industrious believers like himself, Grant was overcome by deep suspicion and resentment of what he saw as partly English snobbery.

In Stamboul, where Asahel Grant landed on May 14, 1841, Mahmud's son Abdul Mejid was pursuing the process of reform with even greater energy. To the south, the Egyptian Mohammed Ali no longer ruled in Syria, thus stabilizing that area for travelers. In July of 1840, the European powers—with the exception of France, which was pursuing its own designs—had delivered an ultimatum demanding the Egyptian's withdrawal from his possessions, with progressively greater consequences for each ten-day interval that he refused. When no submission was forthcoming, at the end of August a combined Russian, Austrian, and British fleet appeared off Beirut, triggering a general uprising by a populace fed up with taxes and conscription. When Suleiman Pasha ("the Frenchman") refused to evacuate the city, bombardment commenced and troops of the Ottoman army were landed to aid in the revolt. By November it was all over: Mohammed Ali's son Ibrahim Pasha and Suleiman had fled south, the Egyptian armies were gone, and the Ottomans had returned to power, ready to impose exactly the sort of taxes that had made the former rulers so unpopular. For travelers and Mosul-bound missionaries like the Hinsdales and Mitchells, the caravan route through northern Syria lay open.

To get to Constantinople Asahel Grant made his way across France to Marseilles, where he caught the next boat going east. Forty-four days had elapsed in the journey from Boston to the capital, ten days less than his passage in 1834, which took him only as far as Smyrna. This shrinkage in travel time becomes even more dramatic when we deduct the weeks he spent in London, Paris, and Marseilles. By contrast, Justin Perkins and family, when they returned to America in the fall of the same year, had to endure a mind-numbing passage of *109 days* from Smyrna to Boston. The difference, of course, was steam. Ships like the brig *Angola*, on which Asahel and Judith Grant had voyaged on their honeymoon, were beginning their long fade into extinction.

It would be another year before Grant could visit his colleagues in Urmia, where the Americans' work was expanding steadily. Five missionaries now resided with their families at the mission, and five miles from the town, 1,000 feet above the plain on the slopes of Mt. Seir, they were building a health retreat for times of pestilence. Grant's medical services were no longer essential. At Erzurum in 1840, while enroute to the States, he had met up with A.H. Wright, who had now taken his place as mission doctor.

The following November came another missionary, Edward Breath, whose arrival had been awaited more keenly than any other. Breath, born in New York City, was a printer who had worked for an Abolitionist newspaper in Illinois where he had seen his editor, Elijah P. Lovejoy, gunned down by a mob. He brought with him, specially manufactured and broken down into transportable pieces, the mission's new printing press. The first press, which had languished so long on the docks in Trebizond, was not transportable on horseback, its smallest piece weighing some 600 pounds. Eventually it was taken back to Constantinople and sold. Breath wrote that the printing press, enroute from the Black Sea, "was a source of *wonderment . . .* some pronouncing it a steam engine, and others a machine for making cannon." With the help of Justin Perkins and a group of locals, he assembled the apparatus and set to work cutting the fonts for their new version of printed Syriac. On March 13, 1841, Perkins wrote:

> The proof-sheet of our *first* tract in the Nestorian language was brought into my study for correction. This is indeed the *first sheet* ever printed in that language and character. As it was laid upon my table, before our translators, priest Abraham and Dunka, they were struck with mute astonishment and rapture to see *their* language in *print . . .* As soon as recovery from their surprise allowed them utterance, "it is time to give glory to God," they mutually exclaimed, "that our eyes are permitted to behold the commencement of *printing books* for our people!"

But at the mission euphoria did not prevail. A letter, dated March 31, 1841, had been sent to Dr. Rufus Anderson in Boston, written by Justin Perkins but signed by all the missionary brethren in Urmia. It was a long letter, bearing unsettling news. To understand its implications, we have to remember the realities of Mar Shimun's patriarchate, a loose organization that was only marginally religious in purpose. Mar Shimun ruled over a church that was a tribe, an army, and a political party; but most of all, the patriarch ran a family business. This was not a business that brought in great rivers of cash—in fact, it paid the House of Shimun very little at all—but it was a business nonetheless, with regular sources of revenue and expenditure and a large, familial board of directors to see that the enterprise remained intact.

It is not clear exactly how many sisters, brothers, aunts, and uncles lived within whispering distance of Mar Shimun's ear, but anyone who looks at the documents soon sees that the number must have been high. Of his relatives, at least five brothers are named: Zadok, a truculent priest who shared Grant's travels in 1841 and was later to be killed by the Kurds; Deacon Benjamin, called "the most evil-disposed of Mar Shimun's brothers"; Deacon Isaac, who after helping the Americans, was excommunicated and a price put on his head by Mar Shimun; and last of all two deacons, Yohannan and Dunkha.

These two, and Yohannan in particular, were the particular subjects of the missionaries' long letter. They had known them for several years. During the Americans' second winter in Urmia, 1836-37, the mission had played host to these two men, and from those first meetings both Grant and Perkins sent back optimistic reports about the encouraging cordiality of the patriarch's family. Yohannan was the younger brother of Mar Shimun and, according to Justin Perkins, his "appointed successor." (He should not be confused with Mar Yohannan, a bishop from Urmia who was one of Justin Perkins's translators.) Every winter Yohannan would descend from the moun-

tains to the plain of Urmia to collect the tribute due to the patriarch, an amount which usually came to $250 to $300. Yohannan
had also visited the previous May, 1836, when he stayed for a
week with the brethren. Grant wrote, "Although there is a certain wildness of expression in his countenance, he is one of the
most noble looking men I ever saw." These words recall Grant's
description of Nurullah Bey, that man of "noble mien," and
they call into question the doctor's ability to distinguish between character and good looks.

When Deacon Yohannan visited Urmia in May 1836, he
brought a letter from Mar Shimun. This was a kind of master-
piece, both in its florid rhetoric and gritty naïveté. Mar Shimun
begins by sending greetings and wishes for everyone's good
health in the name of Jesus Christ, the saints, and all his church,
"Amen." He is careful to include his compliments to "Lady
Judith" and "Lady Charlotte" and their (at that time nonexist-
ent) children. He urges the missionaries to come visit him soon,
and to be sure and communicate the time of their arrival so that
the Kurds, "those children of wild asses, may not come in your
way to do evil." He promises to send escorts to guard the Americans while they are traveling, "Amen." Then, out of nowhere,
"we beseech of you a watch, a very excellent and beautiful one,
the like of which shall not exist. Amen." He concludes by sending the love of all the priests, the deacons, and "the great ones,"
as well as all the brothers of Mar Shimun and all his family
great and small, wishing the Americans to remain "prosperous
and firm" in our Lord, now and forever, "Amen."

These rococo sentiments, coupled with childish greed, were
a pattern that soon became familiar to the missionaries. When
Grant visited Nurullah and wrote of compliments "too Oriental to bear repeating," this is what he meant. This sort of behavior, carried to a much higher degree of deception and venality, was described in the missionaries' letter to Dr. Anderson. As
usual, the patriarch's brother, Yohannan, had spent a good deal
of time in and around Urmia that winter, passing the hat on

behalf of his older brother and extended family. During this time he had been given food and lodging, and his relations with the missionaries remained the picture of cordiality. He had brought a letter from Mar Shimun telling the missionaries about Ainsworth's visit and assuring them that the promises given to Dr. Grant remained valid. But then Yohannan told them that his brother was "conferring by letter" with Ainsworth and Rassam. This raised flags of suspicion on the missionary quarterdeck. Why, if the pact with Dr. Grant remained in force, was the patriarch "conferring" with the Anglicans?

As a counter to this activity, the Urmia missionaries decided to go ahead and authorize Mar Shimun to open schools in four or five villages, with a promise to pay the teachers up to certain limits. This would work as a stopgap until Grant's return from the States. A letter was written at the end of February to give to Mar Shimun, informing the patriarch that as soon as he had opened the schools, he would receive the money to pay the teachers. As parting gifts, offered and accepted with great cordiality, Deacon Yohannan received sundry items, including friction matches and a gold American coin.

Almost immediately after Yohannan left, a letter arrived, purportedly from Mar Shimun, telling the Americans that he had opened schools and asking that his brother be given money to maintain them. The lightning speed with which this had traversed the mountains startled everyone. The reason became obvious when a native informant told the missionaries that in fact the letter had been written by Deacon Yohannan before he left the mission grounds. Needless to say, Justin Perkins and company did not reply to this message.

Two days after his departure, from a village just to the north of Urmia, the patriarch's brother sent back all of the missionaries' gifts, with the exception of the gold coin, which he claimed to have lost. After a short meeting, Albert Holladay and William Stocking were delegated to ride to the village where Yohannan was staying. They met him and asked why he had done these things. He replied that he and his brother, Deacon Dunkha, had not been treated with the respect due them for their position in the church. The room provided had been too small; he spoke ill of the missionaries and "ridiculed" their presents. Last of all, he was offended because the Americans had not entrusted him with the money for the schools.

The two emissaries used all the diplomatic language they could muster to deal with this petty extortion. They assured Yohannan that the funds for the schools would be forthcoming as soon as the schools were opened. But the deacon was not placated. Holladay and Stocking returned to Urmia for another general discussion. Yohannan's behavior was obviously despicable, but he was the designated second in command to Mar Shimun, and no one wanted to make an enemy of him. With great reluctance, the assembled missionaries voted to give $20 to Yohannan and $5 to his younger brother. In 1841, it must be noted, these were not trifling sums. Holladay and Stocking then rode back and presented the money to Yohannan, who accepted it without any sign of gratitude.

That appeared to settle the matter. Once again Mar Shimun's brothers made their way north, and another day's journey brought them to the Nestorian village of Gavalan, in the hills separating the Urmia plain from that of Salmas. But from Gavalan they sent a new note. Yohannan demanded more money, this time to pay for porters. The outraged missionaries found this request "preposterous"; nevertheless, they complied with "a few dollars" more. This, for the time being, marked the end of Yohannan's chicanery. At Salmas, the last town before his party turned west toward the Ottoman frontier, Yohannan wrote a last message, exhorting the Americans to remember the promises they had made "or else." He did not make his threat explicit.

This was the character of the Nestorian patriarch's brother and apparent "appointed successor." Justin Perkins told Rufus Anderson not only about Yohannan's departure and extortions, but about Yohannan's behavior during his stay in Urmia. This deacon of the Church of the East, it turned out, was anything but pious. He took no part during the missionaries' prayer meetings, but stood "aloof." Nor did he attend or take part in the services of his own church. The local Nestorians—another telling sign—refused to invite him to their homes. Last, and most scandalous of all, Perkins wrote, "We will add only that one item on the bill which we had to pay for his entertainment during his last visit was *ten dollars* for wine only; and this sum, as wine sells in Ooroomiah, must have procured more than *100 gallons*." (Having tasted Urmia wine for himself, the author will attest that a price of ten cents per gallon is a good gauge of its worth.) But no matter what the price, seeing a church prelate swill it in these quantities left teetotalling New Englanders like Justin Perkins feeling profoundly betrayed.

Perkins was never a strong supporter of Grant's mission to the mountain Nestorians. He seems to have acquiesced out of respect and affection for his colleague, and because he knew that Grant could not survive in the climate of Urmia. After this incident, Perkins expressed regret to Rufus Anderson for having to pay what amounted to bribes. If Deacon Yohannan did indeed exert a strong influence upon Mar Shimun, this did not bode well for future relations.

But the issue of mountain schools and cash payments had not ended. Having written a long letter about Deacon Yohannan, Perkins was compelled to add a postscript. Just as he wrote his last lines, a letter had arrived from Mar Shimun who, after the usual bowings and scrapings, informed the missionaries that, per their authorization, he had opened *twelve* schools with *thirty* scholars in each school. This he had miraculously achieved within the space of about two weeks, between the time of Yohannan's return and the dispatch of the letter. At twenty-five cents per pupil per month, which the Urmia mission had pledged to pay, Mar Shimun now claimed that the Americans owed him $90. Once again, an obvious fraud was being attempted. The mission had authorized the patriarch to open four to five schools, and told him that they could pay teachers' wages based on no more than a *total of thirty students* in all the schools together. In other words, they had budgeted a maximum of $7.50 per month. When they talked to the messenger who had brought the letter, the missionaries asked him how many schools had actually opened. He replied, of course, that the number was zero.

The response of the Prudential Committee of the ABCFM to this letter can be imagined. Were these, they had to have asked, the sorts of Christians—frauds, cheats, and liars—their missionaries were going to be dealing with in the mountains? Were the pennies donated by American schoolchildren going to be used to pay bribes to local thugs? To make things worse, Perkins's letter also revealed that the route from Persia into Hakkari was especially dangerous that year "in consequence of a quarrel between the Patriarch and the Koordish chief." From Constantinople, Asahel Grant wrote Rufus Anderson that he need not worry about opposition from the patriarch's brother. But the situation did not look promising. The graybeards of the American Board may well have wondered if they should have yielded to to the appeals of Dr. Grant, one of whose principal arguments for the mountain mission had been the imminent approach of papal emissaries, forces to which the Nestorian patriarch was steadfastly opposed. Only the year before, Albert Holladay had written from Urmia, adding his support for efforts among the mountain tribes "lest they fall prey to the wiles of the Catholics." But the behavior of Mar Shimun and his brother now raised the question: what was the real reason for the Nestorian leaders' opppsition to the Catholics? Did they oppose the pope's envoys on religious and doctrinal grounds, or were they simply protecting the family franchise?

No matter how deep their misgivings, it would have been too late by then for the American Board to turn back. It was summer, and Asahel Grant had disappeared into Asia Minor.

Two couples, the Mitchells and the Hinsdales, were in Syria
enroute to the mountains. Like it or not, the station in Mosul
would become a reality, and the mission to the Christian tribes
of Hakkari would go forward. The missions' governing committee, devoted to the principle of Prudence, could only hope
that Dr. Grant knew what he was doing.

ABOVE:
Asahel Grant, M.D.
From a daguerrotype
made in 1841.

LEFT:
Rev. Justin Perkins,
D.D., with his modern
Syriac Bible.

Aladagh Range, Taurus Mountains, Southeastern Turkey. *(Author photo)*

The castle at Van, where Friedrich Schultz copied Urartian inscriptions.
Foreground: footing of ancient Urartian walls. *(Author photo)*

Hakkari town (Julamerk); road descending into gorge of the river Zab; Sümbül Dagh (11354 feet) beyond. *(Author photo)*

Cooper's workshop, Hoshap castle, Van-Hakkari road—Dr. Grant passed
this way twice. *(Author photo)*

LEFT:
Graveyard in Kespiyanish (now Mutluca), former Nestorian (now Kurdish) village, Hakkari province, Turkey. Looking south toward Iraqi border. *(Author photo)*

BELOW:
Anatolian plateau, central Turkey, near Sivrihisar. Typical of the lands through which Dr. Grant traveled, especially on caravan routes to Persia. *(Author photo)*

ABOVE:
Mardin: rooftops and minaret; view south toward Jebel Sinjar. Grant twice escaped death here in 1839. *(Author photo)*

RIGHT:
Monk at Deir-ul-Zaferan, Syrian Orthodox monastery where Grant and Homes took refuge from Kurdish mob in 1839. *(Author photo)*

Hoshap castle: road to Başkale and mountains of Hakkari. *(Author photo)*

Village of Oramar (with terraced fields), Hakkari, looking north toward mountains of Jelu. *(Photo by Captain Bertram Dickson, R.A., British Military Consul in Van, c. 1910)*

Sümbül Dagh, gorge of river Zab. *(Author photo)*

Shrine of Nebbi Yunus (Jonah), and walls of Nineveh, with Mosul and the Tigris in the background. Drawing by Claudius James Rich (1787–1821).

Constantinople (Stamboul; Istanbul) in the early 19th century. Drawing by Claudius James Rich. (On foreshore: the village of Scutari, where Florence Nightingale established her hospital during the Crimean War.)

THE PILGRIM

"Savage life does not bear a near view. Its total lack of privacy, its rough brutality, its dirt, its undisguised greed, its unconcealed jealousies and hatreds, its falseness, its pure selfishness, and its treachery, are all painful on close inspection."
—Isabella Bird, *Journeys in Persia and Kurdistan*

ASHAEL GRANT LANDED IN Istanbul on May 14, 1841. From this point—indeed from the time of his last visit to Waterville—he became a permanent wanderer. He had torn up his roots in Urmia as surely as in New York, and on the one occasion he returned there, though welcomed as a hero, he stayed as a guest. Now instead of a home he found lodgings: sometimes a tent, sometimes an *arzaleh*, at others a rented house or a vacant rooftop, and often simply a patch of earth. In Mosul, though he spent months occupying the same rooms, he never again had a place to call his own.

Physically, Grant was not ready for the task ahead. The black cloud of illness had followed him to the United States, and when he reached Turkey it descended upon him again. As impatient as ever to be off to the mountains, he was struck down by influenza soon after arriving at the Stamboul mission. The disease, a killer today, was even more dangerous in the 19th century. The very name "influenza", Italian for "influence," or an "intangible visitation," reflects the general cluelessness. In the absence of knowledge the doctors could only resort to their usual bag of tricks, with the result that the disease was often fatal. To Rev. Willard Jones, in Urmia, Grant wrote on May 27: "I was to have left last week . . . but the physicians join with the missionaries in urging me to delay another week, and I have reluctantly consented." On the whole he was feeling better, "but I cannot conceal from myself that my hurried visit to America has not so invigorated my constitution but that I ought to be ready for my last change." These last three words do not connote something so innocuous as a change of scenery; they sound a note of fatalism. "Do not think from these remarks," he adds, "that I am dangerously ill; but life is uncertain, and nothing should be risked on the life of one man, and he the tenant of a shattered tenement." Despite his having left Urmia, and his occasional professions of well-being, he is admitting that his physical health is more than "uncertain."

As soon as the "shattered tenement" could move, its owner left Stamboul and took the steamer east to Trebizond. Within days he had crossed the rain-soaked mountains of Pontus and was in Erzurum, seeking a caravan. From there, on June 15, he wrote to his brother Ira, "This is a wicked land; and it is as true now as it was in the days of the Psalmist, that 'The dark places of the earth are full of the habitations of cruelty.'" Grant had just returned from the palace of the pasha. On his way there he saw a Kurd left hanging by the neck for three days as an example to others; at the palace he saw other Kurds "bastinadoed till they were nearly dead." These men were said to be thieves; the hanged man had committed both robbery and murder. But guilt or innocence were dubious concepts: the accused, he notes, usually confessed only after hours of torture. For many years, exacerbated by drought and famine, a general lawlessness had ravaged the East. "Confidence is scarcely known," Grant said, "the traveller goes armed, not knowing but he may be robbed and murdered by the first man he meets."

Enroute to Hakkari, Grant had to veer from the normal caravan route to Persia and strike south toward Lake Van. For safety reasons, the restless American found himself cooped up in a caravan, shackled to its plodding routine. To his son Edwin's guardian, Rev. Wayne Gridley of Clinton, New York, Grant wrote on June 24: "I write you, seated upon the ground, among the mountains of the wild sanguinary Koords." Caravan horses, unladen, were grazing nearby, their necks hung with bells. "My umbrella," he wrote, "sustained by a small pile of merchandise from our caravan, affords a partial protection from the beams of a noonday sun. It is the only shade I can find, as there is not a tree nor a house to be seen." He had been on the road to Van for three days.

The other travelers called him *Hadji,* Pilgrim, because—except for an attendant muleteer—he traveled alone. There were some forty wayfarers in his caravan. "Not one with whom I can exchange a word in my native tongue, but Turks, Armenians and Koords as they are, they all speak *Turkish,* and in this I converse, think, and dream." Grant was not a "loner" by choice; several times in the coming years he would try—in vain— to find companions for his mountain journeys.

Grant's caravan offered more security than solitary travel, but it was nothing like the 600-horse throng that he and Judith had joined in 1835. This group was not well-armed, and Grant, as a matter of policy, carried no weapons. Moreover, there appears to have been no clear leader. The wayfarers and merchants moved at the whim of the head muleteer, who halted whenever good grazing could be found, even if it was after only a few hours' march. His letter to Rev. Gridley was written around noon, and the caravan, having started at 4 a.m., had stopped marching by 7:30 that morning. Eventually, this leisurely pace led to schism, and from that to danger.

In the letter to Gridley, and in his journal, Grant tells the story. The way south from Erzurum led first across the Palandöken Mountains—so steep that their name means "saddle-dumpers"—from which emerge the headwaters of the river Araxes. By the evening of June 24 they had crossed that river and camped on the southern side. During the night some of the caravan horses were lost, and it was assumed that Kurd bandits had made off with them. The drovers had to stay and look for the lost livestock, but about half the travelers could stand the delay no longer. It was, said Grant, a choice between danger and starvation. Because of the famine, no bread could be found enroute, and in Erzurum they had not been able to buy much. Given a choice, they now broke away and rode ahead.

Unencumbered by the caravan, the group (some twenty-two Kurds, Turks, and Armenians, and one American) covered a good thirty miles their first day. But they were now even less armed than before, and their party had shrunk by half. On their first evening away from the caravan, they camped near salt springs in the mountains. In the night Grant was awakened by a scream, followed by others, and leaping up he saw his companions huddled together, terror-stricken in the starlight. "Our company," he wrote, "seemed to have given themselves up for lost." The assumption was that they were being attacked by Kurds. Grant looked for a path of escape; but except that their horses had pricked up their ears in curiosity, he could see nothing. After the first minutes of panic, the travelers started asking one another what the matter was. Nobody knew. After much questioning, it turned out that one of the party, an Armenian priest, had gone to sleep in a state of "great apprehension." When one of the party's horses nudged the priest's bed, he woke up screaming.

The next night found them camped beneath the castle at Malazgirt, a village which, called Manzikert, had served as a Roman and Byzantine stronghold on the eastern frontier. At Manzikert in A.D. 1071, the Seljuk Turks routed a Byzantine army led by the emperor Romanus IV Diogenes. This historic battle effectively opened Asia Minor to Turkish control and played a large part in provoking the Crusades. But Asahel Grant makes no mention of it; he dismisses Malazgirt as "a small town with Roman fortifications." It is as if a traveler had visited Hastings and said nothing about 1066. This seems an odd omission until we remember that Grant was, apart from medical matters, an autodidact who probably knew little of that history. And unlike the green, prosperous village of Hastings dominated by its Battle Abbey, dusty depopulated Malazgirt sat in the middle of nowhere on the road to somewhere worse, a clump of mud-brick huts with a crumbling castle, showing no signs of a battle eight centuries old.

In any event, the doctor had more pressing things on his mind. Malazgirt was not a safe place. In 1829, the Englishman George Fowler, traveling with a caravan far more substantial than Grant's, had been besieged within its walls for two weeks as a mob of Kurdish bandits, both inside and out, tried to decide how to rob them successfully. Only the arrival of a Turkish cavalry detachment saved the day. Fowler, too, does not mention the battle of Manzikert. Grant and his companions left Malazgirt safely, but were now passing through the most dangerous area of their route. For several days they had seen horsemen—Kurdish scouts, they assumed—reconnoitring their position from the surrounding hills, and they sweated every mile. The plain of Malazgirt, desolate enough in itself, gave way to great fields of lava rock and pumice as the group approached Süphan Dagh, the snowy 14,000-foot volcano squatting on the north shore of Lake Van. Except for a few isolated villages, they saw only treeless, empty wilderness. "The want of good government," Dr. Grant wrote, "the ravages of the Koords, and the existing famine . . . have nearly finished the work of depopulation which the Russians began in their late war [1828–29] with Turkey." Besides the Armenians, lured to the Khanate of Erivan by the Russians, many Kurds also had left, "but parties of them occasionally roam about for the sake of plunder and open robbery."

On the 27th of June, while approaching the east end of Lake Van, they received word that a party of some twenty-five Kurds had been committing robberies along that stretch of the road. Descending from the hills, Grant's party came suddenly upon a group of eighteen Kurds on horseback, carrying their long spears and plenty of firearms, and watching them from a ridge between the caravan road and the lake. Terror seized the travelers. They knew that three years before, a party of seventeen men had been murdered on this route, and their killers were never found. One of the Kurds, brandishing a spear, galloped forth on his horse to reconnoiter. Grant's party did not want this, because the closer the robber came, the more clearly he could see what easy pickings lay before him. One of the men wanted to shoot the Kurd as soon as he got within range, but Grant convinced him to shoot over the rider's head while he was still at a distance. When the gun went off the Kurd pulled up and stopped. A basic confrontation ensued, with both sides crouched for action. Voices and fists were raised; Grant drew his rolled umbrella, trying to make it look like a rifle.

The Kurd galloped back to his companions, who rode forward to meet him. When they saw this movement by the main body of Kurds, the men in Grant's party went into a panic, crying, "They're coming! They're coming!" Everyone talked at once and tried to push into the center of the group for safety. Some wanted to flee, but as they were poorly armed, mounted on slow caravan horses, and many miles from the nearest village, this idea was quickly discarded.

Grant urged his companions to "keep boldly on their way, as the least appearance of hesitation or flight would only invite pursuit." A small hill on their left looked inviting to some of the party, who started off in that direction. At this point Grant decided that, foreigner or not, he had to take charge. "I saw," he wrote, "they were sadly in want of a commander, and, for the first time, I assumed the tone and air of one." To dissuade the others from making a hasty, and certainly disastrous, retreat, he pointed to another hill further along the road and convinced them that they could seek refuge there if they had to.

His commanding tone was effective. Re-forming their column, the mixed band of Turks, Armenians, and Kurds rode on as "boldly" as they could. After watching them for a few minutes, the robbers turned and disappeared behind a ridge. Were they retreating? Or merely setting up an ambush further on? The prospects seemed no better than before. Moreover, the travelers were approaching a small river that had to be forded, a perfect opportunity for attack. The water was "deep and rapid," and, hurry as they might, the crossing took an hour. As Grant's company forded the stream, horsemen were seen approaching from the rear. Another spasm of panic engulfed the party, but this time it was not justified. The newcomers were part of another caravan enroute from Bitlis, at the west end of the lake. Not only were they not robbers, they would prove to be allies in the final push to Van. The travelers were "loud in their expression of thanks to God," Grant wrote. The ordeal, "such as I never wish to witness again," was over.

Reaching Van on July 1, Grant stayed with the Armenian bishop in rooms attached to the town's principal church. There they conferred on religious matters, including the city's eminent suitability for a mission station. This bishop, Grant noted, was a considerable improvement over the one he had met the previous year, a "bigoted narrow-minded man" who "had the reputation . . . of caring less for the flock than for their fleece." After talking to Grant, the bishop was surprised and delighted to find out that Protestants were not all atheists, infidels, and Freemasons, as he had been told. One of the topics discussed would become increasingly important to Grant in coming years. "In speaking of their prospects," he wrote, "the bishop [said] that they expect the downfall of the Mohammedan power in 1260 of the Hedgirah [1844]—a belief that is founded upon the thirteenth chapter of Revelations, which they refer to the description of that persecuting power."

Grant had first come upon this prophecy three weeks before, while crossing the Pontic range south of Trebizond. In this, one of Turkey's most beautiful areas, a place climatically similar to the American Pacific Northwest, the doctor found ample opportunity to think of Judith and their passage six years before. He had taken shelter in a post-house at a village called Jevizlik ("Walnut Grove") when a lightning storm, accompanied by drenching rain, stopped him from traveling further. Two dervishes, "pilgrims like myself," had also found shelter there, and the doctor shared with them his supper of yoghurt, fried eggs, and black bread. Later the innkeeper offered him honey, but Grant refused, fearing that it was the same narcotic, poisonous variety—wrought by bees feeding on the Pontic azalea—first described by Xenophon in the *Anabasis*. The year before, traveling with young Henry, he had eaten some of this "*deli bal*," or "mad honey," given to him by a peasant who served with it a raw onion to counter the toxic effects. He did not want to repeat the experience.

The dervishes, or "religious vagrants," as Grant described them, proved to be amiable company, and the three passed the evening together in pleasant religious discourse. The two men did not like the reforms of the sultan, who had broken from the faith, and mendicant holy men like themselves did not receive the same respect as before. "The world, they said, was changing for the worse; the last days were at hand, and the power of Islam was passing away." But Allah had decreed it, and they had no choice but to submit. Grant asked when these events would take place. The dervishes didn't know without consulting their books, but they assured him that the time would be soon—within three to five years. Later the doctor met another Muslim who, like the bishop of Van, told him that the power of Islam would be broken in A.H. 1260, some three years hence. Grant thought that his informant might have gotten this notion from the Armenians, with their belief in Revelation 13:5. In fact, Messianic speculation was already rampant among Muslims: the Shi'a in particular. The year 1844 would mark the thousandth anniversary of the disappearance of the twelfth Shi'ite Imam, and hopes were high for his return. Before the decade was out, the turmoil and rebellions surrounding this expected event would threaten to overthrow the government of Persia.

Thus were "last days" expectations planted firmly in the brain of Dr. Grant, and with them came renewed signs of fatalism. "Whether we ever meet again in this world," he wrote to Rev. Gridley, "is more than I can say. If our lives are spared a few years, it is at least possible." He wrote also to Ira Grant from Erzurum: "The Lord will take care of me while He has work for me on earth. May I then be prepared to enter into rest." Thomas Laurie mentions these "end times" prophecies in passing, but says little about their importance to the doctor. For Laurie, perhaps—and definitely for Justin Perkins, as we will see—such speculations were not to be taken seriously. Almost certainly, Perkins would have thought, they should not get in the way of that "concentrated effort" which alone would produce results. Though Grant voiced as loudly as anyone his disapproval of the "nominally Christian" Eastern churches, with their "dead forms," their "corruption" and "superstition," he chose to take seriously the notion that, within three years, the Muslims of the Middle East would lose their faith and the political power that attended it—an opinion based on a rumor floated by priests whom he did not really respect. To Wayne Gridley, Grant wrote: "I ought in justice to spend some time in a more full development of this important subject." But by July 3 he was again on horseback, and Independence Day found him at the great castle of Hoshap south of Van. In Başkale, having just missed the weekly caravan to Julamerk, he went on alone, accompanied by two muleteers. On July 8, 1841, three months and a week after leaving Boston, Asahel Grant reached the home of the patriarch Mar Shimun in Kochanes.

In that summer of 1841, life in central Kurdistan had become increasingly unsettled, and in the province of Hakkari, especially, plots had thickened to the point of coagulation. The previous year, the emir Nurullah Bey, as we have seen, had bartered his independence from the Ottomans in return for an appointment as governor in the mountains. The emir was not, however, an absolute ruler who could make this decision by himself. He needed the assent, or at least the acquiescence, of lesser Kurdish chieftains in order to make the new order work. Many of those chieftains did not want to give up the Hakkari tribes' independence, especially to the Turks, and one of their faction was Suleiman Bey, Nurullah's nephew and rival, the friend of Mar Shimun and son of the late emir. Like Nurullah, Mar Shimun held his authority only through the consent of the various tribes and their maleks. Moreover, at a time when unity was essential, he had fomented discord by trying to assert his political authority over mountaineers who formerly had regarded themselves mainly as part of his spiritual flock, not as the obedient subjects of a despot. Everyone, in other words, was grabbing for more power: the sultan and his ministers, the pashas of Erzurum and Mosul, the emir Nurullah, his nephew Suleiman, and Mar Shimun, the patriarch of the Nestorians. In the south, Ismael Pasha of Amadiyah was scheming to re-take his capital, while to the west of Hakkari the emir of Bohtan, Bedr Khan Bey, wanted to be king over all of them.

It is understandable that Grant, immersed in this pit of serpents, would hope that God would swoop down, shake the nations to their roots, and install Someone Better on His throne. Evil was seeping like melted snow from the rocks. On July 7, deep in the canyon road that winds from Başkale to Julamerk (close, in fact, to the place where Schultz was killed), Grant, unarmed, had to face down an attempt at extortion by two muleteers who demanded more money after he had already paid them. To the south, Ottoman troops, active again in the district of Amadiyah, were threatening Asheetha and the Tiyari. "Wars and rumors of wars, but fear not—God reigns!" This phrase, ringing with faith and fatalism, would become Grant's mantra in the months ahead.

In one sense the doctor had reason for optimism. After the missionaries in Urmia had written their letter of March 31, detailing fraud and deception, a good deal of tension might have been expected when Grant met with Mar Shimun. But Dr. Grant wrote that nothing could have been more cordial than the words which flowed from the patriarch's lips after their twelve months' separation. All his former promises—of cooperation, security, permission for the opening of schools—were repeated. "The welcome which he gave me," Grant wrote in his journal, "together with his unremitted attentions while I remained with him, were all that I could ask."

To William Stocking, in Urmia, he was less effusive: "The Patriach never seemed more cordial than now; but there is an unsettled aspect to the whole region, which seems to denote changes in prospect." Note the word "seemed" in describing Mar Shimun's cordiality. There is no mention of the larcenous deacons, Yohannan and Dunkha, who were undoubtedly lurking somewhere in the rocks. Zadok, another of Mar Shimun's brothers, a priest who would prove to be as temperate as a sailor and as pacific as Genghis Khan, agreed to accompany the doctor in his mountain travels. Thus, accompanied by Priest Zadok and the patriarch Mar Shimun (who was to travel with them for the first five days), Grant set out on July 10 for the mountains of Jelu, the highest district in Kurdistan.

13

INFERNO

"Travel is a foretaste of Hell."—*Proverb from Turkestan*

WHILE ASAHEL GRANT FOLLOWED a path that led across mountain glaciers, through canyons veined with snow, Americans in the plains north of Mosul were facing a different challenge. There the summer heat was approaching, and with it a time of danger. During his winter in the United States, Grant had warned of this, and in his letters to Rufus Anderson he strongly recommended that the Mitchells and Hinsdales, his new colleagues in the mission to the Mountain Nestorians, should arrive before the "poisonous winds" of summer swept through.

In writing of these winds and their alleged toxicity, Asahel Grant repeated the medical reasoning that led doctors to condemn the atmosphere of Urmia, with its "miasma" and "bad air." His concerns were valid. Disease, he knew, was so prevalent in the East, so deadly and baffling, that any weakening influence had to be avoided, and common sense told him that to bring missionaries straight from North America into the furnace of Babylon would invite disaster.

Thomas Laurie, writing about Mosul summers, leaves little doubt about the trials facing newcomers. From May onwards everyone in the city slept on the rooftops, while during the day, all residents who could afford them would stay in *serdabs*, cellars fitted out as subterranean sitting rooms. Siroccos, Grant's "poisonous winds," sometimes sprang up during the summer, and then "the air is so filled with fine sand, that, however one shuts himself up, it is deposited all around him, and sifts into every drawer, desk and trunk." Inside the stifling houses even "the very air seems lurid and dark, as if impervious to light."

> In July, every dry object communicates the sensation of heat. Beds seem just scorched with a warming-pan, and even the stone floor is hot to the touch. A change of linen, instead of imparting the cooling sensation that it does in other climes, feels as if fresh from the mouth of a furnace; for perspiration keeps the body cooler than the dry substances around it. Such extreme heat deals most unmercifully with furniture. Solid mahogany desks are split; articles fastened with glue fall to pieces; miniatures painted on ivory curl like a shaving, and the ivory handles of knives and forks crack from end to end. An unfortunate piano, that had wandered from England to one of the consulates, was continually wrenched out of tune, and rendered useless.

A tough climate required strong people, and the ABCFM sent the strongest they could find. The Americans who sailed for the Middle East that winter—Colby Mitchell and his wife Eliza; Abel and Sarah Hinsdale—were cut from the same cloth (invariably black) as so many other American Board missionaries. Young, God-fearing, teetotalling, well-educated New Englanders all, both men were Yale graduates and the women as sturdy as any Yankee Protestantism could produce. They all knew hard work, and they had certainly known privation. Colby Mitchell, especially, embodied both the selfless missionary spirit and a gritty determination to succeed. A man of "superior powers," according to A.C. Lathrop, who knew him at Yale, Mitchell had worked his way through college splitting wood and doing other odd jobs for the residents of New Haven. These were not, in short, a collection of dilettantes. Of the four, it was Sarah Hinsdale who proved to be the toughest, and it was she who told their story to Thomas Laurie.

Having sailed from Boston on January 12, the missionaries should have easily arrived before summer. Their ocean passage was rough, but given the time of year, one would be surprised to hear otherwise. In any case, after forty-one days of being tossed about in their barque, the *Emma Isadora,* the Americans landed at Smyrna on March 2, 1841, and two days later caught the Austrian Lloyd's steamer heading south. They reached Beirut on March 12. This great Lebanese port was out of their way; they were going to Aleppo, en route to Mesopotamia. But the newcomers had come to Beirut to connect with another missionary couple, Rev. and Mrs. Elias Beadle, who would serve as interpreters for the journey to Aleppo.

The Beirut sojourn, though pleasant enough, took far more time than expected. In fact, six weeks and a day passed before the missionaries could leave the town. Many obstacles, mostly involving official travel documents from the Ottoman authorities, delayed their departure until April 24. Even then they had trouble, for the journey north to Iskenderun, that could often be done in a day, took six days, as contrary winds kept their ship from making headway. Nevertheless, after passing through Iskenderun and Antioch, the Mitchells and Hinsdales, accompanied by Rev. and Mrs. Beadle, arrived in Aleppo on May 8.

Aleppo was an important city, though as described by Layard—large sections deserted, houses falling into ruin, streets "deep in mud and filth"—it seems even worse than Iskenderun, which Layard called "little more than a heap of ruins." From Aleppo the trade routes fanned out, to Diyarbakir and Antep, to Antioch and the coast, and south toward Homs and Damascus. The Beadles now dropped out of the party; they were staying in Aleppo to establish a mission station. From this point

on the Mitchells and Hinsdales had to secure their own interpreter and muleteers, as the Mosul caravan had left only a few
days earlier. This, of course, meant further delays.

After a long search for an interpreter, the Americans found
a man Hinsdale identifies as "Mr. Kotschy, a German natural-
ist," who joined the company. This was Theodor Kotschy, a
botanist who was born in 1813 in Silesia and was to die in
Vienna in 1866. At the age of 28 Kotschy had already been
travelling in the Near East for seven years searching for and
identifying plant specimens. He travelled from the Sudan to
Egypt, in Cyprus, across Syria and Turkey, and into Persia, and
his name appears in botanical Latin on a wide variety of plants,
including a rhododendron (*r. kotschyi*) and the species *Kotschya*.
From the rivers of Syria and Iraq he sent back to Vienna a large
collection of fresh water fishes, and on Kharg Island, in the
Persian Gulf, he took time off from collecting algae to discover
a new species of sand crab: *Epixanthus kotschyi*. Kotschy was,
in other words, one of those indispensable and indefatigable
19th-century scientist-explorers who, like Friedrich Schultz, did
so much of the hard work on which human knowledge depends.
Besides his linguistic abilities and general experience of the area,
Kotschy possessed considerable medical skills, a definite asset
for the journey ahead.

Around May 21, just when the party was ready to depart,
illness struck. "Intermittent fever"—malaria—kept Colby Mitchell in his sickbed for a week. By the time they were ready to
leave, it was May 28, dangerously late in the season for their
journey. However, if they travelled at a good pace, it was still
possible for them to get to Mosul in plenty of time. Unfortunately, the Mitchell-Hinsdale party now encountered the same
obstacle that had held up Asahel Grant's caravan: green grass.
The spring rains in 1841 must have been heavy, because there
was abundant grass along the route. Their chief muleteer insisted, just as Grant's had done, on taking time to let the pack
animals eat all they could hold, with the result that the mission-

aries spent much of the journey sitting on the ground watching horses graze. After two weeks of pleasant, if dilatory, wandering, they reached Diyarbakir on June 12.

On June 14, Colby Mitchell wrote to Elias Beadle in Aleppo that all was well. The party was encamped in a grove of willows a few miles northwest of Diyarbakir. Their health was not only good; it had actually improved on the journey, and all were fully rested for the trip ahead. That same day they left for Mardin, sixty miles to the southeast. They went so slowly that it took them five days to reach the town, an average speed of one half-mile an hour. This is astonishing, because in July 1839 Asahel Grant and H.A. Homes had done the journey in a day. Even an inveterate plant-hunter like Theodor Kotschy could not have held them up that long. We can only assume that by the time the Mitchell-Hinsdale party reached Mardin the head muleteer's horses were exceedingly well fed.

They now faced the last leg of the journey, over the same ground that Asahel Grant and Capt. Arthur Conolly had traversed in September 1839. But while Grant and Conolly had taken a direct path across the desert and close to the mountains of Sinjar—formerly a notorious lair for Yezidi bandits—the missionaries and Kotschy decided to detour east toward Cizre (Jezirah ibn Omar) and stay closer to the river Tigris. According to Hinsdale, the heat remained moderate, and they could wear their overcoats for three or four hours every morning. When the party arrived at Mardin on June 19, they camped on the plain below the city. Kotschy and Hinsdale rode up to the town to buy provisions, and Colby Mitchell stayed in camp to help set up the tents. A violent rainstorm came up—a highly unusual occurrence for so late in the year—and soaked Mitchell to the skin.

The Sabbath fell on June 20, and of course the missionaries went nowhere on that day. They could not, as it turned out, have traveled anyway, as the malaria returned to Colby Mitchell with a vengeance. One day of fever and shaking lengthened to a second; they set out on Monday morning when Mitchell was feeling somewhat better, and by Tuesday his fever had gone. A series of villages—Haznavur, Chuluaga—marked their progress. Summer heat now set in, and on the 25th they rested until the cool of evening would allow them to go on. That afternoon Mitchell went out on the plain during a sirocco, and when he came back he complained that he could not see clearly. Kotschy gave him an emetic, which brought a bit of relief, and as all the company, including Mitchell, were anxious to go on, they set out at 7:00 p.m. and rode six hours into the night. Colby Mitchell, refreshed by the ride, went to sleep with the rest of them.

By morning, however, things had changed. When Abel Hinsdale woke he found Mitchell already dressed and "evidently deranged." Did this mean the delirium of fever? A permutation of malaria? No one can say. A clue might be found in his blurred vision of the day before, and its possible connection to a neurological problem. For some reason, the man had gone to bed apparently healthy and awakened incoherent and deranged. The party had stopped for the night by a pool of water, but in daylight they could see that it was small and stagnant. With Mitchell in his saddle, supported by a man walking on either side of him, the stricken company rode an hour to a Kurdish village called Mushtafia.

One of the servants had gone ahead to secure a room, and there the sick man was put to bed. Theodor Kotschy now went to work, and of course the first thing he brought out was his lancet. Bleed as he might, however, he could produce no positive results. They washed and rubbed Mitchell's arms, and this revived him somewhat. All other remedies—including, we can assume, more emetics—were tried in vain. Mitchell's feet had gone cold, and a "clammy sweat" covered his body. Like Asahel Grant telling his mother of his "rice-colored" excretions, Thomas Laurie gave his readers the details whether they wanted them or not. "He seemed," Laurie wrote, "much troubled at some great obstacle defeating all his efforts to do good at the very moment of success." What was this thing that possessed him? Even from a distance of 160 years, the illness seems astonishing. There was no fever, no vomiting, and evidently no pain. Mitchell sank, "like a flower withering in the sun," and on the Sabbath morning of June 27, he simply ceased to breathe.

In the mud-brick house by the waters of Babylon, the missionaries could scarcely believe what had happened. The body had to be buried, and quickly, but the Kurds of Mushtafia would not allow a Christian to be buried in their graveyard; nor would they touch the corpse, fearing that it might be contagious. Another village, a Syrian Jacobite settlement called Telabel, lay seven miles away, and there the travelers took Colby Mitchell after strapping him to a horse. At the Telabel graveyard, they dug a grave in the blazing heat. Green branches cushioned the bottom, and flat stones, set on edge, lined the sides. Abel Hinsdale read the burial service. More flat stones, a protection from animals, were laid upon the remains of Colby Mitchell, and the crevices filled with straw. After covering all with earth, they placed two stones on top to mark the place. With this, the desolate band returned to their hovel in Mushtafia.

Through the illness and burial, and even the following night, Eliza Mitchell had held up well. Her body's mental defenses—shock, disbelief, a reflexive numbness—had deflected the blow, but this fragile barrier could not stand for long. It must have seemed to Eliza that they had wandered from the smiling heaven of New England into the earthly equivalent of hell. The world had gone brown with dust; the Assyrian heat pressed upon their shoulders like a stone. In Mushtafia crowds of peasants, their bronze faces scored by years in the sun, gathered to stare.

It happened the next morning, as they were helping Eliza onto her horse. "Grief," wrote Laurie, "could no longer be constrained." He gives no details, leaving us to imagine the nightmare of that day's ride across the plain. By dark they reached Pesh Khabur, a town which stands at the current border between Turkey and Iraq, where the eastern Khabur River winds out of the mountains and joins the Tigris. Rough, uninhabited terrain barred their path along the right bank of the Tigris, and it took twenty men an entire day to float the travelers and their goods across the river on goatskin rafts. The horses were forced to swim, with the result that many were carried far downstream by the current and had to be retrieved.

Leaving Pesh Khabur in the morning, the company rode six hours and spent that night in a Yezidi village. The next day, July 1, they had been in the saddle for only an hour when Eliza Mitchell collapsed. Despair had given way to fever, and even with men walking beside to lend support, she could not proceed. At an Arab village called Bowerea they were forced to halt; and there, after the hellish journey, things turned even worse.

Those who travel in the Middle East know the lack of privacy that accompanies any trip outside the major cities. The very concept of privacy is, in fact, alien. In the Turkish language the word "privacy" does not exist in the Western sense. Village people lead boring lives in any poor country, and when confronted by outsiders they crowd around and stare, unaware of the European desire to be "left alone." In his *Travels and Researches,* Ainsworth described his misery in 1840, when he and Rassam could not enjoy a moment's solitude while they waited for Mar Shimun in an Armenian village near Julamerk. Even an experienced traveler like Isabella Bird, dwelling among the Bakhtiyaris of Persia, found the lack of privacy to be an ordeal. After seven years in the Middle East, Theodor Kotschy surely knew what to expect, but the missionaries did not.

Hinsdale and Laurie left behind no detailed description of Bowerea, so Eliza Mitchell's sickbed has to be imagined. Almost certainly she lay in a mud house with a floor of hard-packed earth. Windows? Not likely. Glass was far too dear, and though the people endured a furnace in summer, their winters brought cold and often snow, so windows served no purpose. Probably the house had a hole in the roof, for the smoke of cooking fires to escape, and a door. For the use of this hovel the

Arabs might not have demanded money, but they seem to have taken payment in other ways.

Day and night, as Eliza Mitchell lay ill, the village women swarmed into her room. In plain view they pawed through the travelers' belongings, carrying off any items that interested them. The missionaries were too demoralized and exhausted to protest. The villagers sat along the walls staring at the foreigners, talking to each other—oblivious to the woman's illness. In their world, after all, sickness and death were common as fleas. The indignities extended even to Sarah Hinsdale, who, while she bent over Eliza Mitchell caring for her, felt the women's hands upon her back as they cut off the hooks and eyes holding her dress together.

On the evening of their fourth day in Bowerea, the travelers could stand it no longer. Come what may, they had to move on. Hinsdale and Kotschy had improvised a litter for Mrs. Mitchell, but they needed four men to carry it, and the men of Bowerea disdained the work at any price. No amount of money could induce them to carry an infidel woman. Only after sending to a distant village could Hinsdale find men who would do the job. The days now were so hot that they could only travel by night. Sarah Hinsdale kept so busy during the daylight hours tending to Eliza Mitchell that she had no time to sleep; Abel Hinsdale was forced to walk beside her on the night marches, supporting her so that she would not fall off her horse. Three years later, Thomas Laurie relates, Sarah pointed out to him a place on the road where she had wrapped herself in her cloak and slept for half an hour at midnight, "amid Arabs clamoring for money, and yet unwilling to earn it by carrying Mrs. Mitchell." Soon after sunrise on July 7, they came within sight of Mosul. For the last two days of their ordeal they had been assisted by a servant of Christian Rassam, who had been British vice-consul in the city since the previous autumn. At last, after the Americans had crossed the bridge of boats into the teeming city, Rassam and his wife Matilda welcomed them to their home.

The missionaries had passed through hell, but now they were in Mosul. In July. As piano frames twisted, mahogany cracked, and heated air thickened into plasma, Abel and Sarah Hinsdale stayed around the clock at Eliza Mitchell's bedside. At one point Abel, after nursing the sick woman to the point of exhaustion, collapsed in a faint while walking from one room to another. For a while Eliza seemed to improve and appeared, as Thomas Laurie put it, to "have unusual enjoyment in Christ." But soon the illness intensified and took a new form, and from then on "reason was dethroned." At the same time, Abel Hinsdale became violently ill and could not leave his bed. Nor could Sarah, whose own health now broke as well. Both were absent when on July 12, deranged and in agony, Eliza Mitchell took her last breath. Among the people gathered for her burial in the yard of the Syrian Jacobite church, there was no one who had ever known her.

Asahel Grant knew nothing about all this—an urgent message dispatched to him by Christian Rassam vanished somewhere between Mosul and Hakkari. As July passed into August and the Hinsdales lingered at the point of death, the weary doctor trekked through hidden valleys, descended cliff faces on trembling legs, mapped peaks and rivers, wrote in his journal, conferred with tribal leaders, preached the Gospel, dreamt of the future, removed trachoma scars, dealt out emetics, and scrambled in his goat-hair sandals over endless heaps of rock. The life, though strenuous, agreed with him. His health improved in the mountain air, and with it grew his plans for a permanent missionary station in Tiyari.

Asheetha, which had so impressed him in 1839, was the obvious choice, despite its southerly location, far from the patriarch's residence and the politico-geographical center of the Nestorian domains. Its advantages were numerous. It lay in the heart of a populous, heavily-cultivated valley. Its climate was pleasant, its water plentiful, and snow lingered the year round within a half-hour's walk of the village. Most importantly, compared to sites on the opposite bank of the Zab, Asheetha offered easier access to the supplies and political contacts of Mosul. As for relations with the patriarchate, Asheetha's distance from Kochanes and Julamerk and their endless political intrigue, might prove an actual advantage.

No one should deprecate the power of hard work and positive thought on human events; but as we look at political forces coalescing in the summer of 1841 the project for this missionary station seems increasingly ill-advised, and especially so when we realize that newcomers like the Mitchells and Hinsdales had been sent to join Grant in the endeavor. No central authority existed in the mountains. The *firman,* an elaborate document on parchment that foreign travelers usually secured from the Ottoman sultan, demanding hospitality, post horses, and lodging for the bearer, carried no weight. The *buyurultu,* a provincial version of the *firman*, was equally uselesss. There were no police and no municipal ordinances: indeed, no acknowledged laws beyond the general diktat of "blood for blood." Grant already knew of the threats from Bedr Khan Bey in the west, Nurullah Bey in the north, and to the south Mohammed pasha of Mosul; but now as he penetrated the valleys the deeper fault lines revealed themselves.

One Nestorian district, for example, the important valley of Tehoma on the left bank of the Zab, had long been at war with a district of Tiyari in the next range to the south. They had buried the hatchet in the 1830s when confronted with Mohammed, the one-eyed emir of Rowanduz; but now that the Turks had taken care of Blind Mohammed, the two Nestorian tribes had again drawn knives and returned to the fight. As with the Kurds, individual villages were sometimes at odds. The tribes and their maleks continued to oppose Mar Shimun's seizure of temporal power. And always there raged blood feuds between families, individuals, or relatives. Of the Hakkari people, one missionary, Rev. George Coan, wrote in 1852: "My very soul was made sick by their endless strifes." Another wrote in 1864: "In these unsubdued tribes, the people are wild and cruel. Murder is no more before their eyes than drinking water." Father Jacques Rhétoré, a Dominican priest who lived in Asheetha from 1908 until 1911, found its people suffused with "greed, deception, duplicity, mutual jealousies, social indiscipline," and "national and religious fanaticism."

This was where Asahel Grant proposed to build a permanent station, complete with a school, a stable, and living quarters for the mission families. Today the hopelessness of the enterprise seems obvious. But miracles, Grant must have believed, could happen, and whether they occurred or not, God's will *would* be done. Grant simply did not care about fear or the threat of disaster. He believed in God, and he believed in himself. Nurullah Bey, Suleiman Bey, and Mar Shimun were "old friends" of his, and he believed in their good will because he knew he deserved it. He had faith that the luck of his thus-far charmed life would carry the brethren over the crevasses ahead.

But besides fatalism and the zeal of the true believer, one overarching cause—anti-Catholicism—provided the extra impetus that drove him forward. At that time Puritan New England seethed with anti-Catholic bigotry, feelings which the missionaries fully shared. In Grant's letters to Rufus Anderson, before and after returning to America, he repeatedly claimed that the Vatican had an immediate interest in the mountain Nestorians. The implication was obvious: "If we don't go there, the Catholics will." For the militant Protestants of New England these fears became the ultimate spur to action, and of all the arguments marshalled in support of the Hakkari mission, this seems to have carried more weight than any other. Nothing aroused the competitive zeal of the Americans like rumors of approaching Dominicans, Lazarists, or Jesuits. If they considered the French consul in Mosul to be a "bigoted papist," they did not hesitate to say so, even though this same consul, Paul-Émile Botta, gave kindly assistance both to them and to the

English, especially to Austen Henry Layard. The pope, purely and simply, was the Antichrist, the "man of sin" and "son of perdition" described in Paul's Second Letter to the Thessalonians, and they detested him and his "reptile" agents from the very depth of their souls. Their urgency and detestation were misplaced. Throughout the 19th century and into the 20th, these same papists, though they nibbled at the fringes and sometimes came offering money, never made any serious effort to establish mission stations in the Hakkari mountains.

After reaching the river Zab on the evening of July 21, 1841, Asahel Grant crossed the wicker bridge to Lezan, the Tiyari village that he had first visited in October 1839. Having exchanged his Oriental disguise for European clothing, the doctor was at first scarcely recognized by the people, and only the full beard he wore "in the latest Paris cut" gave away his identity. After sleeping that night by the Zab, Grant and Zadok set out the next morning for Asheetha, expecting to reach it in a day. But before they could leave, the malek of Lezan, who had been absent when Grant visited in 1839, emerged from his house and insisted that the doctor come in for a visit. Within minutes, multitudes of villagers had gathered to ask for medical aid. "Some who had experienced relief from former prescriptions," wrote Grant, scandalized at their lack of medical prudence, "wanted a supply of the same medicine for themselves and their friends to use at discretion!" The villagers seem also to have acquired a love of vomiting as a restorative activity, for "tartar emetic was in special demand." Thus delayed, Asahel Grant could only progress that day as far as the village of Minyanish. There his former cataract patient, the young man who had wandered blind through the mountains to reach Urmia, greeted him once again with a gift of honey. At noon the next day, Friday, July 23, Grant arrived in Asheetha.

The journey had not been easy, and at one point, in Tehoma, there came news—unconfirmed—that a party of Kurds had been sent to intercept him. Qasha Zadok, the patriarch's brother, complained bitterly of fatigue and especially of the heat, for despite the altitude the sun's rays concentrated powerfully in the narrow valleys. Only love of Dr. Grant and support for his mission, Zadok loudly declared, could have induced him to undergo such an ordeal. Zadok, it would seem, protested too much; although the man was a priest with a high position in the patriarchal family, his religious commitment made no great impression on Asahel Grant. In fact, his character overall appears to bear a remarkable resembalance to that of his brothers Yohannan and Dunkha, the leeches of Urmia. Zadok does not seem to have been much use as a guide. Perhaps he was more like a patriarchal "minder," assigned to accompany Dr. Grant and watch over for the Shimun family interests. At least once on the journey to Asheetha the party was forced to make a midday halt because Zadok had drunk too much wine at the house of a village chief; and later, religious office did not prevent Zadok from urging his brethren to make a sneak attack against the Kurds on the Sabbath. Grant soon began to feel that Zadok and the Tiyari people were not seeking "the pearl without price," but had more temporal concerns in mind.

During his four weeks in Asheetha, Asahel Grant lived at the home of Qasha Auraham, the learned scribe who had entertained him on his first visit. Auraham's house was typical of the mountain Nestorians: a two-story structure with a solid, windowless first floor often built into the hillside, a second floor for summer use with a front wall open to the air, and a ladder leading to the flat roof where everyone slept in summer. Grant seems to have enjoyed those four weeks: Asheetha overflowed with terraced gardens, vineyards, and orchards, irrigated by the waters that tumbled endlessly into the valley. The village offered a bracing, healthful climate, the opportunity to do good works, and overwhelming physical beauty—the time Grant spent there was, in all probability, the closest thing to contentment he could have known.

In Qasha Auraham's upper room the doctor spent his days tending to patients, chatting with visitors, and dining upon the usual mountain fair: millet boiled in sour milk. It didn't take long for word of Grant's presence to get around, and each day the customary horde of patients descended upon Asheetha. Some were emergency cases: one boy had been badly injured when he fell down a mountainside, while another, a shepherd, was mauled by a rockslide that his flock had set into motion. Both were carried in unconscious; under Grant's care, both recovered. Of the other sick villagers, we can assume that many came in for their much-desired swig of tartar emetic. Above all, there was the curse of trachoma and its resulting "cataracts," so-called because, like the waterfall which gives them their name, the masses of scar tissue on eyelids would fall like a curtain across the cornea, obscuring vision. Grant could do nothing about curing the disease (now easily treated with antibiotics), which is highly contagious and endemic in the Middle East. He could, however, excise the scar tissue, a delicate operation rendered even more difficult by the lack of anesthesia. "Most of the blind," he wrote, "I assembled at once, and in a single day I removed cataracts from the eyes of no less than seven men and women, most of whom experienced an entire or partial restoration of their sight."

All this the people appreciated, and though many of the Tiyari tribesmen suspected Grant's motives—he was, after all, known to be a friend of the emir Nurullah Bey—the doctor's kindness soon won them over. Fortune was not smiling upon the valley that summer. A raid by a group of Kurds from Berwar had resulted in the death of twenty Nestorians, the capture and imprisonment of others, and the loss of 7000 sheep. This was followed by a plague of locusts, devouring grain crops and threatening a lean winter. Though the locusts were the result of forces beyond their control, the raid almost certainly was not. It is impossible to point to the prime offender in eternal feuds of this kind, but clearly the men of Tiyari were notorious robbers and raiders who doubtless gave the Kurds of Berwar plenty of reason for their assault.

We have seen Ainsworth's reference, the year before, to a particularly horrendous raid by the Tiyarians. In 1852 in *The Nestorians and Their Rituals*, George Percy Badger refers to the Kurdish raid of 1841 as if it were a single incident, and he surmises that Mohammed Pasha, the ever-scheming governor of Mosul, may have instigated the deed to stir up trouble—as if any such intrigue were necessary. The American missionaries, even with their Christian bias, saw plenty of evidence to the contrary. Thomas Laurie and Azariah Smith, on a visit to Hakkari in 1844, did not hesitate to speak of the Nestorians' "wildness and savageness" and the "provocation" they gave to the Kurds. While touring the area in 1849, Justin Perkins asked his guide, a Nestorian from Duree, whether his village had ever been sacked by the Tiyarians. Yes, the man replied quickly, "five or six times by the Tiyari people; and not our village only, but all the villages of Bewer [Berwar], both Nestorian and Koordish."

When the men of Asheetha lamented their misfortunes, Grant came up with a simple remedy: they should repent. They had departed from God, he told them, and He was punishing them for their sins. Moreover, "I feared they might be chastened yet more severely in the loss of their independence and consequent oppression and suffering, unless they would speedily repent and return to the Lord." The Nestorians nodded their heads in agreement, said, "It is even so," and returned to more practical things, like plotting their next raid.

The demands of his work in Asheetha did not prevent Asahel Grant from remembering his colleagues. He knew that the Hinsdales and Mitchells should have arrived in Mosul by then, and yet he had heard nothing. When July had given way to August, he dispatched a letter asking for word of their progress.

On August 15, his last Sabbath in Asheetha, he attended a council of war. Tribesmen from all over Tiyari had assembled in large numbers to debate their course of action against the Kurds of Berwar. By then two more Nestorians had been killed, and those who counseled restraint were being shouted down by the likes of Qasha Zadok, the patriarch's brother, and the scholarly Qasha Auraham. The latter, Grant noted, called for war with a special vehemence, declaring that if the men of Tiyari did not take immediate vengeance, they were not men and should dress in women's clothing. Zadok turned to Dr. Grant and said he would rise at once and lead the Tiyarians into battle.

"What?" Grant replied. "On the Sabbath?"

Zadok, ever the realist, replied that they could make a surprise attack in the night, when the Sabbath was over, but they had to get going before the men dispersed and went back to their farms. Grant said that he could not give advice on war or peace, but he suggested that, rather than desecrate the Lord's day, they might be better off spending it in prayer for God's blessing and guidance. This led to further spirited discussion, in which the doctor did not take part. At length, however, the men dispersed, having decided to postpone the invasion of Berwar.

By then Grant had heard nothing from Mosul, but his stay in Asheetha had already extended a week beyond the time he had planned. On Monday morning he traveled down the Asheetha valley to the village of Minyanish and stayed overnight. It was there on the morning of August 17, his birthday, that a Kurd arrived bringing word of the Mitchells' deaths and the Hinsdales' continuing illness. The doctor now had no choice but to proceed to Mosul as soon as possible. But on arriving at Lezan, on the banks of the Zab, he found that the Kurdish chief of Berwar, who feared his pro-Tiyari influence in Mosul, would not let him pass through to Amadiyah.

At that point another letter arrived, this one from Mar Shimun. The tone of his message could not have been more urgent. The emir Nurullah Bey, having won the support of the Ottomans in 1840, had spent the previous year attempting to impose tributary taxes upon the patriarch and all the Nestorian villages of Hakkari. In this he had been fiercely resisted. Justin Perkins, writing from Urmia on April 1, noted that the caravan route from Persia into Hakkari was unsafe due to a "quarrel" between the patriarch and the emir. This quarrel, relating to those taxes—indeed, relating to fundamental issues of power and governance in the mountains—was now coming to a head. The letter from Mar Shimun pointed the tribesmen not to the south, where they had been focusing their attention, but to the north, where a combined force of Turks and Kurds, under Nurullah's orders, was advancing upon the patriarch's home. In his letter Mar Shimun, cloaked in the mantle of spiritual and temporal authority, was calling the tribes to arms against the invaders.

With this news Lezan fell into turmoil. The patriarch's brother Zadok urged Grant to remain, to lend the tribes his counsel and medical aid. This kind of involvement, however, was exactly what Grant wanted to avoid. He spent all of Wednesday, August 18, preparing for departure and tending to the sick who came flocking to him for a final time. The next day he wrote a letter to Dr. Austin Wright, a letter that did not arrive in Urmia, 100 miles away, until eight months later. Grant informed Wright of the disaster in Mosul and rejected the idea of staying with the Nestorians as they moved toward war. Even if the Hinsdales had not needed him in Mosul, Grant wrote, he would not have stayed in the mountains, "for to remain with the Patriarch might be to enlist as a military surgeon, an honor to which I do not aspire."

The journey facing Asahel Grant was the most perilous of his career. Somehow he had to make his way over two wild mountain ranges and the intervening Berwar district before he could find safety in the Turkish-held fortress of Amadiyah, and he had to do it at night. Of the dangers he had endured before—blizzards, bandits, even the mob violence in Mardin—none had been directed at him personally. By 1841, however, fame had put its mark upon him, and he had become identified with one side—the Tiyarians—in a feud that was fast approaching total war. The sheikh of Berwar's refusal to let him pass through was not a death sentence; the Kurds, after all, prized

Grant's skills as much as did the Nestorians. Still, in the company of ten heavily-armed Tiyari men—recruited as guides by Zadok—Grant faced considerable danger, especially if a fight developed. As the sun set on the evening of August 19, after saying his last good-byes, the doctor and his companions, including the Kurdish porter who had brought the letter, set off up the mountain toward Berwar.

Night had just fallen when Grant's guides drew aside to talk. Having conferred among themselves, they confronted the doctor, telling him that they refused to go on unless he doubled their wages for the journey. These payments had, of course, been agreed upon by everyone before they left Lezan. By then the only illumination was starlight, and the party had climbed into a wilderness of rock. Asahel Grant was already experienced in dealing with petty extortion. Just a month before, two Kurdish muleteers in the valley of the Zab had tried the same thing close to the spot where Schultz was murdered. But this was different. These men, picked by Mar Shimun's brother, were supposed to be friends. Just before dark, as twilight deepened upon the ranges, they had paused to gaze at the scenery and ask, "Is it not beautiful?" a question with which the doctor could only agree. "[The scene] was tinged with the sombre hues of twilight," Grant wrote, "and was in such harmony with my feelings that I could scarce refrain from tears." His thoughts were full of "the past, present and future, of this beloved people." Now upon a mountainside, in utter darkness, these beloved people were gouging him for more money. The doctor remained calm. He was, he reminded them, totally in their power. They were ten; he was alone and unarmed. If they wished to rob and kill him, he would do nothing to resist them; but he would not give in to their demands. If they decided to go on, their reward at the end would be in proportion to their good behavior. If that did not suit them, they could return immediately to Lezan.

It was a remarkable incident, not only for what it revealed about Grant's courage but for the decidedly negative impression left by the Tiyari tribesmen. To the missionary elders in Boston, concerned with donations and recruitment, the unsavory nature of the confrontation was more significant than Grant's bravery; thus, no word of it found its way into the doctor's journal in the *Missionary Herald*, although Thomas Laurie does not hesitate to tell the tale. The guides yielded: for once in the human experience character triumphed over venality. Before reaching the summit one man, exhausted, gave up, and then another. With the eight remaining guides and his Kurdish porter, Grant crossed from Tiyari into Berwar.

It was the same mountain boundary—now the Iraqi-Turkish frontier—that he had crossed on October 18, 1839, but this time he was moving in the opposite direction and unable to admire the scenery. Berwar contained many Nestorian villages, including Duree, the first he had visited, but in no case could he risk the chief's retribution by asking fellow Christians for help. The ten men proceeded silently, in single file, stopping often to reconnoitre and make sure they were not seen. Occasionally they spied the campfires of shepherds and heard their dogs. They passed one village, then another guarded by a castle. At times only the width of a knoll separated them from the Kurdish guards, whose conversation they could hear plainly. In the heart of the district they came upon a creek flowing eastward to the Zab. A bridge spanned the water, but as it was too greatly exposed they decided to make a ford further downstream. This led to more complications when four of the guides became separated from the main party in heavy thickets edging the stream. Long minutes dragged by as they waited, unable to shout or call attention to themselves, until finally the men appeared. This happened, as Grant determined by feeling for the hands of his watch, slightly after one in the morning. After another arduous climb, dawn found them at the summit of the Chiya Matinah, the mountain pass overlooking Amadiyah, three miles away. Here Grant paid off his guides, who kissed his hand and gave him a few morsels of bread and cheese before parting. They would remain in hiding for the rest of the day until they could retrace their steps after nightfall.

Grant had arrived safely within sight of Amadiyah, but the ordeal had not ended. The Nestorian guides had been gone only a few minutes when Grant and the porter were stopped in their tracks by two Kurds, who emerged from the rocks and made a grab for their baggage. A long dispute ensued between the porter and the thieves in Kurdish, which Grant could not understand. Their import was obvious: the travelers were to stand and deliver. But the unarmed doctor, stubborn as he was, refused, and his Kurd porter backed him up. Only after pointing to the place where his Nestorian guides lay hidden in the rocks did Grant and his companion finally convince the robbers to let them go. Minutes later, having descended from the mountain and walked through the irrigated gardens surrounding Amadiyah, Grant became the honored guest of the town's Ottoman governor. From there to the Tigris it was all riding, sleeping, and weariness. On August 24, after several alarms and one more escape—this time from Arabs of the Shammar tribe, who had used the pasha's absence to begin raiding Kurdish and Yezidi villages near Mosul—the doctor arrived at last at the sickbed of Abel Hinsdale.

14

"INDUCTIONS DANGEROUS"

> "A party of well-mounted men rode down upon us and joined us. Mirza sidled up to me, and in his usual cheery tones, said, 'Madam, these are robbers.'"
> —Isabella Bird, *Journeys in Kurdistan*

THE TIME HAS COME to talk of intrigue, a difficult subject, dealing with dark plots and Byzantine machinations. The best account of political maneuvers in Hakkari and central Kurdistan from 1832 to 1843, does not come from the pens of American missionaries. Asahel Grant, Thomas Laurie, and their colleagues often referred to these affairs, but they tended to write as if their readers were either already intimately familiar with the terrain, or trusted that "God reigns" and thus cared little for worldly affairs. In *Dr. Grant and the Mountain Nestorians*, Laurie leaves facts, characters, and events lying about like so many fragments of rope, expecting that the reader will somehow snatch them up and splice them together; and Grant himself only occasionally delivers a solid nugget of information, as when in 1840 he encountered Nurullah Bey in Van and summarized the political deal that the emir had made with the pasha of Erzurum.

The rest of the time the reader forges ahead, bemused by the intrigue and vaguely excited by the danger, feeling that he, like his pious narrator, is swimming in murky waters indeed.

George Percy Badger, however, tried at least to present a coherent story. After arriving in Mosul late in 1842, this Anglican missionary made it his business to set before his readers all the facts he could find on Nestorian life and politics. The results of his political inquiries are not exhaustive, nor are they always verifiable, but they are the best that we have. This is why Badger's 1852 two-volume *The Nestorians and their Rituals* is a standard reference, and my main source for the following information.

As Badger tells it, from 1832 to 1843 there was increasing discord in the ranks of the Nestorians, along with a steady accumulation of external enemies. Petty enemies, of course, they had never lacked. Feuding, raiding, and sheep-stealing occupied large chunks of their leisure time, with predictable results. One of their enemies was Zeiner Bey, a Kurd of Berwar who specialized in raids against his own people as well as against the Nestorians. Zeiner, though a petty rival, was to play a large part in the events of 1843.

For the development of major enmity, Badger goes back to 1832 when Blind Mohammed, the one-eyed Bey of Rowanduz, pushed his conquests further to the north and west and took the town of Amadiyah. This battle marked the beginning of a long downward slide for that unfortunate place, whose war-ravaged state was described by Layard and Dr. Grant. Ismael Pasha, the hereditary ruler of Amadiyah, whose family claimed descent from the Abbasid Caliphs of Baghdad, was forced to flee, and Blind Mohammed installed one of his brothers as governor of the town.

Ismael Pasha did not flee far away, and soon set about rallying allies for an attempt to retake the citadel. That Ismael's family occupied a high rank among the Kurds is obvious from Dr.

Grant's description when he met him in Urmia: "His dress surpassed all present in richness and elegance; and his countenance and whole appearance would have graced any circle in America." Indeed, since his ancestors had ruled Amadiayah since the 13th century, he would not be expected easily to give up the family seat. It was natural that among his allies, Ismael Pasha would seek out a contingent from the most formidable fighting men in the mountains—the Nestorians of Hakkari. The Tiyarians had already repulsed an attack by Blind Mohammed, and after securing permission from Nurullah Bey, their nominal overlord, they willingly fell in with Ismael. An army of 3000 tribesmen headed by Mar Shimun and including a large contingent of fighting priests, marched off to join in the reconquest of Amadiyah.

Badger is unclear about dates; and sources for these years are sparse. The attack on Amadiyah must have come after 1836, because when Grant met Ismael Pasha in June of that year the Kurd was still on quite friendly terms with his Nestorian neighbors. The campaign probably took place around 1837 or 1838, when another force had become active in that patch of Kurdistan. As Mar Shimun advanced with his tribesmen into the valley of the river Supna, near Amadiyah, he received a private letter from Mohammed Pasha of Mosul, who had occupied the governorship only since 1835, but whose vigor and ruthlessness had already brought him fame. His army, the letter told Mar Shimun, was approaching Amadiyah; if anyone was going to take the town from Blind Mohammed, it would be he, and not Ismael Pasha. As the Ottoman governor of Mosul, he had every intention of extending the sultan's power into that part of Kurdistan, and if Mar Shimun joined with Ismael in fighting for Amadiyah he would very soon find that he was fighting against Ottoman troops.

The note was a prime example of "divide and conquer." Mar Shimun reacted to it quickly. He valued his independence and certainly did not want to fight the Turks. So he told Ismael Pasha that since Easter was approaching, he could not join in the attack because of the severe fasting demanded by that holiest of Christian festivals. The next night, under cover of darkness and without any further word to Ismael, Mar Shimun and his entire army left the siege and crossed the Chiya Matinah into Berwar, enroute to their homes in Tiyari.

It was the grossest kind of betrayal. Mar Shimun had given his word to Ismael, a man as proud as any in the mountains, and he had broken that word in the most public and humiliating way. Of course, with the loss of these forces the Amadiyah expedition could not succeed, and by 1838 Mohammed Pasha's troops had taken the town. Ismael, who was carried off to Mosul as a prisoner, never forgot what the patriarch had done. During the coming years, as he escaped from captivity in Mosul to a wandering exile in Persia, Hakkari, and Bohtan, Ismael, always planning for his return to Amadiyah, continued to nurse his resentment.

The next major enemy acquired by the Nestorian tribes will be obvious: Mohammed Pasha himself. On an elementary level the reason was plain, as the pasha made enemies of everyone. In fact, other than his chief wife, a Greek woman with whom he was very close, it was not known that he had any friends. Like the petty despot that he was, he did not seek friends, he sought accomplices. Western travelers, grateful for a degree of order in Mosul, at first described him as "vigorous," and later as "greedy," "cunning," and "cruel." When George Percy Badger first met him, he found the pasha at his palace perusing a volume of theology. He later found that this was a sham: the Little Ensign could neither read nor write. He could, however, drink alcohol, which he did to excess, and he was reputed to have a fondness for dancing-boys. Having assumed the governorship and subdued the rebellious citizens of Mosul, primarily through assassination, hanging, decapitation, and impalement, he set about squeezing every last piastre from the city and surrounding countryside. Many villagers deserted their homes rather than stay and be beaten—or worse—for not coming up with the taxes. Before long the pasha had appropriated monopolies in such things as soap, raft-building, indigo-dying, tobacco, and coffee, which he then proceeded to sell back to local businessmen at exorbitant prices. And these were only the beginning. For the year 1841, Thomas Laurie puts the total take from his extortions at $138,935, a colossal sum given the place and time. The Little Ensign regularly sent large bribes to the sultan's ministers in Constantinople, and he claimed that the Sublime Porte owed him some £150,000. Still, it was not enough.

No pretext was lacking for an extension of Ottoman authority (i.e., his own) into the mountains, as they were a perennial source of warfare and trouble. However, the Little Ensign faced a stumbling block, in that most of the territory he coveted was not officially his responsibility. Hakkari was nominally subservient to the pasha of Erzurum, who ruled through a governor in Van. The territory of Bahdinan, which included Amadiyah, Berwar, and districts to the west, had traditionally been assigned to the pasha of Baghdad. The rebellious territories to the north of Mosul, including Mardin, Cizre (on the Tigris) and Bohtan, were attached to Diyarbakir, and thus were the domain of Bedr Khan Bey.

All three areas the Little Ensign wanted for his own, and in two out of three he got his way. We have already seen that it was his troops who marched north and put down the revolt in Mardin in 1839. This was an emergency measure, brought about by Diyarbakir's descent into chaos after the Battle of Nizib. By the beginning of 1841, after lengthy appeals by the Little Ensign, who promised increased revenue to Constantinople, the Porte made it official: Mohammed Pasha of Mosul was given authority over Mardin, Bohtan, and Bahdinan, putting him directly at odds with Bedr Khan, the Kurdish tribes near Amadiyah, and the Nestorians of Tiyari. With the stage set, the machinations could begin.

The man who proved to be the Nestorians' greatest foe was Bedr Khan Bey, but it is unlikely that the great Bedr Khan would

would ever have become involved in Hakkari affairs without the influence of the mountaineers' perpetual nemesis, the emir Nurullah. Like Mohammed Pasha, Nurullah wanted more of everything, and in this he had always been frustrated by the independence of Mar Shimun and his flock. His position as "emir but not ruler" of Hakkari was a constant source of exasperation to him. After his official appointment as Ottoman governor in 1840, Nurullah set out to assert his authority by imposing upon his Christian subjects the *kharaj,* a submission tax levied upon all non-Muslim adult males in the empire. This gave him money, but a lot more trouble. The *kharaj* was regarded, understandably, as robbery by the Nestorians. The idea that a government might provide services in return for the payment of taxes lay outside the ethos which then governed the Ottoman Empire. Despite resistance, the emir urged his tax-gatherers to press on, instructing them if necessary to spread their carpets across the altars of the churches, an act of gross desecration, in order to compel payment. He also, to foment dissension, threatened to punish those Nestorian villages that honored Mar Shimun with their allegiance. Lastly, he went to the village maleks and won them over by promising them that portion of the church revenues which traditionally had been set aside for the patriarch.

And so they slowly built the vast machinery of intrigue. By the spring of 1841 its gears were clanking, with no great secrecy, in every corner of the province. The Turks, too, soon played a hand. By becoming Ottoman governor, Nurullah no doubt felt that he had gained in status and authority. But in forming such a direct relationship he gave the Turks what they had never had before: the ability to dictate the terms of political power in Hakkari. In 1841 they took advantage of this. A command came down from Erzurum dividing the emirate into two equal parts, with Suleiman Bey ruling in Julamerk and his uncle Nurullah in Başkale. As a political ploy, it could not have been more blatant; but the neatness of this move, its artistry and cunning, surely deserves some admiration. It was exactly the

kind of manipulation needed to provoke the quarrels and rancor that would lead inevitably to an Ottoman takeover.

Soon new plots were afoot among the Nestorians, chiefly a
movement to get rid of Nurullah and raise Suleiman to the post of
emir. Here George Percy Badger relies upon the testimony of two
Nestorian priests, Qasha Audishu and Qasha Kena of Lezan. These
men, says Badger, played a prominent role in the village councils.
They were also literate, and one of them, Qasha Kena, wrote a
critical letter at the behest of their leaders. They are, for better or
worse, our principal sources for the events of that summer.

According to Badger's informants, feeling against the emir
Nurullah Bey had grown among the Nestorian villagers into a
deep and bitter hatred. Many were determined at any cost to get
rid of him. The maleks, despite having been courted by the emir,
professed to take the side of the people. Two of them, Malek
Ismael of Chumba (related to Mar Shimun by marriage) and
Malek Berkho, from Salaberka, a village east of the Zab, went to
see the patriarch, who was staying in a village near Lezan. They
told him the plan straight out: they and the people wanted to kill
the emir. Mar Shimun reacted with shock. He told them that he
could in no way support a plot to murder Nurullah; he did everything in his power to convince the maleks not to go ahead. Berkho
and Ismael, seeing the depth of the patriarch's opposition, fell
back upon a second idea. The Christian tribes, as tradition dictated, had exercised their votes in the election of Nurullah as
emir. Now, since he had begun to oppress them, they had a right
to advocate his expulsion by a vote of all the Hakkari tribes,
followed by the elevation of his nephew to the emirate. In this
they knew that they would have the support of many of their
Kurdish neighbors. Mar Shimun, forced to make a decision, and
knowing that they were serious, decided to go along with the
explusion plan. He promised that he would tell Suleiman Bey
about the scheme, and this he did soon after.

There matters remained for several months, into the summer of 1841. Except for the continuing pressure from Nurullah's

tax-gatherers, nothing was happening. Nurullah soon found out about the movement against him, but since he did not have enough power to defeat the Christians in battle, he was reduced to fomenting dissension among the principal actors. The rebellious tribes, growing impatient, came to Qasha Kena in Lezan and asked him to write a letter. This letter told Mar Shimun very plainly that they were tired of waiting and intended to attack Nurullah within a few days. Warriors had been recruited from across the mountains, and arms distributed. Nothing he could say would make any difference. It was time for the patriarch to join them or get out of the way.

When he received this letter, Mar Shimun at once sent a confidential messenger to Qasha Audishu in Lezan, asking the priest to come to him immediately in Kochanes and consult about the best course of action. The patriarch, deeply perplexed and troubled, needed the advice of someone who lived closer to the plotters. Audishu would have set out immediately, but basic needs got in the way. Human beings cannot live without salt, and the priest's household was running low. Audishu knew that a short trip to Kochanes at such a critical time might easily turn into a long sojourn, and so he decided to replenish his salt supply first.

This involved a journey to Berwar, and so with his mule, his gun, and a companion from Lezan, Audishu set out across the mountain to buy salt. Near the village which supplied their needs, the two Nestorians were approached by a Kurd, who asked what was going on in the mountains. Audishu told the Kurd what he knew. Then came the surprise. The Kurd told Audishu that only a few days earlier his village had been visited by the Nestorian elders from Tiyari, who had gone to the village mullah and asked him to write a letter to Nurullah Bey. (Such a letter would have required a different language and another alphabet, and so another kind of priestly scribe.) On its surface the message the Kurd told to Priest Audishu seemed to be an outright betrayal. The elders offered to deliver Mar Shimun personally into the hands of the emir Nurullah and let him do with the patriarch what he would. Henceforth, they would recognize only Nurullah as their chief, and to this letter each of the Nestorian elders affixed his seal.

Only God knows, Badger notes, whether this offer was sincere or simply a ruse to make the emir drop his guard. Audishu himself was thunderstruck by this news. He lived in Lezan, not far from the men involved, and he was evidently not even aware that the elders had made a journey to Berwar. Immediately he went into the village and found the Kurdish mullah, who confirmed the story in all its details. With this information Audishu started immediately for Kochanes and Mar Shimun. Nothing more was said about his load of salt.

When Audishu says that he "hurried" to meet the patriarch, those of us in the modern world may think little of it. But one must remember the terrain. Only a Kurd or a Nestorian could "hurry" over such mountains, and we can only imagine the endurance it must have taken to walk that far under those conditions. In Kochanes, Mar Shimun and his household greeted the news with alarm. Who were these men who had dictated the letter? Were they serious? He knew all the village leaders in Hakkari, and the thought that a group of them might betray him to Nurullah must have left him dumbfounded. In the absence of evidence to the contrary, there seemed no choice: Mar Shimun had to believe that the traitors' intentions were genuine. On that same night, the patriarch took his gun, gathered his attendants, left his home, and fled south toward the peaks of Jelu.

As it turned out, he had acted none too soon. Unlike his Christian vassal the patriarch, Nurullah the emir of Hakkari had not spent the past months in dithering and vacillation. Nor did he limit himself to fomenting dissension among his enemies. He took advantage of the fact that his castle lay much closer to the Ottoman garrison at Van than did Kochanes, Julamerk, and Tiyari. Wasn't he the officially designated governor of Hakkari? Wasn't it his obligation to call for help if his position was threatened by rebels? As Mar Shimun fled into the mountains, a combined force of Ottoman troops and Nurullah's Kurds descended upon Kochanes and the patriarch's home.

In the desperate letter which arrived in Lezan on August 17, just as Asahel Grant was preparing his escape to Mosul, the patriarch appealed for help against this impending assault. By then it was already too late for such an appeal. By the time Grant arrived at the sickbed of Abel Hinsdale, Nurullah's forces had taken Mar Shimun's home and "burnt it with fire," and were going on to ravage Nestorian villages in the district of Diz, across the river from Kochanes. In the south, the men of Tiyari soon made good on their vows of vengeance, invading Berwar, sacking Kurdish villages, and making off with more sheep than they had lost earlier in the summer. By the end of September 1841, as the Pasha of Mosul awaited his chance and the vengeful Ismael of Amadiyah lingered in the castle of Bedr Khan Bey, the political framework of Hakkari, that teetery *arzaleh* of thin promises and cruel realities, lay shattered like kindling on the rocks.

15

DEMONS AND ANGELS

"I existed before, I exist now, and shall remain to the end of time."—Kitab al-Jalwah

IN THE WAKE OF THIS ONSLAUGHT Mar Shimun became a wanderer among his own people, a man without a home to call his own. In a letter to Dr. Grant that arrived in Mosul before Christmas, he appealed for help and lamented the "bitter persecution which has befallen us." Not until 1849 would he return to the residence in Kochanes; however, with Malek Ismael of Chumba acting as intermediary, Nurullah Bey and Mar Shimun reached a truce in the autumn of 1841, allowing the patriarch to move about in the mountains without fear of pursuit. At the beginning of October, Christian Rassam and Dr. Grant visited Mohammed Pasha at his fortress south of Mosul. There the pasha told them about events in the mountains and announced that the independence of the Nestorian tribes had come to an end. Although this was not the case—except for the burning of Mar Shimun's house and the attacks against Diz, the rest of the tribal domains remained intact—Grant felt that the Nestorians would do well to make peace with their enemies, and especially with the Turks, though with typical scrupulousness he refrained from giving any political advice to the mountaineers.

The missionaries, meanwhile, were at a loss. Grant and the Hinsdales had been sent to work in Hakkari, but they could not reach their mission field. To occupy their energies they might have approached the Chaldean Christians of the plain, but it would have been useless, because these people were the particular domain of the Catholics, specifically the French Dominicans. With the Chaldeans spoken for and the mountains full of danger, the Americans concentrated their efforts upon the Syrian Orthodox (Jacobite) Christians of Mosul and the surrounding area, making contacts with their clergy, opening schools, and of course working with the sick. Even this violated an agreement made with the Episcopal Church of America, who had proposed (after the visit of Horatio Southgate in 1838) to work amongst these people. But in 1841, with no Episcopalians in sight, the ABCFM missionaries set to work anyway.

In August, when Grant arrived, Abel Hinsdale lay on the brink of death. With the approach of autumn, however, he had recovered, and on November 19 the two men (without Sarah, who stayed behind with the Rassams) set out for a two-week tour of the villages closer to Mosul. For Asahel Grant, this was a first. Never before had he been able to share his mountain travels with an American friend.

Hinsdale and Grant's autumn tour covered new but familiar ground. The mountains, not so high as those of Hakkari but nearly as rugged, made traveling both difficult and scenic. As in the Tiyari country, the residents hacked a living from the unlikeliest of places, with "rich fields of rice, cotton, and barley, and groves of oaks, pomegranate, and olive trees" hidden amidst the barren rocks. Here, in houses of stone laid in mud, the two men sat upon hard-packed dirt and ate from "tables" made of coarse sacking. Grant was called upon to treat, besides the usual illnesses, a case of snakebite, as well as a young man severely traumatized by his close encounter with a bear. The missionaries did not miss a chance to probe deeper into the hills, even if it meant backtracking to take a different way. Atop one summit they looked out at "nothing but barren mountains piled upon mountains, if possible still more rugged, each towering cliff seemed to endeavor to out-rival every other in forbidding grandeur."

Mostly they visited Nestorian and Kurdish settlements, but those of the Jews drew their interest as well. The residents of Shoosh, situated at the base of a perpendicular cliff, claimed to have lived there since the time of the Babylonian Captivity. When Grant asked the rabbi if he knew where Nineveh was located, the man told him without hesitation. The Americans found that the Nestorian villages, many degraded and without priests, were fast yielding to the bribes of papal missionaries. In one village a priest told them that he had received fourteen *cherkis*, about $1.75, to turn Catholic, but after three days, during which he spent the money, he had renounced the pope and gone back to the Nestorian church. All complained of oppression, but Grant and Hinsdale urged upon them "the importance of a reformation of life, and turning from their iniquities unto the Lord, as the only means by which they might expect deliverance from Mohammedan tyranny." To this Grant received the same response given by the men of Tiyari: "Deliver us first, and then we will reform and serve the Lord." As for the Jews, they were at least spared such pious platitudes, although they lived in terror of everyone, no matter what the religion.

For Grant, none of these groups offered the fascination of the Yezidis. Even today, 160 years after they first gained the attention of Europeans, much about the Yezidis and their religion remains a mystery. In the first place, no one knows where the name Yezidi came from. Many theories exist; so many, in fact, that their very multiplicity is surely proof enough that none is valid. In the 21st century, Kurdish nationalists claim the Yezidis as their own. This they can easily justify, since all Yezidis speak Kurdish and have done so as long as anyone can remember. Moreover, there is a new-found respect for them, as some Kurdish intellectuals feel that Yezidism, which predates Islam and contains elements of Zoroastrianism, Mithraism, and Christianity, may represent a more purely Kurdish faith than the imported creed of the Arabs. However, for many centuries the Yezidis were not respected by the Muslim Kurds who surrounded them; in fact, because of their religion they occupied a rank even lower than that of Christians and Jews. Concentrated among the rocks and hills in the Sheikhan district northeast of Mosul, with populations near Mardin and Diyarbakir, in the Sinjar mountains west of the Tigris, and as far away as Russian-held Armenia, the Yezidis did not fit neatly into the system of *millets*, the officially sanctioned religious and ethnic minorities, which made up the Ottoman Empire. By advice of the Prophet, Muslims were bound to show respect to *ahl al-kitab*, the "people of the book": those Ottoman subjects whose religious traditions were based upon the revealed, transcribed word of God. With their Torahs, Talmuds, and Testaments, Christians and Jews easily qualified. The Yezidis, having no books or scholarly tradition—at least, none that anyone knew of—did not.

Through the centuries, with no status as a *millet,* the Yezidis suffered from regular episodes of persecution. In his brief, murderous career Blind Mohammed of Rowanduz hit them hard and often, a campaign that culminated in 1832, when a vast crowd of fleeing Yezidis was massacred by his troops on the east bank of the Tigris opposite Mosul. The people of the city, cut off, like the refugees, by high water and the subsequent withdrawal of the bridge of boats, could only look on in horror. The Yezidis, however, were not sheep, and they shared the independent spirit of the neighboring Kurds, as well as the Kurdish penchant for quarreling and blood feuds. This does not mean that their reputation matched that of the the mountain Nestorians; still, in the Jebel Sinjar, west of Mosul, it came close.

The Yezidis of Sinjar reaped the rewards of a good business plan and a prime location. At that time trade goods took three routes between Diyarbakir in the north, and Mosul. Rafts on the Tigris, as we have seen, carried a substantial portion of the southbound cargoes, but they could scarcely be expected to carry all of it. Much more passed back and forth by caravan. From Diyarbakir to Mardin travelers faced a short journey, which most could do in safety. Past Mardin, however, they had to make a choice. Of the two possible routes to Mosul, neither was easy; the safer of the two still involved fording the Tigris at a point where it is deep and strong. But there was a third, simpler way. This was the route ultimately taken by the Istanbul-Baghdad Railway. It involved a direct strike to the southeast, with no rivers, no settlements enroute, and no place to get supplies.

Though shorter, this route was far more dangerous. W.A. Wigram, writing in 1912, referred to this land as the Chôl (*Çöl* in modern Turkish), which means "desert." He spoke of its scrubby plains, its dullness and desolation, and of the abundant ruins testifying to its ancient prosperity. He also warned of the "Poison Wind" that Dr. Grant spoke of, "a faint invisible eddy of scorching air, which will pick out a single man or beast from the midst of a caravan and strike him down instantly senseless, sometimes even killing him on the spot." Asahel Grant and Capt. Conolly chose to travel via the Chôl in 1839, and it was virtually the only possible route for bigger caravans, which could not take the risk of forcing large numbers of animals—difficult enough with horses; impossible with camels—to swim across the Tigris at Pesh Khabur. The Chôl was thus a primary highway for commerce, and for many years it provided the Yezidis of Jebel Sinjar with a plentiful harvest.

Jebel (or *Jabal*) means "mountain" or "mountain range" in Arabic. Jebel Musa, the mountain of Moses, is, not surprisingly, the Arab name for Mount Sinai; Gibraltar also takes its name from this Arabic word. The *jebel* of Sinjar is an anomaly, a slim line of peaks thirty miles long, rising like an island from the Chôl some eighty miles west of Mosul. Writers have compared it to a pirate ship riding upon a barren sea, and it is an apt comparison. Its highest peaks—approx. 4800 feet—do not approach those of Hakkari, but they are high enough to catch rain (and, occasionally, snow) and rugged enough to give refuge to those who seek it. They also make excellent vantage points from which to scan the surrounding desert.

For centuries the Yezidis of Sinjar used these observation posts to facilitate their specialty: caravan robbery. We should note, of course, that they were capable of doing other jobs. They raised sheep, for one thing, and Austen Henry Layard, who visited in 1847, admired their clean, whitewashed houses, their neat terraces of fig and olive trees, and their grapevines. Sinjar was noted for its exports of dried figs. But it was robbery, not figs, that made their reputation. Over centuries of banditry the Sinjaris had acquired a fortune in booty; it was rumored that most of this was hidden in a vast cave somewhere in the mountains.

Given the centralizing tendencies of the Ottoman government during the 19th century, it is not surprising that this life of plunder had to come to an end. In his history of the Yezidis (*Survival Among the Kurds,* 1992), J.S. Guest quotes the account of an English traveler, Dr. Frederick Forbes, who visited Sinjar in 1838. On the north slope of the mountain Dr Forbes came upon a village called Kirsi, whose inhabitants seemed to have sunk to the depths of idleness and misery. When Forbes asked why the people were not working, his guide, a Yezidi from Bashiqa, pointed to a hill opposite the village. "Do you see that hill?" he asked. "Before Hafiz Pasha came here, the whole employment of the people of Kirsi was to sit on top of it all day, looking out for travellers and caravans, in order to plunder them." Now, he said, there was nothing for them to do.

Hafiz Pasha's sword had fallen upon them the previous year. The governor of Diyarbakir, two years before his dreamy debacle at Nizib, was pushed beyond the limits of patience when the Yezidis of Sinjar attacked a government caravan and made off with a large shipment of military uniforms. This theft seems to have been a silly mistake. In return for a load of hot, uncomfortable garments which only a miserable draftee would have worn, the bandits faced two hostile armies, one, Hafiz Pasha's, marching at them from Diyarbakir on the west, the other from Mosul on the east. By the summer of 1837 the Sinjaris and their chieftain, a man named Lula, were surrounded and under attack. William Ainsworth and Christian Rassam, having finished with the Euphrates Expedition, witnessed the spectacle at the invitation of Hafiz. A long struggle ensued, with much bloodshed on both sides, while the pasha took heart from a dream that predicted victory. After three months of warfare this dream came true: the bandits ran out of ammunition and Lula agreed to surrender. Much booty—including the purloined uniforms—was discovered. From one cave alone 516 people emerged. It is not clear whether the Turks recovered all of the Yezidis' treasure. Some say they did; others that the Yezidis showed them only part of it and kept the rest hidden.

Though the fate of the Sinjar treasure remains uncertain, the secrecy surrounding the Yezidi religion has lifted somewhat. It turns out that the Yezidis do indeed possess religious books, though they claim that those remaining fragmentary manuscripts—notably the *Kitab al-Jalwah,* or "Book of Revelations," and the *Meshef Resh,* the "Black Book "—are only a fraction of the total lost in various persecutions over the centuries. Knowledge of Yezidism has advanced considerably since Asahel Grant made his tour in 1842; but he was one of the first Western travelers to visit these people and their shrines and to make serious inquiries about the substance of their beliefs. At the time they were regarded as "devil-worshippers," a name which Grant repeats and which has stuck to them to this day, but which should certainly be obliterated once and for all. Unorthodox believers have long been libeled as fellow travelers with the Devil, or worse. It is a standard technique employed by the dominant over the weak. Jews, of course, were, and still are, the frequent targets of these calumnies, especially the "satanic" claims—which led to many persecutions, notably in Damascus in 1840—that they require the blood of freshly killed victims to conduct their services. As followers of a religion hidden from everyone outside their circle, it was to be expected that the Yezidis would come in for more than their share of such slander.

The charge of devil-worship was abetted by a peculiarity of Yezidi beliefs. Their neighbors generally knew that the Yezidis would not pronounce the name of Satan (*Shaitan*) in conversation, nor would they willingly say words that resembled it. Because of this "Satan-avoidance" it was supposed that they worshipped the Evil One, or that at least they revered him so highly that they avoided taking his name in vain. In fact, the Yezidis could be more correctly called "angel-worshippers," since they worship the spirit of God as represented in his seven archangels, and especially the highest angel of them all. In Christian tradition, Satan occupied that highest position, but after asserting his independence he fell from grace and began a second career as the great tempter of mankind. The Yezidis reject that story. They believe that the angel Azaziel, who became known as "Satan" (an insulting name, meaning "enemy" in Aramaic), remains in favor with God, is not associated with evil, and is in fact more properly called Melek Taus, or, the Peacock Angel. "Giving him a bad name is unjust," said Kawal Suleiman, a Yezidi priest interviewed in 1990. "It is like calling a great, honourable man a thief. We recognize his real name, not this ugly one."

Melek Taus is central to Yezidism. Though the Yezidis believe in one God (called *Khuda* in Kurdish), who created the universe and governs everything in it, the focus of their worship is the Peacock Angel. Prayers are directed to him; poems and songs are composed in his honor. In Grant's time Melek Taus was represented by seven identical brass figures, called the *sanjaks,* stylized depictions of a peacock guarded by a special caste of priests. These priests, called *kawals,* were divided into teams that carried the images from village to village throughout the lands where the Yezidis were scattered. For these peasants the arrival of a *sanjak* was a great occasion. It linked them with the rest of their brethren; its priestly guardians brought them news; its coming allowed them, through monetary contributions, to contribute to the maintenance of the central Yezidi shrine in the village of Lalish.

After Ainsworth's visit in 1840, Lalish (or Sheikh Adi as it was also called, after the 12th-century prophet of Yezidism) became a standard destination for explorers in Kurdistan. Eventually it would figure in Grant's and Hinsdale's itinerary as well, but on that first night they slept in Bashiqa, a Yezidi village surrounded by olive groves, some four hours' ride from Mosul. Rising above the olive trees were the square whitewashed tombs of Yezidi sheikhs, some fifteen to twenty in number, each surmounted by a fluted conical spire. (Bashiqa, according to a current account, has become a town of some 20,000 inhabitants, including Muslims and Christians, but the forest of olive trees is still there, as are the Yezidis, the whitewashed tombs, and the persistent rumors of devil-worship.) Upon arrival the Americans found that one of their horses had gone lame, and so, while Hinsdale returned to Mosul to procure a new one, Grant spent two days exploring Bashiqa and its neighboring village, Baazani.

Grant had visited Bashiqa before, in 1839, on his first night out of Mosul. Then, thinking that he was a Turk, the villagers had shunned him. Only after finding that he was a Christian did their attitude change. This was not surprising: since the two groups shared a common enemy, Muslims, and a common saint, Jesus, Yezidis generally got on well with Christians. At one of the tombs of Bashiqa, whose unlighted interiors made them "meet temples for the worshippers of the Prince of Darkness," the chief priest answered Grant's questions about his people. The priest told Grant that the Yezidis were descended from the Beni Halil, a tribe of desert Arabs. This assertion the visitor found incredible, especially since the Yezidis uniformly spoke

Kurdish, had always done so, and continued to speak it despite their close intercourse with Arab peoples.

That night Grant's host, Abdul-Kiyah, a "very intelligent Yezidi," told him that their ancestors had been Nestorian Christians living in Hakkari, and thus they were the brethren of those remaining. One of their religion's alleged founders, "Adde," probably corresponding to Sheikh Adi, bore a resemblance, Grant thought, to Thaddeus, one of the apostles, and St. John (Mar Yohanna) was also claimed as an early teacher of the Yezidis. Soon Grant was brought back to End Times speculations, as Abdul Kiyah, with an anxious look, asked "if the day was not near when Christianity would triumph, or when Christians would rule the world." He concluded with a fervent prayer, recited in the direction of the rising sun, for the imminent arrival of Jesus.

Since so much of their religious tradition was oral, it is not surprising that Grant heard conflicting stories from the Yezidis themselves. In a conversation the next day, his host ("after looking about to see that no one was within hearing") told the missionary that they were descended neither from the Beni Halil nor the Nestorians of Hakkari, but that, in reality, they were "Beni Israel" (sons of Israel) and believed in the Pentateuch, the Psalms, and the Gospels. Previously, in the presence of Muslims, Abdul-Kiyah had claimed that they possessed no religious books, but now he told Grant that the Yezidis in fact had a book called the *Fourkan*, known only to themselves. How much of this Grant believed he does not say, but it is unlikely that he believed very much. Indeed, he soon came to the conclusion that no straight answers were to be had from the Yezidis concerning their beliefs and origins. Those men who thought they knew the facts were wrong; those who might really know weren't telling.

Grant and Hinsdale had spent ten days among the mountain villages when winter's approach forced them to turn back. Two days' ride from Mosul they arrived in Lalish, the vale of

Sheikh Adi, home of the saint's tomb and a place of pilgrimage for all the Yezidi diaspora. Indeed, this was the Holy of Holies, and in virtually every published account the valley's magic seems to reach out and hold the traveler in thrall. In early descriptions of Sheikh Adi, its Western visitors, despite the enchantment and beauty surrounding them, assume that the inhabitants are all adherents of a foul and evil demon, or, as George Percy Badger puts it, worshippers of the Evil Principle. The classic description of Sheikh Adi comes from Henry Layard, who in the fall of 1846 took time off from his dig at Nineveh to attend the Feast of the Assembly, the annual gathering of the Yezidi clans. Layard, who was not a clergyman and had no official need to pass judgment on devil-worshippers, simply recorded what he saw: a festival abundant with beauty and devoid of debauchery, with oil lamps sparkling among the olive groves by night; the music of flutes and tambourines and the chanting of priests; crowds of white-robed Yezidis; dancing maidens with their black hair plaited in glass beads and gold.

Grant and Hinsdale, arriving two months after the the Assembly, found the site nearly empty. Still, viewed in the slanting light of December, as beetling cliffs walled off the valley from the outside world and ancient olives shaded the path toward the shrine, Lalish held them in its power. "Surely," Grant wrote, "if any place on earth is haunted by evil spirits and wizards, judging from the scenery, one might be led to infer that they have selected it as their sacred place." The two missionaries were struck with awe and reverence, "not for infernal powers, but the power divine, whose handy work was so strikingly displayed." Divine or demonic: the American could not decide. At last, in a direct contradiction of his opening statement, Grant wrote that "surely this is a proper place for the tabernacle of the Great Jehovah!"

Grant and Hinsdale spent only three hours at the sanctuary of Sheikh Adi. They saw the spring of Zemzem, named identically with the well of Mecca, in which all Yezidis washed them-

selves before entering the sacred precinct. They inspected the
saint's bare whitewashed shrine with its fluted spires and animal figures carved into the stone. For a few minutes they felt
the magic of the place, and then moved on. Compared to the
researches of Henry Layard, their experience with the Yezidis
was no more instructive than a programmed stop on a package
tour, and yet for the biographer that is hardly the point. In the
context of Grant's life, so often a Chôl of poison winds and
danger, this visit to Lalish is a respite, a blooming violet in a
wall of naked rock. Two years later, in the last letters home
before he died, a crack opened in Grant's piety and resolve.
With a few sentences he made clear the degree of hardship that
his labors required; and prominent among the trials, along with
warfare, danger, and discomfort, was a constant, though un-
spoken, loneliness. "One must be strong," wrote Freya Stark,
"to place oneself alone against the unknown world," yet in this
last mountain tour before the onset of winter, Grant was relieved of that burden. For once he had a colleague in his travels.
He was absorbed in the work and surrounded by physical grandeur. His health was no worse than normal, and no one threatened his life. All these constituted his modest reward.

"Wars and Rumors of Wars"

"We must prepare for a severe struggle—the last great battle. The political elements also look threatening. Every thing is in a transition state, and great commotions may attend the yet greater change that will follow. So dark is our horizon at times, that our only consolation is the blessed truth, the Lord reigneth, and that all his glorious promises will be fully verified."

—A.G. to Rev. Wayne Gridley: March 15, 1842

NOT UNTIL JUNE 6, 1842, did Grant leave Mosul for the mountains, and then once more he rode alone. His departure came after a winter spent teaching and medicating, as well as soliciting aid for his "poor Nestorians" through the British consul in Baghdad, Col. Robert Taylor, to whom he forwarded portions of Mar Shimun's letter. The Mosul station, still in its infancy, began to build up its forces. From Boston, Grant ordered books of history, philosophy (including Emerson's works), and biblical commentary, as well as writing supplies, quantities of medicine (principally quinine, laudanum, and emetics), and a "small, portable electric machine" (he had left his first one in Urmia) for administering shocks to his patients. Until the beginning of

June the doctor hoped that Hinsdale—despite a severe attack
of cholera in February, which he barely survived—might join
him in his labors. Both men desired to make the journey that
would involve final arrangements for a mission station in the
mountains, but bad luck and male chivalry would not allow the
partnership to happen. Christian Rassam, in his dual roles as
British vice-consul and burgeoning business mogul, had been
called away to Baghdad, and no one knew how soon he could
return. This meant that Matilda Rassam and Sarah Hinsdale,
who was newly pregnant and could not make the journey, would
be left alone if Abel Hinsdale and Dr. Grant traveled to Hakkari
together. No matter what they might have thought about the
strength and spirit of these women, the missionaries would not
allow the only two foreign ladies in Mosul to remain alone and
unprotected. So Abel Hinsdale was compelled to stay.

But the route that Grant projected led him to hope that a
missionary colleague from Urmia might yet join him. Normally
this would have been impossible, but war and upheaval in the
mountains compelled the doctor to take a path far different
from the usual road through Amadiyah. That fortress town, so
often bludgeoned and ravaged during the previous decade, had
changed hands yet again. In the spring of 1842 Ismael Pasha,
returning from exile, had attacked and, with the collusion of
the Kurdish governor, taken the citadel from its Albanian garrison. Given the Albanian irregulars' usual problems—malaria,
boredom, and drunkenness—such a raid could not have been
terribly difficult, even without help on the inside. Still, the capture required an immediate response, and Mohammed Pasha
did not hesitate to deliver it. Even as Grant rode across the
bridge of boats, the Little Ensign was marching with his troops
to besiege Amadiyah, an action that blocked that way entirely
for the missionary. Grant decided to make a great circular detour. After bending southeast and north, in order to enter Persia via Rowanduz, then riding north to Urmia, he would make
his way back into Hakkari by taking the caravan road north to

Salmas and then west across the passes to the headwaters of the Zab. From there Grant could follow the great river south by west to Başkale, Julamerk, and the Nestorian domains.

All this looked like a good way to avoid the battle for Amadiyah; however, it ignored another reality: the imminent war between the Persian and Ottoman empires. Close to bankruptcy, and having been fighting without victory almost constantly for the first forty-two years of the 19th century, the Ottomans might have been expected to avoid this sort of activity. From 1821 to 1823 they had fought a war with the Persians in which they were saved from defeat only by sudden, widespread epidemics of cholera that decimated Persian armies that had advanced past Van, as well as to Erzurum and Baghdad. The Treaty of Erzurum (1823) put an end to that quarrel; but now another was raising temperatures in Stamboul and Tehran. The long undefined border along the spine of Kurdistan lay at the core of the conflict. Neither country possessed the power to patrol it, and Kurds from both sides were constantly making raids and escaping unpunished. Bad fences made bad neighbors, and these problems were exacerbated by the perennial Sunni-Shia rivalry between the Turks and Persians. In the summer of 1842, open war was expected at any moment.

Far off in Central Asia, another drama was playing out, unknown to anyone until months later when an eyewitness brought the news to India. On a morning in June Capt. Arthur Conolly, Grant's "kind" and "amiable" traveling companion of 1839, sank to his knees in the great central square of Bokhara. A great crowd had gathered. The emir was there; so was a man with a long and very sharp sword. Beside Conolly knelt Col. William Stoddart, the officer he had come to rescue some eight months before. The British retreat from Kabul that January and the ensuing massacre, sealed their fate. Both men, half-starved and in rags, had spent their final months in a deep pit filled with vermin and filth. They were alone, in the middle of nowhere. No help was expected, and none arrived.

Grant knew nothing of Conolly, but he certainly knew of the dangers waiting in Kurdistan. He had gained too much, however, to throw it away because of his own fears. On June 6 and 7, the doctor enjoyed for a few hours the company of two fellow travellers. Abel Hinsdale and Athanasius, a Syrian Orthodox bishop from Malabar in India, had come along as far as Bashiqa and Baazani to inspect several mission-sponsored schools. Two others, Mohammed Pasha's personal physician, an Armenian from Stamboul, and the pasha's personal banker, probably also an Armenian, joined them for the ride. On the plains opposite Mosul the peasants, sickles in hand, were reaping the harvest, and each offered a fistful of wheat as a token gift to the passersby. At the threshing-floors, ox-drawn sledges, their runners embedded with flints, cut the grain from the stalks. This abundance of Biblical activity did not fail to arouse the interest of the missionaries.

For Grant, the afflictions of summer began early. A chilly night's sleep on the roof of a house soon "brought on a cold," according to Thomas Laurie, and the doctor became so sick that for two days he considered calling off his trip. The next morning the Yezidis of the village were roused to excitement by the arrival of one of the images of Melek Taus, a sight the missionaries were not permitted to witness. Night cold was succeeded by blistering heat, and after a midday stop at Bertullah, where they inspected another Syrian school, Grant's friends bade goodbye to the ailing doctor and a young Syrian servant named Baho.

After he crossed the Zab on a *kelek*, Grant took the road bearing east by south to Erbil, a collection of mud houses surrounding an ancient mound crowned by a citadel. Here the path turned north by east toward Rowanduz, home of the late Blind Mohammed, who, Grant discovered, was still beloved by his people. The reason was simple: security. During the Bey's reign of terror, not a scrap of bread was taken without his permission. Petty thievery was commonly punished by the loss of a hand, and Mohammed seemed especially fond of gouging out eyes in retribution for various crimes. So thoroughly did he monopolize the gallnut trade that two Kurds who had gathered them without paying the required share to Blind Mohammed, were hauled before the ruler and each suffered the immediate loss of an arm. The region round Rowanduz, says Thomas Laurie, was noted for its hatred of Christians, especially Franks. Evidence of this antipathy was on display when Grant tried to pay a call upon the governor, a brother of Blind Mohammed. That eminence, presented with the doctor's *firman,* refused to greet him or even to treat him with ordinary civility. After three hours' wait outside the governor's room the doctor got up and left, "rejoicing that, unworthy as I was to suffer for Christ, all this scorn was poured upon me for his sake."

For Rowanduz and its romantic setting, Grant nurtured fonder sentiments. The caravan route of that time involved a steep zig-zag to the pass of Sar Hasan Bey, where the traveler was rewarded with a splendid view of the town 1500 feet below, and a sea of mountains filling the horizon to the Persian border and beyond. Here Grant happened upon an "unlooked-for feast": the missionaries' hired messenger, returning with mail from Urmia, was just riding up from the town, and at that remote rendezvous the doctor was rewarded with letters to assuage his loneliness. Grant gave the man a note to carry back to Mosul. It arrived safely, but this messenger was not so lucky. Sometime later, the man was murdered by Kurd robbers in the same section of road that Grant was about to traverse.

In Rowanduz, Grant found a caravan leaving immediately for Persia, and he did not miss the chance to join. That night Grant and others slept on the ground beside the horses, where they were in danger of being trampled, because the animals were huddled together tightly to protect them from thieves. At Sidek, a village reached on June 11, Grant stayed with a Kurd who sent two men to escort him safely to the Persian border. Murders had recently been committed on the road, and the imminent war between Turkey and Persia was making the robbers even bolder.

Half an hour from Sidek, at the top of a mountain, he came upon a stone pillar with cuneiform inscriptions, probably a marker of Assyrian origin. When the doctor stopped to examine it, the people of the caravan tried strenuously to dissuade him, an attitude that Grant ascribed to the usual paranoia: the writing, the Kurds thought, was in the language of the Franks, and if discovered this would allow the foreigners to come and lay claim to their country. That night he slept in the lee of a rock at an elevation of 8,500 feet, and he estimated the next day's pass into Persia, reached only after treks across glaciers and a torrent bridged by snow, at 10,000 feet. At the summit, Grant reported, "a vast sea of mountains was spread before me," with Lake Urmia glittering in the sun and the plain of Mesopotamia in the opposite direction. After safely passing the last camp of nomad Kurds, usually identified as the culprits when robbery was afoot, Dr. Grant hurried ahead of the caravan to Ushnu. For the first time in two years he had come home to Persia.

Two days later, at the mission compound in Urmia, the Americans assembled and voted unanimously to send one of their own to the mountains with Asahel Grant. William Stocking, the most enthusiastic supporter of the Hakkari mission, was the logical choice, and he readily agreed to go. Two Nestorians of Urmia, native helpers of the Americans, also signed on for the trip. One other member, sober by nature and conspicuous by his absence, might have made this collective enthusiasm more difficult to achieve. But Justin Perkins, the senior and most highly respected missionary in Urmia, had left Persia with Charlotte and their two surviving children in July 1841. They would not return until 1843.

The governor of Salmas, Yahya Khan, had taken up residence at his ancestral castle, Charreh, an imposing structure built atop a rocky pinnacle west of that town. Here Grant migrated with his party, to consult with the khan concerning their proposed journey. Beside the castle some 200 tents were pitched, as the Kurdish tribes gathered for a council of war. Yahya Khan was an important man, widely known for his honesty and good character. Besides being governor of Salmas, he was chief of a branch of the Hakkari tribe. He had married one of Nurullah's sisters and given the emir one of his own in return, while another of his sisters resided in Tehran at the harem of the shah. Yahya greeted the Americans cordially, but he could give them no encouragement for their proposed journey until he had talked with Nurullah Bey, who was expected to arrive shortly from Hakkari. The news from the mountains was bad: so bad, in fact, that Grant and Stocking were ready either to postpone their attempt or give it up altogether. War between Turkey and Persia had never seemed so close. Orders had gone out from the shah recalling all Persian subjects from Ottoman territory, and the Turks were threatening a punitive expedition against Persian nomads northeast of Başkale, thus disturbing the border region even more.

The missionaries' trepidation evaporated with the arrival of Nurullah and his nephew Suleiman. From these all was cordial welcome, as they inquired after the doctor's health as well as that of his young son Henry. Nurullah repeated his assurances to Grant in the presence of Yahya Khan: he would grant the missionaries protection, and they would indeed be allowed to erect whatever buildings were needed for themselves and their schools. The emir strongly urged Grant and Stocking to accompany him on his return to Julamerk, and he promised to send the missionaries on to Tiyari from there. Laurie writes that Suleiman Bey earnestly seconded this request, and this "warm friend" of Mar Shimun promised to accompany Grant to Tiyari.

All this was extremely gratifying, and in the case of this American doctor, whose presence might actually benefit Nurullah, there is little reason to believe that the emir was not sincere. But Grant states clearly the purpose of the emir's visit to Persia, and those facts leave a different impression. Grant had last met Nurullah in 1840, when that ruler was returning from Erzurum as the Ottomans' new governor and ally. Since then Nurullah had cracked down hard, imposing the *kharaj,* suborning the Nestorian maleks, and joining with Ottoman troops to burn the house of Mar Shimun. In fact, had that prelate not received advance warning of the raid, he may well have been killed. Now that war was threatening to break out at any moment, Nurullah had come to Persia fully prepared to betray the Turks and make a deal with the shah. With Suleiman Bey at his side, well-watched and, as it were, securely leashed, the emir now bargained for the use of his forces in the upcoming war. Nurullah and the other mountain chiefs were also sending men to Amadiyah to help Ismael Pasha retain his ancestral seat against the Turks. Negotiations were underway to persuade the Nestorian tribes to join in this siege, and if they agreed, the victory, everyone assumed, would be assured. The hope was expressed that this fight in a common cause— for the fortress of Amadiyah was of great symbolic importance— would allow the Kurds and Nestorians to settle their differences and put the past to rest.

At this point the "miasma" reasserted its power. Urgent word came from Urmia telling Grant that one of Albert Holladay's childen was gravely ill. Presumably, Austin Wright, the physician who took Grant's place, was in attendance, but the Holladays sent for Dr. Grant, who had attended at the death of their first child, Catharine, in 1840. The doctor agreed to return, hoping that he could see the patient through the crisis and return in time to accompany Nurullah to Hakkari. Unfortunately Grant, too, had taken sick. That old enemy, the malaria of the plain, now revisited him, and as he mounted his horse he found himself growing worse. In this condition he rode all night, a twelve-hour, sixty-mile journey, and in the morning arrived thoroughly enfeebled. In that condition he could do little good, and by the time the child began to recover Asahel Grant was resting under the care of his friends.

No sooner had Grant regained his strength than William Stocking fell ill. It was the same story of incessant, overlapping illness that had driven Grant to the mountains in the first place. At this time work was nearing completion on the mission's health retreat on Mt. Seir, five miles from Urmia and 1000 feet above the level of the plain. This compound of houses, located near a spring of pure water, would eventually prove a boon to the mission families; but in 1842 it could not help Stocking and Grant. The two men decided, however, that Stocking was not so ill that travel might not benefit his health; therefore, on July 14, after several days of quinine and recuperation, they saddled up again and rode north.

By this time they had abandoned the thought of accompanying Nurullah Bey to Amadiyah. Their journey north carried them near the shore, where they visited mission schools, talked with local priests, and several times found relief by swimming in the brackish waters of Lake Urmia. On the second day out of the city, at the house of Mar Yohannan—a bishop who had gone to visit America with Justin Perkins—Asahel Grant was again stricken by fever, further delaying the journey. Not until two days later, with Stocking still ill, were they able to resume their march. Five days from Urmia they reached Khosrowa, near Salmas, the same distance that Grant had previously covered in twelve hours.

Here William Stocking's illness proved too much for him. Undoubtedly he wanted to continue the journey, and the mountain air might have helped him. But there were other considerations. Stocking's wife, Jerusha, remained behind in Urmia, where their infant daughter Harriet had died only four months earlier. They had already lost a son, Charles, in February 1840, before he reached the age of two. Had William Stocking continued into the mountains and perished of disease or misadventure, his wife would have been left alone. Asahel Grant might have been able to justify taking that kind of risk, but Stocking could not. The two men decided that the junior missionary must turn back.

This loss fell hard enough upon Asahel Grant, but now the two Nestorian assistants, men of the Urmia plain with little affinity for their mountain cousins, refused to go on. Their reason was simple fear, as a trip perilous in the best of times had been rendered doubly dangerous by the imminence of war. Here no discussion was possible: the men had volunteered, and no one could make them proceed. With these defections Grant's party of five had been reduced to himself and Baho, his Syrian servant from Mosul. The doctor wondered if he should travel at all that summer. The danger was obvious, but he did not want to lose the momentum already gained. He believed in Nurullah's assurances as well as the importance of his own mission. He must also have known that, had he returned to Urmia, he would have ended up in a sickbed sweating with fever one day and shaking with chills the next.

At this point his indecision received a nudge from two quarters. Dr. Austin Wright and Edward Breath, the mission's printer, providentially arrived in Khosrowa and were able to advise their colleague. More important, Mar Yusuf, a Nestorian bishop of the village, volunteered at the last moment to accompany *Hakim* Grant into Hakkari. Thus was the decision made to proceed. Early in the morning of July 21, forty-five days after his departure from Mosul, Grant parted ways with his fellow missionaries and set out again for the mountains.

Charreh, the castle of Yahya Khan, lay on the route, and there Asahel Grant sought a private interview with its lord. As they talked Yahya Khan seemed uneasy at the prospect of Grant's journey, and the doctor asked him if he felt assured of Nurullah Bey's friendship. The Kurd replied that he had no doubts whatsoever; in fact, he offered to send along letters guaranteeing the American's safe return. He had seemed worried, he told Grant, not because of Nurullah but because of the Turks, who were threatening retaliation against the border nomads.

Yahya's concerns were soon supported by evidence, as the travelers saw with their own eyes on the morning of July 22. Grant, Baho, and Mar Yusuf got up at dawn and, accompanied by two "rough-looking" Kurdish guides, pointed their horses toward Ottoman territory. As the sun rose, their movement was soon slowed to a crawl, for everywhere they looked the road was packed with refugees, their animals, and their belongings, all fleeing from Turkish troops who were marching from Van to punish them for their raids. Flocks of sheep and goats, bullock carts heaped with baggage: a moving terrified mass of people and livestock spread across the hills to the horizon. Though the young—and formerly bold—Baho begged Grant to turn back, the doctor pressed on, countering these pleas with soothing speculations about what they might do if they met the approaching army.

At length the travelers found that they had waded through the principal mass of refugees, and as they approached the border, they had the road more or less to themselves. A stray colt, an orphan from the refugee horde, began to follow their party, and the two Kurds eagerly seized it as a prize. But Grant took charge of the colt and insisted that they return it to the last party of refugees they had passed. The Kurds, of course, objected, but Grant did not give in. Riding back to the last group, he presented the colt to them and explained the situation. When he returned to his party he was violently abused by the two Kurds, who claimed that the animal was rightfully their property. Perhaps they were correct, at least according to the code of the mountains, perhaps Grant's action revealed as much meddling self-righteousness as moral strength. Certainly there is no evidence that the Kurds with whom Grant placed the colt had any more intention of restoring it to its rightful owner than did the two ruffians who had first grabbed it. But the doctor's conscience could not let the situation stand. The difference is, that by returning the lost animal Grant at least opened the possibility that restitution might be made. Had he left the situation as it was, he would have been a party not so much to theft as to indifference. For Asahel Grant this was not an option.

At the pass into Ottoman territory (an easy ride, some 8000 feet high) their luck held. No Turkish forces were in evidence, and the nomads who might have threatened them had all fled into Persia. The region, its pastures, and the nearby mountains were known as Albagh (also Ali Bagh and Al Bakh). This pass, then regularly traversed by caravans, has long been abandoned for legitimate commerce. No motor road has ever been built over it, and the railroad from Van into Iranian territory runs fifty miles further to the north. Grant noted the place where, in 1840, he had slept in the snow with his son Henry in his arms; then, with a pang of regret, he passed over into the headwaters of the Zab.

In Turkish territory, however, the danger had by no means disappeared. After spending the night at Surb Bartolomeos (Kandi Kilise), an Armenian monastery at the foot of the Albagh range, they pushed on past Başkale. At a Kurdish village called Zarany, where they asked for shelter but were refused, the travelers spent the night sleeping on the ground before a door. In the morning Grant rose with an empty stomach but felt grateful not to have been robbed—the villagers probably felt the same from him. Two hours' ride brought terrible news. A caravan proceeding to Persia from the orpiment mines of Julamerk had been set upon in the night and plundered, and five men lay dead. Word of this attack came to them just as they were entering the gorge of the Zab. At that point one of the murdered men was carried past on a mule, and faced with this horror, young Baho again pleaded for a delay. Grant argued that since the robbery had just been committed, the bandits had surely scattered with their loot. Moreover, the chances for a robbery were lower in daylight with the entire country in a state of alarm. His reasoning was sound, as was the instinct telling him that they were no worse off forging ahead than turning back. What followed was a long and very tense day in the shadows of the Zab gorge, a place Stygian and threatening even in the most peaceful times. By nightfall they had reached the patriarchal seat at Kochanes and the welcome of Nestorian friends.

The long, frightening detour was over. But Mar Shimun was absent, having long before fled to his house south of the river, subsequently burned in the assault of 1841. At this time he was living with Malek Ismael in Chumba, where Grant resolved to go as soon as possible. Nurullah had removed to his summer camp at Berchullah, a *zozan* two hours' march above Julamerk, where he was preparing for a move south toward the battle for Amadiyah. The next day Grant followed, and there midst mountain pastures found the war party in full swing.

It was a war party in both senses, for besides the marshalling of forces, the Kurds used the occasion for war games and displays of manly bravado. Ismael Pasha of Amadiyah had arrived, having temporarily left his besieged fighters so that he could appeal for support. Ismael, together with Suleiman Bey, was about to depart for Chumba to enlist Mar Shimun in the fight. Both men urged Grant to accompany them, presenting him with an opportunity for mediation and political action that could conceivably have changed history. But Grant would have none of it, excusing himself because Nurullah had taken ill with malaria. The emir then promised to send the doctor on to the patriarch as soon as they had travelled south to the rendezvous point in the mountains.

By now Grant, at his host's request, had donned Kurdish costume. Thus attired he sat down to dinner in Nurullah's tent and then spent the night in a rock shelter roofed over with boughs. On July 28 Nurullah Bey and his warriors set out down the mountain to Julamerk, first stage on their trek south. At the *zozan* Asahel Grant lingered with friends, including the mother of Suleiman Bey. This woman, who in 1840 had lavished so much attention upon the young Henry Martyn Grant, was a consistent friend to the doctor. More than once she warned him to beware the treachery of the Kurds, especially Nurullah Bey. Grant, who knew the emir's suspicion of her son, did not need the warning, but, having no real alternative, continued to work with Nurullah anyway.

At Julamerk castle the games continued, as the guards at the gate pretended to repel an "attack" by the emir's men. Much homemade black powder was expended, and a good time was had by all—with the exception of Dr. Grant, who apparently looked upon the proceedings with a disapproving eye. As usual, it is unclear whether he was disturbed more by the violence, or by the enjoyment that it clearly engendered. He had noted with approval the Kurds' sober avoidance of alcohol, as opposed to the Nestorians' happy tippling. Since the next day was Friday, the Muslim holy day, Nurullah refused to travel, and Grant seized this opportunity to request that his Sabbath be recognized as well, a favor that was granted. It is a measure of Grant's self-confidence that he could make such a request, and an equal indication of the expedition's lack of urgency that it could be granted so readily. At noon on Saturday, when the stars were propitious, the expedition set out down the steep path to the Zab. They spent their Sunday in the Nestorian district of Tal, with Nurullah feasting while the doctor saw patients.

By Monday night the emir and his army had crossed the river and were encamped in an upland valley in the heart of the Hakkari mountains, far from any village. This was to be the rendezvous point for forces gathering against the Turks at Amadiyah. The villages of Tal, a narrow slit of a valley whose waters emptied into the Zab, paid tribute to the emir, a concession which earned them constant robbery and harassment from their neighbors in Tehoma, the adjacent tribal district. Such thuggery and in-fighting was to Grant yet another sign of the mountaineers' disunity, and more evidence of this would soon appear.

Having no taste for life in a military camp, he now left for a four-day tour of Jelu and Baz, districts even wilder and more remote than those he had previously visited. On his first night out of camp Grant and his companions found themselves marooned on a high inaccessible ledge, unable to descend in the gathering darkness. The next day, in the shadowy gorges below, men swarmed out of the rocks at his approach, firing guns and threatening murder. Only when they recognized that under his native costume was the famous *hakim* of Urmia did the Jeluwaye extend a welcome. Jelu, notorious for its bandits and itinerant confidence men, was a district that was never conquered, even in 1915. When Grant passed over the mountain to Baz, the men of Jelu could not guide him, for the way was blocked by a blood feud between the two tribes. Here as elsewhere he treated the sick, and with Mar Yusuf, his companion from Salmas, preached the gospel to people who seemed to care more about swallowing medicines and being bled than about the Word.

Returning to the emir, Grant watched as groups of fighters arrived and were dispatched to Amadiyah. Far to the southwest they could see evidence of the fighting in columns of smoke rising from burning houses. Some men, including Nestorian fighters, returned from the siege carrying the ears of Turks that they had killed, battle trophies rewarded with money when presented to Nurullah. Grant found this revolting, and soon asked leave to visit Mar Shimun in Tiyari. The emir of course granted the request, but not before trying to persuade the doctor not to build his mission house in Asheetha. Nurullah wanted Grant's services closer to hand. Already on their journey the doctor had treated the emir, suffering from a fainting spell, with a dose of peppermint followed by bleeding, as the emir desired. If the doctor would settle closer to his home, said Nurullah, he would order the house built to the American's specifications, and Grant would want for nothing. Grant, of course, resisted these blandishments. A mission outpost was already established in Mosul, and Asheetha lay far closer to that supply point than any place Nurullah could provide. Nurullah then requested that Grant put off building until he could see him again, and the missionary agreed. On August 9, after leaving the emir with a supply of

medicines and instructions for their use, Dr. Grant set out for
the village of Chumba, in Upper Tiyari.

Grant met Mar Shimun at the *zozan* on August 14, having
arrived in Chumba the previous evening. This is where we began Dr. Grant's story, where he woke swollen and in pain. He
had spent five days on the march from Nurullah's camp, a journey as difficult as any he had made. In one harrowing mountain passage, the doctor came very close to falling into the abyss.
The bridge over the Zab at Chumba—three feet wide and 150
feet long, with no railings or supports of any kind—we have
already seen on Grant's first visit to Chumba. In the mountains
the mules often had to be carried or pulled past obstacles. On
the Chumba bridge the men hauled them up bodily whenever
their hooves punched through the wickerwork.

The morning before he reached Chumba, Dr. Grant went
out of his way to meet Heiyo, a Nestorian outlaw and robber
who was the most dangerous man in Tiyari. Only the need for
propitiation made this meeting necessary. Heiyo hated Mar
Shimun and was living under his anathema, but Grant did not
want mission families living close to such a man without an
attempt at friendship. In this he seems to have succeeded. When
Heiyo announced that he could easily dispatch the missionary
with a stroke of his blade, Grant simply replied that, as his
host, the outlaw could do with him as he wished. In the end he
was grudgingly allowed to leave, having impressed the bandit
with his sang-froid, if nothing else.

From the *zozan*, Grant set out for Asheetha, accompanied
by Mar Shimun and the malek. There the rendezvous had been
arranged, and with Suleiman Bey, Ismael Pasha, and all the tribal
leaders expected to attend, a decision about Amadiyah would
at last be made. Grant now learned the patriarch's real plans.
He told Grant he had no intention of making peace with the
emir or taking part in the battle for Amadiyah. In fact, he had
established a secret correspondence with the Kurds' enemies.

Mohammed Pasha of Mosul, ever the Machiavellian schemer, had sent several friendly letters to Mar Shimun in an attempt to open a dialogue. Although this strategy—divide and rule—is as old as the human race, the Nestorian patriarch took the bait. He was now in regular contact with the Little Ensign, whom he had told the details of Nurullah's collusion with Ismael and Bedr Khan Bey. Mar Shimun apparently believed in the pasha's offer of friendship. He also believed that if he were going to lose his independence, he woud be wise to lose it to the Turks, who were susceptible to foreign influence. The recent attention paid to his people by the missionaries, along with the expedition of Ainsworth and Rassam, had led him to conclude that the English and other European powers would come to his aid.

It was a fatal error, and not his only one: Mar Shimun had also deluded himself about the extent of his power. An accident of birth had put him into a position where only someone with a mind of the greatest subtlety and courage could have won through, and the patriarch did not have these qualities. Unfortunately, he was also ambitious. He wanted to be to the Nestorians what Bedr Khan was to the Kurds: the leader of leaders, in battle and at the baptismal font. We have already witnessed the doltish behavior and petty criminality of his brothers; possibly a good portion of his self-delusion sprang from their counsels. In any case, the tribes did not want him to reach for power. They wanted to be left alone.

Overestimating his ability to lead and unify, Mar Shimun went on to deprecate the threat posed by the Kurds. Their newfound unity and enmity was embodied in their main leader, Bedr Khan Bey, the emir of Bohtan. Even today it is hard to know what to make of him. To Kurdish nationalists he is an important figure, having made one of the first attempts to forge a truly independent Kurdish state in the midst of Turkish domains. Bedr Khan's power extended from Van to Diyarbakir, and he even went so far as to strike his own coins. Blind Mohammed of Rowanduz though independent and powerful, had been little better than a thug, hated by all who knew him. Bedr Khan, though never reluctant to spill blood, won others' respect and allegiance through strength of character. Other chiefs—Nurullah, Ismael, and Khan Mahmud from north of Başkale, to name a few—rallied to Bedr Khan's banner. Kurdish villagers praised his equity and fairness; they spoke of the peace that prevailed in his domains. Christians, however, were of quite another opinion, and for this, as we shall see, they had good reason.

Two days' journey brought Grant and his companions to the mountain overlooking Asheetha. Here Grant paused to take detailed compass bearings, a task he took seriously; unlike his first visit, he could now feel safe gathering geographic information. Near the bottom of the descent, a priest, acting as official welcoming party, walked up from the village swinging a censer on a chain, and with this escort they proceeded toward the outskirts of Asheetha. Soon Grant and Mar Shimun were engulfed by a crowd of villagers, then led to a nearby house overlooking the valley. Here, where a stream shaded by walnut trees turned a small mill, the doctor spent a week seeing patients and watching the crisis play out.

The crowd that greeted doctor and patriarch was only part of the assembled multitude. Indeed, Asheetha had become an armed camp, for in addition to the expected Christian tribes, over 400 Kurds had gathered for the rendezvous. The bargaining seems to have begun almost at once. Suleiman Bey and Ismael Pasha had already arrived and stated their case. The chiefs of the Nestorian tribes then met in council to talk about the proposed alliance with Nurullah, and when he discovered that many seemed to regard it favorably, the patriarch immediately went on the attack. He informed them of his unmovable opposition to the plan and threatened anathema, the deadliest of curses, to anyone who opposed him. Those whom he could not turn against the alliance, he convinced to attach conditions so troublesome that the Kurds would not agree to them. In all this, no one seems to have realized the high stakes involved. Neither Grant nor Laurie mentions anyone who looked beyond the moment, who saw the looming figure of Bedr Khan, and questioned the implications of insulting Nurullah once again. Mar Shimun had already betrayed Ismael Pasha at Amadiyah five years before, and there was no reason to think that he would be given a third chance. Now, unbeknownst to all, he was trying to effect an alliance with the Turks. The situation was a disaster in the making, a sleepwalk to the cliff's edge.

Once Mar Shimun announced his opposition in such implacable terms, the deal was doomed. Ismael Pasha, no doubt disgusted anew with Mar Shimun, now left Asheetha. Several of the clans expressed a willingness to join Ismael Pasha, especially those from Tehoma, a tribe long at odds with the Tiyari. But these were few. In the aftermath, with the alliance defunct, the cry went up among the Tiyarians that they should immediately attack the remaining Kurds and drive them out of the valley. That this was a direct violation of all the laws of hospitality did not stop some hotheads from proposing it. After a strenuous effort by the patriarch, the attack was thwarted. Still, in the general hubbub some five of Ismael Pasha's mules were taken by order of Mar Shimun and Malek Ismael. Thus was injury added to insult.

Had the patriarch been a political genius, he might somehow have threaded his way between Scylla and Charybdis and emerged unscathed. But he was not a genius, and the one man who might have counseled him sat beneath his walnut tree seeing patients and, despite repeated invitations, did not once join the assembled chiefs. Asahel Grant had said nothing when Mar Shimun told him his plans, and beyond a vague admonition for the parties to make peace with each other, said nothing now. Strict neutrality in political matters was the official policy of the American Board, and Grant rigidly adhered to this. But in any case, it is hard to see what else he could have done. He could not advise the Nestorian patriarch to ally with Nurullah against the Turks. Such counsel would have been madness, an

action leading to expulsion—or worse—for himself and his colleagues immediately upon his return to Mosul. Nor could he
tell Mar Shimun to trust that scorpion in the boot of humanity,
Mohammed Pasha, the Little Ensign. One could argue that the
doctor was in the wrong place at the wrong time and should
not have gone into the mountains at all; but that would be to
argue that he should not have been who he was: a man who
took enormous chances in a cause that he felt was bigger than
himself, bigger than the petty quarrels of men.

As for Amadiyah, as everyone predicted, without the
Nestorian forces there was little hope. In fact, the humiliation
of Nurullah and Ismael could not have been more complete.
Before the end of August, hungry and outnumbered, their warriors gave up and returned home. With the town in ruins and
the Turks again in control, the emir of Hakkari had one more
reason to hate Mar Shimun.

The House in Asheetha

"When a man builds, he lives."—*Turkish proverb*

ON AUGUST 29, GRANT watched first the men of Tehoma, then the main Kurdish force, return from Amadiyah. By then he was in Chal, a Kurdish district across the Zab from Lezan and Asheetha, where Nurullah Bey had moved his camp. When he arrived on the 27th, he found the emir gripped by the ague—the chills of malaria—and thus in a state to welcome his services. But the welcome was tinged with suspicion. As Grant measured out his medicines, Nurullah must have been thinking that this English *hakim*, after all, had just come from the camp of his enemy, Mar Shimun. Nurullah trusted no one, so why should he trust this man? It was a common question in the mountains, where neither patriarch nor emir would touch a drop of coffee until someone else had tasted it.

Nurullah's mood worsened on the 29th, when the warriors came straggling in. Amadiyah occupied an immensely strong position, and Laurie reports that during the five-month siege, despite the thousands of rounds of ammunition expended, only eleven of the defenders died of gunfire. Yet if an army marches on its belly, this one was retreating on an empty one. In one voice the men blamed Ismael Pasha's "commissary," which basically did not exist. Except for fruits and roots, the defenders of Amadiyah had eaten nothing for weeks. As virtually none of these men were natives of the town or compatriots of Ismael, it is hardly surprising that they would not want to starve and die for him. This did not stop Nurullah from accusing the leaders of cowardice. He was so chagrined by this humiliation that he could scarcely speak. The Kurdish chief of Chal was singled out for blame: after imposing a fine, Nurullah stripped him of his rank. Only a year before this man had taken part in the burning of Mar Shimun's house; now, spurned by the emir, he went over to the patriarch's camp.

Asahel Grant wanted to leave as soon as possible. A sick, suspicious despot is no one's idea of a good companion; nor did Nurullah seem to want him there. Grant had come on specific business: to secure from the emir written authorization to build a mission house in Asheetha, and having secured this document, he could return. After the departure of Ismael Pasha and the Kurds, the people of Asheetha were eager to proceed with construction, especially in view of the cash wages they would receive. Before he left, Grant, wanting no misunderstandings, no possible reason for suspicion, insisted on a final visit to the emir: Nurullah had already tried to convince him to build closer to Julamerk, and Grant had promised to do nothing until he had seen the emir again. This honorable act exemplified the doctor's character, yet in retrospect his precautions seem irrelevant. As Grant would find, Nurullah's jealousy was a monster that could proliferate in unimaginable ways.

From the emir's camp Grant hastened to Tiyari. At Lezan he took off his boots and crawled across the bridge, while his mules were forced to swim the Zab. Back in Asheetha, he set to work at once building a future for the mission. Within days a school was organized, with one of the local priests acting as teacher, and more were planned. Most importantly, the doctor set about finding a place to build his home. This act, the siting and construction of the house in Asheetha, now became the defining endeavor of his existence. That it would cause problems, let alone provoke a festival of paranoia and fantasy, Grant never dreamed. From beginning to end, he believed that if he conducted himself like the open and honest person his mother had raised, all would turn out well. If it did not, the decision was in the hands of God.

To understand Grant's choice of a building site, we must look at Asheetha and its landscape. For this was no ordinary mountain village. In Jelu, Baz, Tehoma, and Chal—indeed, in all the districts of Kurdistan that he visited, the settlements were clusters of houses, packed together and often stacked like blocks of mud or stone against the mountainsides. The villages from Asheetha to Lezan, in the valley of the Izani River, presented quite a different situation. Here a combination of factors—sheer rock barriers on three sides plus the ferocious reputation of the people—produced a climate of security, where people felt no need to huddle together for safety. And there was the configuration of the land itself. Unlike a typical river valley—broad and flat, with ample room for crops of wheat, as in Amadiyah—the Izani was chopped up into hills and ridges, down which dashed a multitude of mountain streams, each in turn directed to a massive system of terraces needing constant cultivation, attention, and repair. These two factors, a secure environment and an enormous array of terraced fields stretching the twenty miles from Asheetha to the Zab, meant that the houses were widely separated, thus allowing the farmers to live closer to their plots of land. It was in one of these places that Asahel Grant chose to build his house.

The project created a sensation. Before he purchased a building site, men were already clamoring for work, and at Zawitha, further down the Izani toward Lezan, the people urged Grant to make his home among them. But the doctor insisted upon

Asheetha. Eventually he found his spot on a ridge, one of several that swept into the valley near the center of the village. At its end, on an eminence overlooking the stream, with cultivated terraces stacked about it on three sides, someone long ago had built what the people called a "castle," probably a large house or mansion. The structure had long since disappeared, leaving in the scattered rocks only a hint of what had once existed. But the name had stuck, and here Grant decided to erect the mission compound.

It was a beautiful site, a place where the air was pure, the torrent's deep rumble never ceased, and snow lay within walking distance even in summer. Grant bought the castle and an adjoining lot for fifty piastres, about $5.00. Payment was made in *cherkies,* the mountaineers' name for their most common currency, a Turkish coin minted in Baghdad. The price was low because of the plot's total barrenness. Later, when the doctor bought a cultivated terrace (eight by eighty-two *dhraa,* or cubits) nearby for a garden, the price was fifty piastres for a considerably smaller area. The title-deed for his patch of rock reads like cuneiform exhumed from a crypt. The usual flowery greetings open the document, along with lawyerly loops and swirls giving "ye who meet with this which we have written" the news that "in the year 2153 of the Greeks (era of the Seleucidae)" the purchase had been made by "Hekim Grant, the Englishman, from the country of America." The use of a calendar dating back to the time of Alexander the Great's successors is startling enough; the sellers—"Deacon Shlimon of the house of Raban," "Newiya from the house of Dadeh," "Yogannis of the house of Bajeh"—present an image even more Biblical. In conclusion, says the deed, Grant and "his associates, the English," shall dwell in Asheetha "even until the resurrection," and all this is done with the permission of the emir, the *mudebbir* (Suleiman Bey, also called the *mutesellim*), and "Mar Shimun Katolika, Patriarch of the East." Having made this document on "the sixth month of summer" in the year 2153, Mar Shimun and Priest Auraham of Lezan affixed their seals.

At last Grant was getting somewhere. His hosts, fractious and violent, with only the fuzziest notion of the difference between Americans and English, had sold him the one thing that could anchor his life. Since he could not get the building completed before the onset of winter, he was forced to take a house in Lezan; furnishing it took up even more of his time. After the fall of Amadiyah, the mountains had gone silent, and for the time being all Turco-Persian conflicts had been staved off by the mediation of the European powers. On September 13, during this lull, Grant dispatched his young servant to Mosul, with a letter to Abel Hinsdale that asked plaintively, "Can you come and spend the winter here with me?"

Baho took only four days to reach Mosul with the letter, and two days later Hinsdale wrote to Dr. Rufus Anderson in Boston. "Had we associates here now," he said, "I should leave without delay, taking Mrs. H. with me to settle in the mountains." But the two missionaries who were expected, Thomas and Martha Laurie, were still in Stamboul, and Sarah was some four months pregnant. Under these circumstances, Hinsdale resolved to go alone to Asheetha and return before the onset of winter. On the last day of September, accompanied by eight mules loaded with books, medicines, and other supplies, Abel Hinsdale crossed the bridge of boats at Mosul and set his course for Tiyari. Baho stayed behind. Though Dr. Grant had fully expected him to return, he had experienced enough of Hakkari and its people for ten lifetimes. Once in Mosul, the young Syrian quickly announced that he was not coming back.

On October 7, after a trouble-free passage through Amadiyah, Hinsdale met with Grant fifteen miles out of Asheetha. The joy Asahel Grant felt was incalculable. "For the first time in four years," writes Thomas Laurie, "the one enjoyed the society of a Christian friend, in this scene of hardship and danger." This is no reflection on people like Mar Yusuf, the bishop who had faithfully accompanied Grant through the mountains. With Hinsdale, Grant could speak English again; and speak it with a real friend from a similar background. It must have been one of the happiest meetings of his life.

Hinsdale, received cordially by the Asheethans, expressed in turn his desire to "live and die" among them. Of Asheetha itself he wrote, "Upon reaching the summit of the hill overlooking the village, the prospect is one of singular beauty. Far below, in the quiet vale, the village extends perhaps to the distance of a mile and a half, with numerous plats of grain and vegetables interspersed among the houses, and the whole variegated and enlivened with shade trees of several different kinds." Seduced, like Grant, by the glories of the setting and the friendliness of the people, Hinsdale foresaw an unlimited future for the station. The field was "white to the harvest," he wrote, and only the "enemy" is awaiting the chance to "scatter his tares." Of course, this enemy was not one so palpable as Nurullah Bey or Mohammed Pasha. Quite another foe occupied Hinsdale's mind, one of great subtlety and infinite wiles—many of which had been learned in Italy.

With winter only two months away, the Americans set to work. When Hinsdale arrived one school had opened, and planning for the mission house was underway. Rock had to be gathered for the walls, beams and branches for the roof. In a land where even dirt was scarce, the mud which would mortar the rocks together and pave the roof was probably as valuable a commodity as anything else. Slowly but surely, with Mar Shimun's help, the project took shape.

By the end of the month, another quite different group showed up in the valley. It was, in fact, the "enemy" himself. Before leaving Mosul, Hinsdale had been told by P.E. Botta, the French consul, that two more emissaries would soon be arriving from Rome. Such proved to be the case. In Urmia, Mosul, and elsewhere, the Americans had regularly come in contact with the "reptiles of Rome." Never, however, had they been so close to their operations as Grant and Hinsdale now found themselves in Asheetha. On October 27, 1842, the papal delegation arrived, the latest effort in the ongoing battle to win over Mar Shimun and his people to Catholicism. Included in this group were the Chaldean—Catholic—bishop of Amadiyah, an Italian priest, and Eugène Boré, a French layman who had been entrusted with 2000 francs by the Society of Lyons. Boré's money had one clear purpose: to persuade Mar Shimun to "return" to the Church and bring his people with him. More boxes packed with gifts remained at Diyarbakir.

The delegation must have known that their task would be difficult. Remember that Grant had heard the epithet "Catoleek" thrown at him in 1839 when he first entered the Tiyari country. What was an insult then was surely no compliment now, as with traditional hospitality and considerable wariness, the people of Asheetha greeted these Catholics bearing gifts. Despite the mountaineers' reputation, Boré and his associates entertained high hopes for the mission. They knew that if Mar Shimun were swayed, his flock would follow, and they probably also knew about his brothers' love of cold cash.

The encounter lasted from a Thursday until the following Tuesday, with the visitors addressing large and skeptical audiences. The two Americans did not go to meet the Catholics, whose reception lacked cordiality. Mar Shimun at first deflected their requests for an interview, but after delaying for three days he permitted them to make their presentation on a Saturday before the assembled Nestorians. Dr. Grant attended the conclave in the company of Mar Yusuf, the bishop from Persia. A vigorous debate ensued, which continued into the Sabbath. Every conceivable point was argued over, including auricular confession, the power of the pope and his ability to forgive sins. As an apostle of Christ, the patriarch claimed full equality with the Vatican. Both he and Mar Yusuf vigorously defended "these English," as Mar Shimun called the Americans, saying that by taking the Bible as authority they were "the best Christians in the world." The conclusion was never in doubt. Boré and his associates, meeting a massif of resistance, tarried until Tuesday morning. They reserved their final efforts for several private interviews with Mar Shimun; Dr. Grant and the bishop were not present. When these interviews failed, and the patriarch not only returned their gifts but forbade them to travel anywhere in the mountains, the papal delegation gave up and left.

In all, this could be considered to be an impressive reflection of the mountaineers' independence, obduracy, and zeal. The argument could be made, though admittedly it is a weak one, that Mar Shimun's submission to the Vatican might have given him a political advantage in the years ahead. The pope, after all, exerted far more temporal power than did the American Board or the Archbishop of Canterbury. But such submission was as inconceivable as that Asahel Grant should give up his mountain dream and return to his children. Character was destiny, and that destiny was leading both men elsewhere.

It was not only Baho who had grown tired of Hakkari. With the departure of the Catholics, Mar Yusuf of Salmas decided to return to Persia. Far from his home and family for the first time in his life, he had become seriously ill, and he had to get back before the roads were snowed in. The bishop had been an immense help to Grant, joining his party in July when it seemed that the American was doomed to enter the mountains alone. Yet Mar Yusuf, like Baho, had found nothing congenial in the character or life of these mountain Christians. His home lay among the peaceful farmers of Urmia and Salmas, not with people whom he regarded as savages.

Work on the mission house now pushed forward, and with it came more evidence of how difficult these "savages" could be. The main problem was *money*: not the lack of it, but its presence. In the mountains of Kurdistan when someone arrived with coin enough to buy land without, for example, sending over a bride as major compensation, or to pay wages without the need for barter, this was big news.

Asahel Grant brought this kind of money, and even in the small amounts that he proposed to spend (some twenty-five cents—perhaps two *cherkies*—for a day's labor) its mere presence made a major impact. Daily at the "castle," the scene grew to resemble a union hiring hall, but with a difference. Here the men carried knives, and they clawed for advantage in the job hunt without the benefit of seniority or, indeed, rules of any kind. The result was anarchy, as "men of all ranks quarrelled with each other for employment in the severest drudgery." Bidding wars broke out, as men offered to carry timber free for one day in return for half wages the rest of the week. At one point the uproar became so serious that Grant had to stop the work, dismiss the entire company, and retire to his house in Lezan for peace and quiet. When he returned, he laid down the law. He took one man from each clan in turn, thus equally dividing the work, but he told them that unless calm and order were preserved he would shut down the site completely. This did the trick, and from then on he had much less trouble.

By the end of November, Mar Shimun had migrated north to Chumba, while Abel Hinsdale took the mules and made his way back to Mosul. Thus Asahel Grant was left alone once again, and this time soon after a bout of fever and ague had all but eaten his strength. Winter was approaching, and, like the tribesmen, he retreated to his burrow to wait it out. But he had just settled into his house at Lezan when a message came from Mar Shimun. A last squall of discord was rattling the rocks of Hakkari before winter: Nurullah and Bedr Khan Bey had met, and they were joining together for a final attack against the Nestorians. The men of Jelu, having suffered the loss of a caravan to Nurullah, had made up this damage with a raid of their own, and Mar Shimun had ordered a retaliatory strike in another sector. Equally disturbing were rumors about Dr. Grant's house. In view of all this, and especially the alliance between the two Kurds, the patriarch asked to see the doctor at once.

What is interesting here is that anyone, especially Mar Shimun, should have been surprised. It was already an open secret that Nurullah had made an alliance with Bedr Khan Bey, the emir of Bohtan. After the debacle at Amadiyah, it must have been obvious that the emir of Hakkari would do everything in his power to bring down his enemy, the patriarch. Grant, weary and weakened by malaria, had no choice but to set out for Chumba.

Just before he reached the village, a message arrived from Nurullah himself. The note, short but friendly, asked the doctor to come at once on medical business. When Grant told this to the patriarch and Malek Ismael, their reaction was immediate. Under no circumstances, they warned, should Grant heed the emir's demand. It was almost certainly a trap set by Nurullah, as portended by, in Laurie's words, "the proverbial treachery of his race." Grant faced a hard decision. He was not well, and December was almost upon them. Since June 6 he had been traveling on foot and muleback—and even on his knees—through war, banditry, and a thicket of personal hatreds. His stomach still troubled him, and the little food he could retain was of the coarsest kind, with millet boiled in sour milk considered to be a delicacy. He knew the emir to be friendly; he knew him to be a murderer. But he also knew that, like himself and half the people in the mountains, Nurullah suffered from malaria and a dozen other complaints. After arguing the case with Mar Shimun and spending the Sabbath in prayer, Grant made the Hippocratic choice. On Tuesday morning, November 29, he crossed the wicker bridge at Chumba and set out for Julamerk.

All of Grant's journeys were difficult, and with bad food and unceasing tension, wore him down in ways we can barely begin to comprehend. Yet the next weeks were in a class by themselves. As he made his way upriver from Chumba, over tracks impassable for mules, Grant was repeating virtually the same journey he had first made in October 1839, but with a difference. This time everything was darker, both metaphorically and physically. Four November weeks had lowered the sun to the brink of solstice, and a permanent chill dwelt in the shadows. Freya Stark has written of the Zab gorge as a descent into hell, and it is easy to see why. There is no softness here, and little light. Everything seems hacked from rock, whether it be the riverbed, the villages, or the narrow crack of sky. It engenders awe, but little optimism. And so it was with Grant. The vista was beautiful. The peaks reared straight up from the foaming river; the low sun hit the mile-high cliffs with a shaft of brilliance; but nothing could erase the knowledge of a destination he did not desire to reach.

Two days' hard climbing brought Grant to the castle of Julamerk. It was December 1 when he arrived, and dusk was thickening as Nurullah's guards swung open the big iron-bound gates. Down a long, unlighted passage they walked, at the end of which Grant found himself alone in a dark, unadorned room that looked uncomfortably like a cell. In his description of the scene, the doctor for once makes no mention of his belief that he is protected by a higher power. In these brief moments the solitary traveler seems genuinely frightened.

The situation, to his relief, did not last long. Within minutes a lamp was brought, and familiar faces from the emir's household appeared. Kurdish voices bade him welcome, and within the hour he was taken to see his host. Nurullah was then residing in the harem, and to his surprise Asahel Grant received the rare privilege of meeting a Muslim ruler in the presence of his women. The room was warm and inviting, with the finest Persian carpets; the walls were hung with a profusion of guns, swords, and porcelain plates. Nurullah sat upon a divan covered in yellow satin and bolstered with heaps of yellow satin pillows, while about him were ranged a dozen of his closest advisors, including his nephew Suleiman Bey.

The emir, says Grant, had never been more welcoming. Everyone was cordial and solicitous; Suleiman in particular came forward to express his regards. When Grant asked after Nurullah's health, his host replied that in spite of recent illness he now— thank God—was much better, and held out his arm so that Dr. Grant might take his pulse. And you, asked the patient, what have you been doing? Grant replied that he had been building, with the emir's permission. Nurullah said he had heard that the doctor was building a castle. Was this true? How many rooms did he have? So here it was: the wild rumors returning home; this was the real reason for his summons to Julamerk. Grant replied with simple candor. His house would have four rooms, with walls of loose stone laid up in mud, no higher than a man could reach. Real fortresses, as Nurullah knew, were much higher than that and were made of stone mortared with lime. And if he really were building a castle, Grant asked, how would he defend it? Had the emir ever seen him armed?

Nurullah turned to his retinue and smiled. Didn't I tell you, he asked, that this was a true man? He had heard the rumors and decided to summon the doctor: if they were untrue, he knew Grant would come at once; if he did not come, they would investigate further. What, Nurullah asked, are the big holes in the sides of the house? He had also heard about these. They, of course, were windows, a feature lacking in the hovels inhabited by the Kurds and Nestorians. To the Kurds they looked like ports for cannon, or, odder yet, merchants' stalls. Taking a piece of paper, Grant drew the house with an explanation of its features: windows to let in light; stoves to come from America, with chimneys to get rid of the smoke; no shops or guns anywhere.

Nurullah was delighted, but he repeated the question he had posed earlier in the summer: why did the doctor have to build his house in Asheetha? Let him come to Julamerk and the emir would build it for him. Of course the doctor wanted to work among the Christians; but there were Christians in Julamerk too, and even more would come if the doctor settled nearby. Like the villagers of Asheetha, Nurullah was willing to press hard to get what he wanted. In the end he asked for and received a note from Grant promising that he would not build a bazaar or take part in government, and that he would always respond when the emir requested medical assistance.

Soon came the dinner: a huge plate of pilaf, followed by coffee. On that night at least, Grant could forget about millet boiled in sour milk. For the rest of the evening, the American was honored by the company of the women, unveiled, after the normal Kurdish custom. Nurullah appears to have kept two wives, the elder being the mother of his heir. This boy had been a playmate of Henry Martyn when the Grants passed through the area in 1840, and he now asked after Grant's youngest son. To the doctor the place began to seem like home. The women, of course, wanted the doctor to take their pulse, but they were so heavily adorned with bracelets of gold and silver coins that this proved very difficult.

Grant passed seven days in the household of Nurullah Bey, where he was treated as both honored guest and oddity, a jester whose tricks—reading English, taking the pulse, expounding on religion—enlivened the otherwise stultifying days. But he soon discovered that behind these pleasant domestic scenes, plots were being laid and alliances cemented even as winter closed in. In one part of the castle Ismael Pasha was closeted with Zeiner Bey, the notorious Berwari outlaw, planning a series of raids against Turkish-held territory near Amadiyah. Grant also discovered what he must have long suspected, namely, that the emir himself was intimately involved in much of the brigandage that went on in Hakkari.

This was confirmed when Nurullah, in Grant's presence, passed a death sentence on one of his most prominent local governors, a man imprisoned in a distant castle. Immediately ten of the emir's "most reckless robbers," in Laurie's phrase, were dispatched to carry out the sentence. When the gang of assassins returned, Grant met them. Fresh from the kill, totally candid and boastful to a sickening degree, they treated the American to a long and vivid account of their raids, robberies, and murders. One of them said that he had just plundered a caravan between Mosul and Amadiyah. They even described their methods of operation, with small groups going out to find who was traveling so that they could swoop in for the attack. Villagers who might warn the travelers were threatened with retribution if they did not keep silent. All in all, this did not present a pretty picture. Thomas Laurie does not make a direct accusation, but it seems obvious that if Nurullah was not controlling the activities of these men, he was at least doing nothing to stop them. We can only assume that he was sharing in their booty or receiving protection money. It was only in July, after all, just after Grant and his party had crossed the border, that a Persian caravan from the orpiment mines had been attacked and five men lost their lives. Even in the rocks of Hakkari, with its countless avenues for evasion and escape, it is impossible that Nurullah could not have known about this.

In the middle of his stay, Grant took an overnight trip to Mar Shimun's former residence, where a few of the patriarch's relatives remained near the burnt-out ruins. After the attack of 1841 these people were poverty-stricken but defiant, and had recently struck back at the emir from their side of the river. This act, as Thomas Laurie points out, was more brave than prudent, especially when their very existence was at stake. No sooner had he returned to Julamerk than Grant was afflicted once again by the parasites swarming in his blood. This time the malaria struck so hard as to leave him almost senseless. Medicine and the kindness of his old friend, the mother of Suleiman Bey, restored him to what passed for health, and once again this woman dared to warn him against the treachery of Nurullah Bey.

On December 7, to his great relief, Grant said goodbye to the emir and his castle. The next day, after spending the night in a Kurdish village, he forded the Zab and began to retrace his steps toward Chumba, where the patriarch and the malek were overjoyed to see him, and he was able to arrange release of the five mules stolen from Ismael Pasha in August. The next night he stayed with Heiyo, the Nestorian murderer and outlaw who had become "much attached" to him. The winter snows continued to hold off, and Grant, worn out with sickness and fatigue, was lucky to arrive in Asheetha without incident, on December 11, 1842.

By now the exhausted doctor had only one desire: to spend a quiet winter at his house in Lezan. On November 8, in a letter that Abel Hinsdale carried back to Mosul, Dr. Grant wrote to Thomas and Martha Laurie, who were just then arriving by caravan from the Black Sea. In a previous letter to a friend on November 3, he had expressed the hope that Thomas Laurie might be persuaded to spend the winter with him in Lezan. Now he had to apologize: he could not welcome the young couple to the mountains, since no accommodations were yet available. The depth of his loneliness is apparent, if only because he refers to these feelings so dismissively. "I will not dwell on my lonely situation," he wrote, "though I have learned that, in these mountains especially, 'it is not good for man to be alone.'" Still, ignoring all the portents about him, he promised a hearty welcome when the Lauries arrived in the coming year.

No peace, however, was possible for Asahel Grant. No sooner had he settled into winter quarters when his plans received a last fatal blow. On December 13, an urgent message arrived from Mosul. Abel Hinsdale, whose arrival he had greeted with such delight just two months before, was dangerously ill. Immediately upon their arrival in Mosul on November 12, both Thomas and Martha Laurie had taken sick, and Hinsdale, working himself to exhaustion at their bedsides, had allowed an illness of his own to gain the upper hand. Now his life was threatened by a disease, that, Grant said, had assumed "a typhus character." Once again, delay was not possible, because the winter snows might begin at any moment. On the morning of December 14, Grant, with infinite weariness, mounted his mule and set out for Mosul.

Mr. Badger Drops In

"The English are Christians, and have churches; but they only go to them once a month, and take the Lord's Supper once in twenty years. On the latter occasion the Priest stands on a high place, that he may not be torn in pieces by the crowd who rush tumultuously forward, snatch the consecrated bread out of his hands and scramble for it. They are also allowed to marry as many wives as they please, and some of them have more than twenty."

—a Chaldean priest of Mosul, quoted in
J.P. Fletcher: *Notes from Nineveh* (1850)

FOR A STORY-TELLER, EACH death among the missionaries is as appalling as the last, each small and sad and saturated in piety. In a literary sense one longs for the majesty of *War and Peace,* where Prince Andrei lies dying, the Russian earth holds her breath, and the cadence of mighty words rolls across the page. But here we are left with middle-class Yankees meeting a mournful end in a desolate place, and for the writer who seeks balance, there seems no way to thread the narrow bridge between hero worship and pathos. To many, these selfless Christians will always be the noblest of beings, rising heavenward to their reward, while to others they are naïve meddling fools, lost in a world they cannot begin to understand. The argument is as old as altruism, as new as the latest delusion, and there is plenty of evidence to support both points of view. Most of all, however, these are human beings, and one cannot deprecate the kindness they embodied or the legacy of knowledge they left behind. Their personal courage midst a hundred calamities is reason enough to grant them respect.

By December of 1842, Sarah Hinsdale had seen her share of missionary deaths. Colby Mitchell, robed in straw and dust, shielded from jackals by the weight of stones. Eliza Mitchell's fevered body on the mud floor, her brow pouring with sweat, while chattering crones cut the hooks from Sarah's dress. And now Sarah's husband, father of a child soon to be born. "If any of the saints are in heaven," said a Syrian Orthodox deacon, "Mr. Hinsdale is there." The words were spoken on December 26, after Hinsdale's wasted body had given up its last breath. The *Missionary Herald* reprinted Grant's clinical account of the illness: fever of a "decidedly typhus form"; heavy involvement of the lungs and head; hemorrhage from the nostrils, throat, and bowels; delirium and death. The end came at 4:30 on the morning after Christmas. Sarah, "deeply afflicted," was there, as were Thomas Laurie and Dr. Grant. Abel Knapp Hinsdale was thirty-five years old.

He was buried in the courtyard of the Syrian Orthodox church of Mar Toma (St. Thomas), the oldest church in Mosul. Eliza Mitchell was buried there, and other Americans would follow. "Oh, what a loss!" Grant wrote to a friend. One more colleague had passed on, and again he was alone. Never had his earthly allotment of days seemed more unsure, and it was not only illness that threatened him. No sooner had he returned to Mosul and received cordial greetings from the Ottoman gover-nor, than he found out the truth: just a few days earlier this same man, Mohammed Pasha, had sent out a message while Grant was still in the mountains, ordering his immediate assas-

sination. The order had gone to a Kurdish chief in league with
the Turks, and it stemmed from the pasha's desire to keep all
foreigners well away from the scene of his machinations. Only
the news of Hinsdale's illness and Grant's sudden departure from
Lezan, had saved the doctor's life. But what, after all, was a
failed assassination between friends? And what could one man
do against a pasha? Relations remained almost legislative in
their warmth and sincerity, and during the coming winter, whenever the Little Ensign required a dose of tartar emetic or a good
bleeding, the doctor was always ready to oblige.

A host of dignitaries turned out for Hinsdale's burial, including all the Christian clergy and members of the tiny foreign
community. All, that is, except one. The Rev. George Percy Badger, representative of the Church of England and a newcomer
to Mosul, stayed away partly because of illness but mostly out
of principle. Quite simply, he had decided that the American
"Dissenters" (his name for the Protestants) were not the sort of
people with whom he, as a representative of the Anglican
Church, should associate. Their theology was more than sus-
pect; it was heathen. Their clergy, installed without reference to
an apostolic succession, were not properly ordained, and their
services lacked liturgical validity. In short, though the Americans as people were pleasant and kind, he thought it best to
avoid their company.

It was a familiar snub. When W.F. Ainsworth and Christian
Rassam had passed through Urmia in the summer of 1840, they
ignored the Americans completely and remained in their tents
outside the city walls. Afterwards, they excused themselves on
the grounds that they (1) had no proper clothing in which to
greet the ladies and (2) preferred sleeping on the ground. No one
believed this in 1840, though of course the missionaries were careful to smile and turn the other cheek; and two years later no one
believed the doctrinal rationalizations of George Percy Badger.

Eventually Badger was to enjoy a long and distinguished career in the East, including service as a mediator and chaplain in

India, Zanzibar, and Aden. As a scholar and linguist he made important contributions, and in later life knew Sir Richard Francis Burton, who made flattering reference to him in the introduction to his translation of the *Arabian Nights*. But it seems fair to say that, during the years 1842-43, Badger was a thoroughgoing religious bigot or a man driven by snobbery to act like one. Like Christian Rassam, he had embraced High Church Anglicanism with the impulsiveness of youth and the enthusiasm of the new convert. At that time Puseyism—Tractarianism, or the Oxford Movement—enjoyed a great vogue, and it seems to have given Badger a feeling of being among the Elect, as opposed to the more proletarian appeal of the evangelicals. He was born in 1815 on Malta, the son of a sergeant in the British army. His sister Matilda, already established in Mosul as the wife of Christian Rassam, had proved a true friend to the missionaries and would remain so to the end. His mother, who had migrated to Mesopotamia with her daughter in 1840, also plainly disapproved of her son's anti-Americanism.

Badger had begun his working life in the service of two groups that he would later oppose. First was the Church Missionary Society, those Anglican evangelicals whose president, Rev. Josiah Pratt, had been so kind to Asahel Grant when he was in London in 1841. In his late teens, Badger, who had joined the Methodists, went to work for the Missionary Society in Malta as a teacher. Some years earlier Daniel Temple, another Massachusetts missionary, had given him a job at the printing office of the American Board of Commissioners for Foreign Missions. When the American Board moved its press to Beirut, Badger followed, and there he remained for two years honing his Arabic skills. The year 1836 saw the youth, still a layman, back in Malta at the printing office of the CMS, which in 1838 published his first book, a guide to the islands of Malta and Gozo.

Badger's brother-in-law had by then made his fateful visit to William Palmer at Oxford, and, under Rassam's influence,

Badger began to correspond with Palmer and take an interest in ordination. After applying to the CMS and being accepted, Badger sailed to England in July 1841 to receive formal training at the society's college in the London borough of Islington. A five-day visit to William Palmer in Oxford fully confirmed the young acolyte's High Church views. In February 1842, George Percy Badger was ordained an Anglican priest.

By the time of his ordination, he already knew his future home. Badger and a layman, James P. Fletcher, had been assigned an educational mission to the Druze of Lebanon, a heterodox non-Islamic sect, who were considered a promising field by Badger. But events soon changed the prospect. The two oldest Anglican missionary organizations, the Society for Promoting Christian Knowledge [SPCK] founded in 1698, and the Society for the Propagation of the Gospel in Foreign Parts [SPG], founded 1701, had granted money for Badger and Fletcher's mission to the Druze. In late 1841, word came of fighting between the Druze and the Maronites, the primary Christian sect of Lebanon. Badger's mission was put on hold. Since Ainsworth and Rassam had visited Mar Shimun in 1840, both men had urged the societies to make closer contact with the Church of the East. In Constantinople, Horatio Southgate, the Episcopalian missionary who had visited Urmia in 1837, was making the same recommendations. With the collapse of the Druze mission, the leaders of the SPCK and SPG decided to send their delegates and money elsewhere. That "elsewhere" was Mosul and the mountains of Kurdistan.

For Badger the change could not have been more welcome: both his mother and sister were living in Mosul. On April 2, 1842, the new emissary left London bound for Malta via the continent. Accompanying him was his wife, née Maria Christiana Wilcox, who, in typical Victorian fashion, scarcely receives a mention in his history of events. The couple stayed two months in Malta, part of which time was spent waiting for J.P. Fletcher to join them. These weeks provided a preview of strife to come, as the quarrelsome Methodist-turned-Puseyite managed to make himself unpopular with his former employers, the CMS. J.F. Coakley, the principal historian of these events, quotes an Anglican Bishop who, after two months' forced association with Badger, ended up congratulating the CMS on having got rid of him. Next the Badgers moved on to Constantinople, where it took three months to procure a *firman*, the elaborate parchment document which ordered—ineffectually, in most cases—all local officials to provide them with lodging, horses, and protection. After a long overland ride from Samsun, on the Black Sea—a journey which included their aforementioned encounters with the leech hunters of Tokat and Amasya—Badger and his companions reached Mosul just before the Lauries, in early November 1842.

Once in Mosul, George Percy Badger began his career in a typical missionary posture—flat on his back. Like the Lauries and their predecessors, he was immediately struck down by a fever that kept him in bed for the next two months. When Asahel Grant returned from Tiyari to attend the deathbed of Abel Hinsdale, he called upon the young Englishman and his wife, who was also ill. While Badger was grateful for the medical visit, he made it clear that he had nothing ecclesiastical in common with Grant and his colleagues. Further medical help was not needed: he bled himself with his own lancet. Social contacts were neither possible nor desired. In Constantinople Badger had snubbed even Daniel Temple, the American who had first given him a printing job in Malta. He did not approve of the Americans' actions in Mosul; even on his bed of pain he was laying plans to bring the churches of Mesopotamia closer to his heart's desire.

One of his first actions was to drive a wedge between the Syrian Orthodox (Jacobite) Christians and their American guests. He had of course been given no authority to deal with this church. From the first visit of Horatio Southgate in 1837-38, the American Episcopal Church had, like a conquistador planting his flag on a beach, laid claim to the Jacobites of

Diyarbakir, Mardin, and Mosul as its own field of missionary endeavor. In the absence of Episcopalians in Mosul, Grant and the Hinsdales had taken it upon themselves to open schools for the Syrians. This they regarded not as a permanent alliance but as a constructive use of their time until they could move to the house in Asheetha. Now Badger arrived with letters from the Syrian Orthodox hierarchy, whom he had met in Constantinople and Mardin, ordering that all the schools be suspended until further notice, and forbidding the Jacobites of Mosul to accept books from either Badger or the Americans. This was ostensibly an even-handed measure, but Badger had no books to give. Badger further offended the Americans when, after their funeral service for Abel Hinsdale, he took it upon himself to translate portions of the Protestants' burial rite and explain to the Jacobites why it was essentially pagan. The Syrians of Mosul, however, were not easily seduced. Their bishop had sent a letter to his deacons warning them against Badger, and, despite the latter's efforts, relations between the Americans and the Syrian Orthodox community remained warm.

Young Mr. Badger now moved on to the Chaldean Catholics. This branch of the East Syrian church had been allied with Rome since 1553, and year by year, aided by French and Italian missionaries, had been steadily encroaching upon the territory of Mar Shimun's Church of the East. No organization could have seemed less ripe for manipulation, and of course Badger's superiors at the SPCK and SPG had given him no such mandate. Here his brother-in-law was helpful: Christian Rassam, brought up as a Chaldean Catholic, had now lost all affection for the Church of Rome. He was part of a Chaldean faction that wanted to break off from papal control and become independent. From him Badger learned that the new—since 1840—Chaldean patriarch, Mar Zaia of Mosul, was not popular. There was, however, another Chaldean bishop, Mar Elia of Alqosh, the nephew of the late patriarch. On what J.F. Coakley calls the "amazing pretext" that the young bishop would "restore the patriarchal dignity," Badger urged Mar Elia to claim the patriarchate for himself and declare the Chaldean Church independent of Rome. Then in February the industrious Badger even went so far as to draw up plans for a reformed Chaldean Church, complete with new buildings and schools, all paid for by the Church of England. This brazen meddling by the 27-year-old Englishman quickly produced results. The Chaldean patriarch sent off an indignant letter to the British ambassador in Stamboul complaining of Badger's interference. Mar Elia, meanwhile, refused to go along with the project, which consequently went nowhere.

Two churches, two failures. By February 1843 George Percy Badger's efforts were not bearing fruit. But there remained the Church of the East, the principal focus of his mission. He had been sent to make contact, find out all he could about their beliefs and rituals, and generally to offer the support of the Church of England in maintaining their independence. Of course, his ambitions so far outstripped these modest instructions that he now made a rash move indeed.

February is not a good month for alpine travel in any part of the northern hemisphere, and certainly not in Kurdistan, where there are few trees to break the wind or provide wood for fires. Dr. Grant, for example, never left for the mountains before April. Even then, as witness his crossing of the Dahar Pass in 1839, the results could be terrifying. The zeal of George Percy Badger, however, would not be denied.

Early on the morning of February 20, Badger slipped out of Mosul with a mule-load of gifts for Mar Shimun, including a telescope, a canister of snuff, twenty pounds each of soap, coffee, and incense, two pairs of red boots, two red cloaks, fifty each of pipe bowls and flints, and a host of other small articles. Of course, even without this bulging grab bag no one could really "slip out" of Mosul unnoticed, since the bridge of boats was out of service at the time, and crossing the Tigris meant undergoing the cumbersome, noisy ordeal of loading three mules and their baggage into the high-sided boats that served as ferries. Nevertheless, by 9:00 A.M. Badger and his party were on the river's eastern bank heading for Tiyari.

Badger explains the reasons for his sudden departure: one reason was that war was expected with the spring thaw. This is true enough, though it was unlikely to happen before summer. Mar Shimun was reported to be in lower Tiyari then and therefore more accessible. Actually, the patriarch was in Chumba, upper Tiyari, two days' farther march. For these reasons, and with "as much secresy [sic] as possible," Badger prepared to make his lightning journey. And why secrecy, one may ask? He certainly was not keeping anything secret from Mohammed Pasha, who supplied him with a passport and guards. No secrecy was possible in his dealings with the bazaar, where he had to procure mules, supplies, and a guide—Da'ud, the same gall merchant who had accompanied Ainsworth. So the question remains: from whom was he trying to hide his departure from Mosul?

Once on the trail, Badger's strengths as a traveler begin to assert themselves, as he supplies fresh details about a world whose complexities never failed to astonish. He does not hesitate to note the errors of those who have gone before him, notably Grant and Ainsworth. Such geographical sniping—pointing out the misnaming of a river or mountain, for example, by another author—occurs often between Badger and his missionary rivals. For example, Badger, a relative neophyte in Kurdistan, tells us that Dr. Grant gave the wrong name for the *zozan,* the summer pastures in the mountains. This even though Grant had been speaking Syriac and Turkish—and sometimes Kurdish—almost every day since 1835.

Taking a longer route to avoid the high mountains, Badger found little snow between Mosul and Amadiyah, but evidence of devastation and tyranny was everywhere. On his second day out of the city he met a party of fifteen Jews from Amadiyah, enroute to Mohammed Pasha to make a desperate plea for relief. The men said they were sorely oppressed by the governor of Amadiyah, who, following the siege of 1842, was now seizing the villagers's few possessions. The Anglican emissary found conditions even worse as he progressed. Hours after meeting the desperate Jews, he encountered Qasha Mendu, the Nestorian priest of Amadiyah—whose father, as Grant described, had been forced to "eat stick" when he refused to join the Chaldean Church. Qasha Mendu was traveling to Mosul in answer to Badger's invitation, and their meeting was a happy coincidence. The Nestorian priest, who now joined Badger's party, recounted the woes of Amadiyah and the valley of the Supna.

The town itself, as Badger soon witnessed, was little more than a heap of rubble inhabited by cave-dwellers. Seven years before, said Mendu, fourteen Nestorian villages were flourishing in the Amadiyah district. Now the majority lay empty and in ruins, inhabited by fewer than one hundred families. Badger gives no figures for the Muslims—neither he nor the Americans spill much ink on their behalf—but it seems likely that they suffered the same depredations. No doubt the Little Ensign's siege army had performed its mission in the usual fashion, supporting itself at the expense of people who were already raising barely enough to feed themselves.

After Amadiyah, there were no easy routes. High mountains and a "sea of snow"—in some places more than twelve feet deep—confronted the travelers. By this time they had left the mules behind, and Nestorian porters humped the loads across this wasteland on their backs. On the second day out of Amadiyah, after hours of toil, Badger came upon what seemed an impossible prospect. Above them stretched an immense peak, the Ras Kadoma, covered in snow; before them was an abyss. At the bottom of the cliff, thousands of feet below, lay the village of Asheetha. "It made one giddy barely to look down the precipice before us," Badger wrote. A narrow twisting path, nearly perpendicular, coated with ice and bounded by a deep gorge, presented the only way down. The porters, however, did not hesitate. Each man took off his load, bound it with rope, then sat down behind it, knees bent, upon a patch of felt. Holding tightly to the rope, with their feet pressing upon the packs, the men slid off one by one. It was terrifying, but it worked, as each tiny figure in turn tumbled from the rocks onto the snow-field below. The Englishman was given no felt pad. After one false start, when the last-second grab of a Kurd saved him from a plunge into eternity, he set off down the chute. Thus did the Rev. George Percy Badger, emissary of the Church of England, slide into Asheetha on the seat of his pants.

The date was February 26, 1843. In the *kellaita,* the public meeting-house of the village, Badger found Deacon Isaac, Mar Shimun's youngest brother, seated before a fire with a dozen of the local leaders. Badger and his companions were too tired to continue on toward Chumba, so Deacon Isaac and the others decided to send for Mar Shimun the next morning. After a two-day wait, Badger was in the *kellaita* when word came of the patriarch's approach. "For two hours," Badger writes, "the village was in a complete uproar" as the peasants scurried about bringing fresh straw for the patriarch's bed, producing firewood, a ewer, and coffee service for his use, and generally making themselves presentable for his arrival. When Mar Shimun appeared on the mountains overlooking Asheetha, a thousand people gathered at the church, while another delegation, which included Badger, climbed the path to greet him as he descended. Badger kissed the patriarch's hand and was, in turn, welcomed warmly to the valley. "The group," writes Badger, "was one of indescribable interest, and the scene around grand in the extreme. Mountains upon mountains hemmed in the secluded valley on every side, the village poured forth its tenants from the scattered dwellings, who flocked from every quarter, some leading a son or daughter through the deep snow, whilst mothers were seen bearing in their arms their infant offspring."

Thus did the people embrace this Mountain Pope. In the meeting room Mar Shimun huddled immediately with the village leaders, and before he knew it George Percy Badger, sitting nearby and listening, found himself immersed in the realities of mountain politics. The patriarch, he discovered, had not come only to bring greetings to the foreigner. Other matters occupied his mind, and he launched himself into these at once. They concerned Mohammed Pasha of Mosul and that noted outlaw, Zeiner Bey. Scarcely three months before this, Asahel Grant had attended Nurullah at his castle, where he learned that Ismael Pasha and Zeiner Bey, also resident, were plotting raids upon areas near Tiyari that were under the Little Ensign's control. Since then the raids had gone forward, and now in a letter to Mar Shimun, Mohammed Pasha vented his anger. According to accounts that had reached Mosul, men of Asheetha and Tiyari had joined with Zeiner Bey's forces for the sake of plunder. Mohammed Pasha threatened retaliation, not only against Zeiner Bey but also those who abetted him. An army would be on its way soon to punish Zeiner. If Mar Shimun did not take action against those who were in league with that outlaw, the army would proceed against his people as well.

To this threat the Nestorian patriarch reacted vigorously and not wisely. Angrily confronting the men of Asheetha, he directed his primary concern not to soothing his immediate neighbors, Bedr Khan, Nurullah, and Zeiner Bey, whose alliance he knew to be coalescing, but toward palliating Mohammed Pasha of Mosul. A lengthy colloquy ensued, with protracted pauses and much muttering. How, the patriarch asked the Asheethans, could they have risked ruin by provoking the Turks? Were they loyal to him or not? Yes, yes, the Asheethans replied, we are your slaves. Walk upon our necks. We will do anything for you. Then why, asked Mar Shimun, did some of them risk all by selling their services to the highest bidder?

After a long pause to allow the guilty parties to contemplate their sins, the patriarch proposed a solution. The people

of Asheetha should immediately assemble a force, some 300
strong, and march against Zeiner Bey, who was installed to the
west, in a castle on the Khabur River. With a raiding party of
that size they could easily rout his forces and perhaps take him,
dead or alive. This would remove Mohammed Pasha's cause
for complaint and convince him of their sincerity. For sheer
naïveté this idea must win some kind of prize. Indeed, it seems
incredible that a man who aspired to temporal power could
have been so ignorant, not only of the pasha's character but of
political reality. "Divide and rule" has been standard government policy since men emerged from caves, and to propose a
raid against one of Nurullah's chief henchmen seems the height
of stupidity. And so it proved.

At this point, as if by divine signal, another reality intervened. Word came that two armed Kurds had been seen descending the mountains from the northeast. "Watch if no more
follow," the patriarch ordered. Within half an hour they arrived, accompanied by a priest from a nearby village to assure
their safe passage. The Kurds (Badger refers to them as
"sheikhs," or "chiefs") brought a letter from Nurullah which,
after bowing low, they laid at the feet of Mar Shimun. As a
gesture of respect the patriarch stood, picked up the letter, and
held it for a moment before breaking the seal. The emir, it appeared, was making yet another offer for peace. He asked the
patriarch to name a suitable place half way between Chumba
and Julamerk, where they could rendezvous and work out their
differences.

Sincere or not, this offer at least seems reasonable. Yet it did
not sit well with Deacon Isaac, Mar Shimun's youngest brother.
When he heard the letter's contents, Isaac boiled over. Why, he
asked, after Nurullah had burned their home and forced them
to wander for nine years [sic] in the mountains, should they
believe anything that the emir had to say? Wasn't it he who had
oppressed them and sullied their honor? Nurullah would of
course have retorted that Mar Shimun was plotting to set up

his own power as a rival to the emir's, and had been implicated in plots against the emir's person. Nurullah, in truth, did not want to deal with the patriarch at all and preferred that political matters be left to the maleks. Isaac raged on. In the midst of his fulminations the young deacon turned to Badger, who was seated nearby. The land, he told the Kurds, did not belong to the Nestorians or to Nurullah, but "to these." With that, he picked up Badger's red fez from the floor and placed it unceremoniously on the Englishman's head. This headgear, which Badger wore as part of his regular traveling attire, was the new symbol of Turkish power. Badger assumed that by placing it on his head, Deacon Isaac meant the Kurds to believe that the missionary was a Turkish official. It is far more likely that Isaac was referring to the English themselves or to foreigners in general. In other words, Why should we bow down to Nurullah when it is the foreigners who are taking control?

The Kurds, says Badger, met Deacon Isaac's tirade with "mute astonishment." Mar Shimun, meanwhile, spoke calmly. He did not approve of his brother's vehemence, he told the two men, but it was true that the emir had treated him and his people badly. Still, his flock loved peace and wished to be friendly with all men. Here, says Badger, the Kurdish messengers broke in, proclaiming solemnly that their ruler had the greatest respect for the patriarch and wished only "to establish a lasting treaty of friendly alliance" with him. This bilateral feast of hypocrisy settled tempers somewhat. The discussion went on for two hours, during which neither the patriarch nor his brother wavered from their respective prudence and spleen. At length the two Kurds were given lodging for the night, with strict instructions that they should want for nothing. And Mar Shimun settled down with his tribesmen to decide what message to send back to Nurullah.

Here Badger ends his account of the parley with the Kurdish messengers. As he is the only witness to have written about the encounter, we have to accept his account as far as it goes. But there is another, albeit second-hand, report. In early September

1844, Thomas Laurie and a fellow missionary, Dr. Azariah Smith, visited the summer camp of Nurullah Bey at Berchullah, in the mountains above Julamerk, where they met one of the sheikhs who had brought Nurullah's letter to Asheetha eighteen months before. To Smith and Laurie the man said: "I see you are very different from other Englishmen; for you wish to maintain peace with all men. But when I delivered my message to Mar Shimon in Asheetha, in the presence of Mr. Badger, as soon as it was translated to him he recommended the patriarch not to seek the friendship of the Kurds, but to apply for aid, if he needed it, to England, which, he said, was able and willing to grant him the fullest protection—and so the emir could not get the ear of the patriarch."

The words are of course a paraphrase of a translation, but it is hard to believe that this Kurd would have invented such a story just to blacken the name of George Percy Badger, a man he had met only once. In fact, the purported remarks strongly suggest the Badger we know: meddlesome, contentious, eager to push his own agenda no matter what the cost to general amity. There is another issue, and that is the translation itself. For the translator of September 1844 is the same man—Da'ud, the gall merchant—who accompanied Ainsworth and Rassam in 1840 and Badger himself in 1843. A simple question to Da'ud—What exactly did Badger say?—might have done much to clear up the mystery, but Laurie and Smith apparently did not ask it. Or if Da'ud confirmed the Kurd's statement, they do not note that.

In the end, however, no one can doubt that Badger had come to promote the cause of the Anglican Church, and that he was more than willing to use the British Government to assist him. Moreover, as with Grant himself, his very existence is statement enough. Once again, Ainsworth's 1840 encounter with the angry Kurdish chief springs to mind. "You are the fore-runners of those who come to take control of this country," the Kurd had said, and by 1843 no one in the mountains would have disagreed.

The two Kurds started back for Julamerk the next morning. With them Mar Shimun sent compliments and regrets, explaining that because of the mountain snows, the approaching Lenten season with its necessary fasting, as well as the presence of a foreign guest, he could not meet with the emir at that time. It was not an impolitic message, and the two messengers, who had taken seven days to reach Asheetha from Julamerk, certainly knew the obstacles to travel. But it left Nurullah, always suspicious, with reason to believe that the visiting Englishman was a person of prime importance, one whose presence boded ill for the emir and his plans.

With the Kurds gone, George Percy Badger could get down to work. Mostly this meant private conversations with Mar Shimun, accompanied by dissertations on the doctrines of the Church of England and its points of difference with other churches. All this was translated by the faithful Da'ud, a man whose interest in gallnuts no doubt exceeded his concerns about the trinity and apostolic succession. Badger, like the Americans and Catholics before him, took pains to make his church seem as Nestorian-friendly as possible. The Church of the East detested idolatrous images; so did the Anglicans. Neither practiced auricular confession. Badger had brought an Arabic translation of the Book of Common Prayer, but of course Mar Shimun could not read it. Badger also raised the subject of schools, and the patriarch promised to open ten of these as soon as it could be arranged, but he added that "unless something [could] be done for the Nestorians in a political point of view, it was useless for the English to talk of schools." Nurullah Bey had "virtually robbed them of their independence, and unless timely assistance be rendered to the Christian population, we may soon expect to see them entirely subjugated by the barbarous and lawless Coords." Mar Shimun was asking for British support as the price of his cooperation.

After hours of talk, they inevitably came to the Americans. Grant's house was being constructed at Asheetha, and a school had opened there as well. "I did not fail," wrote Badger, "to acquaint the Patriarch how far we are removed in doctrine and discipline, from the American Independent missionaries, and this I did not so much by exposing their system as by unfolding the principles of our own Church." Having done this, Badger threw down the gauntlet. "I showed [the patriarch], moreover, that it would be injudicious, and would by no means satisfy us to have schools among his people by the side of theirs, and pressed upon him to decide what plan he would pursue under existing conditions." In other words, as blood feuds boiled, beys and pashas schemed, and war threatened from every quarter, Badger was telling the Patriarch of the East that he could play with English marbles or American, but he could not take both. And he had to decide on the spot.

Not surprisingly, Mar Shimun dodged the question. And lied. As for the Americans and their doctrines, he told Badger, "I hold them as cheap as an onion." Badger did not take this at face value; he knew the affection in which Dr. Grant was held among the mountaineers. Still, it was a promising sign, as "I am convinced that there is hardly a Nestorian in the mountains who sympathizes with the doctrine or discipline of the Dissenters." But the American missionaries, he noted, spoke most eloquently with the language of money. "I am sorry to say," Badger wrote, "that the mountaineers, from the highest to the lowest, appear to be an over-reaching and gift-loving people." Of this he had ample proof, as wherever he went he found himself dunned for handouts and baksheesh. The Nestorians looked for these, he said, "as a matter of course, and are not only disappointed but even affronted by a refusal." The many gifts Badger brought from Mosul, he notes, satisfied Mar Shimun at the time, but soon after the Anglican's return to the city he received a letter from the patriarch demanding £120 (an enormous sum in 1843) for "school expenses," as well as "a mare, a silk girdle, and a string of coral beads." All this recalls Mar Shimun's initial demand in May, 1836 for "a watch, a very excellent and beautiful one, the like of which shall not exist. Amen," along with the incident in1841, when the patriarch and his brothers attempted to gouge "school money" out of the missionaries in Urmia, as well.

Thus Badger became quickly acquainted with mercenary mountain ways, and he soon made another discovery. If he were to open schools for the Nestorians he must have schoolbooks, which did not exist in Syriac. Moreover, the only written form, ancient Syriac, was understood by no one. These were problems already confronted by the Americans, whose press in Urmia had by then begun to churn out arithmetic, geography, and natural science books by the thousands, to say nothing of countless tracts and Biblical translations, all in Syriac fonts cut by Edward Breath. Badger knew little or nothing about this.

Still, Badger must have felt great exhilaration and pride as he concluded his sessions with Mar Shimun. In the middle of winter he had penetrated to the heart of Tiyari, beating the Americans there by almost two months. He had made contact with the Nestorian patriarch, convinced him of his church's friendship, doctrinal affinity, and power, and prepared the ground for the seed-time to follow. On March 3 he set out to climb the mountain from Asheetha. By March 7, after an absence of eighteen days, Badger crossed the Tigris into the safety of Mosul.

HOLDING BACK THE TIGRIS

"As the day waned, we seemed to be entering a prison between the beetling crags. Their summits led towards what looked like gulfs of a dark conflagration . . ."

—Freya Stark, *Riding to the Tigris*

TO MAR SHIMUN, BADGER was as good as his word. By March 22 he was writing to Sir Stratford Canning, the British ambassador to the Sublime Porte, conveying the patriarch's wish to be recognized as both religious and civil authority for his people in Hakkari. At the same time Badger, reporting his actions to the SPG, included a request for resources to counter the efforts of the Americans. This must have surprised his superiors in Islington, who had given him no authority whatever to enter into competition with the American missionaries. Moreover, by his letter to Canning Badger was now involving the British Government. The Puseyites did not lack for enemies within the Church, and these actions soon aroused their attention. By the summer of 1843 the young clergyman had become a center of controversy: articles in an Anglican newsletter, citing his unwarranted meddling and opposition to the American missionaries, roundly accused him of besmirching the good name of the Church of England. The controversy did not have time to develop, however, for soon events in Hakkari turned the schemes of George Percy Badger into a feeble joke.

The situation began to develop in March, after Nurullah's messengers returned from Asheetha and told the emir about the latest stranger to visit Mar Shimun. News of yet another foreign presence, this time a representative of the powerful British, could only prod Nurullah more urgently in his intrigues. The Kurds had long been milling about, muttering with resentment and wondering how to get back their own. Nurullah, a local ruler governing at least partly through consensus, could never have marshalled their anger; but Bedr Khan, the emir of Bohtan, definitely could. Bedr Khan had been outraged by Mar Shimun's attempted collusion with Mohammed Pasha of Mosul, an offense which could not be tolerated. Bedr Khan wanted no less than an independent emirate, and to this ambition and outrage, he added a vein of Muslim extremism. As the winter of 1843 passed into spring, the long-contemplated alliance of Bedr Khan and Nurullah began to cohere.

But one point was still missing from the triangle. As the two emirs looked south toward the mountain fortress of Tiyari and the other Nestorian domains, they saw not only the tribes they wished to subdue but another reality as well. The Ottoman Turks, having secured their hold on Amadiyah the previous summer, sat on the edge of Berwar and the tribal territories. Bedr Khan and Nurullah knew that Mar Shimun had corresponded with Mohammed Pasha, who said that he would protect the Christians in the event of a Kurdish invasion. Could this be believed? The Kurds had to know which way the pasha was leaning.

The Little Ensign, as always, was leaning toward self-aggrandizement, and both sides were trying to placate him and his fellow Osmanlis. Mar Shimun had informed on Nurullah and Ismael

Pasha when he told of the Kurds' alliance to retake Amadiyah, and now, as the patriarch had urged them to do during Badger's visit, the men of Tiyari sent a raiding party against the outlaw Zeiner Bey in an attempt to win favor with Mohammed Pasha. This won them nothing but the undying hatred of Zeiner Bey, who would return the favor a hundredfold by the end of the year. Meanwhile Nurullah had delivered a pack of lies concerning Dr. Grant's house to the pasha of Erzurum. The doctor, he told the Turks, was building a castle in the mountains, an action which so enraged the people that they had risen in revolt and would have killed Dr. Grant if he, Nurullah, had not intervened. Whether from Nurullah or Mar Shimun the implicit message was the same: You need me to subdue and spy upon the other factions, who are the real problem.

But to the Turks all the tribes were outlaws, whether it was the forces of Bedr Khan, Nurullah, Zeiner Bey, Ismael Pasha, or Mar Shimun. None of them paid taxes; none contributed men to the Ottoman army; all spent scandalous amounts of time raiding, robbing, and killing their neighbors. Mohammed Pasha wanted the lot of them crushed and peeled, no matter where they lived or what kind of prayers they chanted. He did not, however, possess an army big enough to do this, so he was delighted to hear of the upcoming Kurdish alliance. In fact, far from honoring a pledge to protect the Nestorians, he did nothing to prevent the onset of war. During the winter of 1842-43, in a series of exchanges with Bedr Khan, Mohammed Pasha assured the Kurd that he would keep hands off in the event of an attack. And of course he meant it. He had nothing to lose if the Kurds and Nestorians went to war, since he was quite ready to come in and pick up the pieces after it was over.

On March 24, Asahel Grant wrote a letter to his brother Ira in New York, summarizing the actions of George Percy Badger, who had the audacity to shun the Americans "while the Papists, with all their abominations, are acknowledged as breth-

ren!" But Grant said also, "I have been more particularly indisposed of late, and have written this upon my bed." The words
"more particularly indisposed" make a fine euphemism, one
which could mean anything from a bunion to brain cancer. They
come, however, from a man who two years before had referred
to his body as a "shattered tenement." Not only had he poisoned himself with calomel, but the malaria parasite in his bloodstream was being replenished in ways he could not conceive.

However, he told his brother that he had begun to feel a bit
better and would soon leave for yet another tour in the mountains. Knowing what we know of Kurdistan, a place where the
annual vengeance festival arrived with the swelling of the Tigris,
this can only seem the utmost folly. Grant realized the danger
ahead. He knew about Nurullah's treachery and Mohammed
Pasha's plot against his life; of the raid against Zeiner Bey and
the plans of Bedr Khan. But "God reigns" remained his motto.
A letter from Mar Shimun, replete with words of love and hospitality, had come in March urging his return; yet even had it
not, nothing could have kept the doctor away.

The party left Mosul on the morning of April 4, 1843, with
young Thomas Laurie replacing Abel Hinsdale as Grant's traveling companion. Once again Da'ud the gall merchant, who seems
to have secured a monopoly in the missionary-guide business, came
along. After enduring the ferry crossing, the men rode out into the
full glory of an Assyrian spring. Fields of wheat and barley stretched
toward the Kurdish hills, wildflowers crowded the path, and ga-
zelles bounded away at their approach. The next day, following a
night at a Kurdish village, Grant and Laurie visited Khorsabad,
where the French consul, Paul-Émile Botta, welcomed them and
gave them a tour of his excavations. Botta had once been labeled a
"bigoted papist" by Abel Hinsdale, a label Hinsdale retracted before he died. Thomas Laurie makes it clear that, although Botta
naturally did all he could to assist their bitter rivals the French
missionaries, his friendship to people of all faiths was simple and
sincere. In fact, Laurie goes out of his way to contrast the

Frenchman's "amiable character and unaffected kindness" with the very different behavior of a certain English missionary.

As Grant and Laurie move on, signs of illness speckle the narrative. At Ain Sifneh, a Yezidi village, Grant went to bed "too hoarse to speak." Was this a virus? A result of the dense smoke of peasants' huts? Or had indigestion inflamed his throat? On that as on the previous night, swarms of "nocturnal visitors" tormented them. Thomas Laurie could barely stand it; yet in the morning Grant declared himself improved, and credited the insects for this. Their assault, he told Laurie, had been as efficacious as a prescription. Whether the vermin had achieved this through therapeutic blood-sucking or plain torture, he does not say. Again, faith in "harsh medicine," the ideology of unpleasantness, ruled the physician's mind.

In Amadiyah, which they reached on April 8, Thomas Laurie was appalled by what he found. Of the shattered town and its roofless hovels he gives a vivid account. Seven hundred soldiers, gangs of whom insolently accosted them in the streets, enforced a system of extortion and slave labor. Many of the people had died of hunger, others of plague; some had committed suicide. One Jew had killed first his wife and then himself to end their misery. In the synagogue, a filthy, dripping ruin, forty rolls of beautiful Hebrew manuscripts were rotting into pulp. Amadiyah's governor was the same brandy-swilling malcontent—now reformed—whom Grant had met at Aqra in 1839. But sobriety had not brought him compassion, and in Amadiyah evidence abounded of systematic cruelty, oppression, and greed. In fact, as Laurie points out, Mohammed Pasha had given the man no incentive to govern decently. The Little Ensign wanted immediate revenue by whatever means possible, and had the governor not provided it, he would have been unemployed—or worse—before the year was over.

Grant did what he could in Amadiyah, visiting patients, dispensing medicines, and uttering words of comfort to people slack with despair. He and Laurie were relieved when, after two days' rain delay, the road again opened to the north. The rain, rather than dumping more snow on the hills, had actually melted much of it, and they found the trek to Berwar both easier and slushier than expected. But Grant's health was not improving. Neither man dwells upon symptoms, but we see the truth when Laurie notes, at one point, that his companion was, "as usual," worn out by the journey.

In Lezan, where they arrived on April 12, friendly crowds turned out to welcome them, and Grant set to work immediately seeing patients. But since Mar Shimun was anxiously awaiting the doctor in Asheetha, they were obliged to push on the next morning. Not only was the Izani, swollen by melted snow, too deep to ford, the normal path was snowed in, forcing them to take a high route that hugged the mountains on tracks barely wide enough to walk. Thomas Laurie soon gave up his mule, preferring to trudge the long miles on hair sandals rather than trust to an animal in such a dangerous place. But Dr. Grant was too weak to walk, and as the mule stumbled along, occasionally losing the path, he was forced repeatedly to mount and dismount in order to save himself from destruction.

At Asheetha, in the *kellaita* next to the church, they found the patriarch seated upon a silk cushion amid the smoke from a fire and a roomful of tobacco pipes. As usual, little of this smoke found its way to the roof-hole but instead added another layer to the creosote sheen of the rafters. When they walked through the door the missionaries found themselves blocked by a heap of straw just inside, that was meant to shut out the winter winds. They had to stumble around it before they could see anyone through the fumes. Mar Shimun was cordial and welcoming, writes Laurie, as were the pipe-puffing men who attended him, but it soon became obvious (through asides to Da'ud) that Badger's visit had awakened in the patriarch a willingness to use the competing missionaries against each other in order to gain money and gifts. To the rumor of Grant's castle-building, others even more extravagant had been floated, including a report that the Little Ensign had chopped off the doctor's hands.

Both missionaries were exhausted, and to this were soon added other—and worse—complaints. After two nights in the *kellaita* they moved to the half-completed shell of the mission house, where they set up shop on an earth floor that was, wrote Laurie, "*almost* as smooth as a muddy road after a hard frost." On it they sat cross-legged to write their journals and letters. The walls were of rock laid up in mud, which continually oozed from the cracks. On the other side of these walls the snow lay two feet deep. The room's northwest corner, built to be entirely open in the summer, was fenced off with a wicker barrier that kept out neither the wind nor the snow. In the center, only five feet from their beds, a tray-shaped platform of earth served as a fireplace, while in one corner lay a heap of wood, found after a full day's march into the mountains and brought into Asheetha on the backs of porters.

"This was a poor place for an ague-fit," wrote Thomas Laurie, "but it was the best we had." Both men now wilted under a full-blown attack of malaria. While they huddled beneath their blankets sweating and shivering, a foul sky threw its worst against the mud roof and stone walls. Laurie quotes his journal: "April 27, rain and hail, nearly all day, covering everything with ice. 28, rain, turning to snow. May 1st, rain and hail; 2nd, rain and very cold wind; 3rd and 4th, rain, hail and snow, each day." And this, they were assured, was a relatively mild year.

There are times when, as Freya Stark wrote, "All fragilities glow . . . in the light of their own annihilation." So it was with the missionaries in Tiyari. Amidst storm and sickness, the spring of 1843 warmed the poplar buds, and violets sprouted next to dying snowdrifts. On April 23, after fifty days of fasting, the people of Asheetha celebrated Easter: the village came alive as throngs of people trekked in from the surrounding valley and crowded the narrow paths between the terraces. "It scarcely seemed possible that the village contained so many," Laurie wrote. They covered the roof of the *kellaita* and the field near the church; the graveyard became a mass of people. And the noise! The tribesmen had grown up using their voices to call from hill to hill above the sound of waterfalls and torrents: this permanently set their conversation at full volume. Amid the uproar children scurried, aging greybeards rested on their canes, and under a walnut tree a group of young girls, twelve years old at the most, joined hands in a circular dance. At last the feast began with the arrival of the giant wooden bowls of millet boiled in buttermilk. Undoubtedly there also flowed a good deal of wine, a fact that Thomas Laurie chooses to ignore. The Easter feast continued for two more days, and was followed by the feast of St. George, patron saint of the village. All this merry-making did not sit well with the missionaries. Few people, says Laurie, spoke of anything but the present day's amusements.

Yet sober reality soon set in. On a Sabbath morning in May, the two Americans woke to find five armed Kurds sitting on the floor staring at them. This startling sight was followed by a greater surprise. The Kurds bore a letter stating that Bedr Khan Bey, emir of Bohtan and the most powerful man in Kurdistan, wished to see Asahel Grant on medical matters. Since the ailments were not named, and there seemed no emergency, Grant and Laurie wondered about the real motive behind the request. To visit Bedr Khan would not be easy. He lived at Derguleh, a castle eighteen miles northeast of Jezirah (now Cizre) on the north side of Judi Dagh, the mountain believed by Kurds—as well as by Jews, Christians, and Yezidis—to be the resting place of Noah's Ark. That was three days' journey away through territory that Grant had never seen. But Bedr Khan could not be refused outright, so Grant promised the five messengers that within the next month, when he had more time, he would visit the emir. No sooner had the Kurds departed than the headmen of Asheetha rushed in, asking worried questions. Most agreed that the men were spies, and some wanted to run after them and kill them. This, forbidden by the rules of hospitality—and common sense—did not happen.

With this strange and unsettling summons in the back of his mind, Grant turned his attention again to the mission house. The plan called for a building sixty feet square, to house three mission families, as well as a schoolroom, chapel, and stables. This would be a substantial compound, though it came nowhere near the exaggerated accounts that were already spreading abroad. Because of the Lenten fast, work had stopped until after Easter; but now it resumed between storms. Almost immediately the missionaries ran into problems. The previous autumn's labor troubles came back in a new way, as the villagers decided to strike for higher wages.

This certainly tried the patience of the missionaries. Had the men not agreed to the wages after open negotiations? Had they not eagerly sought to have the mission house erected in their village? Grant's house was the only wage-paying construction project outside of Mosul. In Amadiyah, men rebuilding the town were being press-ganged into service and given neither money nor food for their work. Where, the missionaries might well ask, were the men going to make more? And—with equal relevance—where were they going to spend it? Faced with a mob of fifty men chanting and shouting outside the mission house, some of the doctor's friends advised him to give in. But Grant brought out a sheet of paper and a pencil and began to write down the names of the ringleaders. This schoolroom technique, combined with a renewed threat to shut down the project completely, caused the revolution to fold like a leaky goatskin. After a few grumbles and shrugs, the men returned to earning their twenty-five cents a day.

But of all unfinished tasks, the heaviest lay upon the shoulders of Mar Shimun. So far he had shown few political skills, and his brothers' teeth-gnashing truculence only made matters worse. Now the man's secular ambition, his lack of self-knowledge and political sense, were about to exact a terrible price. With winter weather and the Lenten fast aside, Nurullah's invitation—overheard by Badger in February—could be put off no longer. This spring parley presented a genuine, if slender, opportunity for peace. No one had forced Nurullah, traditionally regarded as the villain in these events, to make the gesture, and yet he had done so. With a diligent effort at mediation, something positive might have emerged. But neither Grant nor Laurie gives this eleventh-hour meeting more than a passing mention.

John C. Joseph, the principal historian of this Christian people, lacerates Asahel Grant for his failure to do anything to avert the impending disaster. Prof. Joseph has a point. After Mar Shimun had gone north to meet the emir Nurullah in Chumba, he sent back a message, surely with the emir's knowledge and assent, asking the doctor to come and attend the negotiations. Before he left, Mar Shimun had been advised by the doctor to "Follow peace with all men," the same vague admonition often made before. Now Grant refused to go to Chumba, on the grounds that the patriarch wanted him "only for political business." Note the phrase. The mountains were set to explode. Thousands of human lives were at stake. And it was "only political business."

Grant could of course have given plenty of familiar reasons for staying aloof. His superiors in Stamboul and Boston would not have been pleased with his involvement; nor—especially—would Mohammed Pasha in Mosul. Participation in such an affair might very well have jeopardized the entire ABCFM effort in Turkey. And would Grant's negotiating skills come anywhere near the level required? The tangle of Hakkari intrigue would have daunted any man; and after all, he was only a country doctor from Waterville and Utica. However in retrospect these seem more like excuses than reasons. Grant was there, at the right place and time. He was a political figure whether he liked it or not. He spoke excellent Turkish and Syriac and some Kurdish. Both Nurullah and Mar Shimun held him in high regard. In sum, he might at least have attended the meeting. Despite pressures, policies, and realities, one feels that a good man missed a chance to save lives—more lives, in fact, than he could with any of his purgative potions. And with that failure our respect for him is diminished.

But there is a deeper reason for Grant's refusal, and it goes to the heart of who he was and why he was there. The American Board had sent for a "pious physician" not so much for the good he could do as for the good will he could produce. Solitary missionaries were spat upon and shunned, while missionaries accompanied by doctors were accepted. The ultimate goal was not to do good in this world; it was to win souls for the next. Thus Asahel Grant, though the kindest of men, at times seems almost indifferent in his dealings with people. A diaphanous film—the veil, as it were, of religious detachment—separates him from the mass of men. Has the pasha delivered a hundred strokes of the bastinado? Jesus loves you, he would answer: nothing else matters. Does your district suffer from robbery and misgovernment? It is your sins that have brought this upon you. Has your enemy murdered your best friend? Pray to God for forgiveness. Everywhere he went Grant found cruelty, rumors of apocalypse, and feelings of futility. Muslim power, said Revelation 13, in his reading, would soon be overthrown; in so many years and so many days, all would vanish. On May 5 Grant wrote in a letter to Rev. Wayne Gridley in Utica, "God is first preparing the way by his movement among the nations. We see it in these Mohammedan lands . . . The storm that may be needed to purify the atmosphere may prove most trying to our faith and courage." Like the physician he was, Grant saw the coming cataclysm as a harsh purgative for a sick land. Politics were irrelevant: "God rules" was the watchword. So he rode on, lancet at the ready, bleeding his way toward the Kingdom of God.

Evidence of man's imperfection abounded that spring. Without Grant's mediation, the meeting between Nurullah and Mar

Shimun proved a complete failure. Following the abortive strike, the men of Asheetha began once again to fight over who should get the construction jobs. In a violent storm, the new mud roof sprang a leak and had to be repaired in the middle of the night. One old priest, Laurie relates, having received payment for five poplar trees, insisted that he had been paid for only four. Later that same priest sold twelve wooden spoons to the missionaries, and after he pocketed the money, proceeded to steal the spoons.

Above all, there was violence. One of Mar Shimun's brothers—probably Zadok—led yet another raid from Diz into Julamerk, burning the bridge over the Zab and angering the Kurds even more. An Asheethan, offended by encroachment upon his pasture grounds, attacked a Kurdish village single-handed. This madman was carried in to Dr. Grant mangled from a multitude of knife wounds and barely alive. After Grant sewed him up the man recovered, much to his friends' surprise. Another Asheethan, having killed his cousin the year before, still owed twenty dollars in blood money; and even though his life was in danger, he refused to sell his goods for less than their value to retire the debt. Disquieting stories, surely, but what could the missionaries expect? They were living, in fact, in a den of thieves. "The men of Asheetha," writes Thomas Laurie, "had a reputation for robbery that made them the terror of surrounding districts. This ungoverned temper, and the passion for plunder, led to the drawing of daggers, in plain sight of our door, over so trifling a matter as a few stalks of fennel." In the latter case, only the arrival of Dr. Grant prevented bloodshed.

But it would be wrong to say that May brought only strife and blood. At the house in Asheetha, life began to assume a kind of normality. A school, taught by a village priest, met in one room of the growing structure, and on sunny days the teacher took his pupils to the rooftop for lessons. The missionaries' home became first a clinic, filled with the lame and blind, and then the common lounging-place for the entire village. Around the smoky fire, in the corners, and beside the Americans' beds, villagers gathered to smoke their pipes, gossip, and sometimes take their siesta. "There was no being alone," wrote Laurie, "even in our own home."

On May 11, Thomas Laurie departed for Mosul with the intention of bringing back the mission families: his wife Martha, Sarah Hinsdale, and Sarah's infant son, Abel Abdullah. Today the plan seems impossible, if not absurd, and at the time the missionaries thought long and hard before going ahead. No one wanted to take unnecessary risks, but neither did they want to run away after having made a commitment to their hosts. Moreover, it was thought (hoped? dreamed?) that the presence of the mission families would allay the suspicions of the Kurds, who, as Grant noted, believed that "our visit and prospective residence in their midst is the harbinger of their downfall."

In his saddle bags Thomas Laurie carried letters in which Asahel Grant revealed the depths of his foreboding. To the wife of Willard Jones, in Urmia, he confessed his increasing dread. "I can only see the light by looking up," he wrote. His brother Ira was ill, and the "pressing wants" of his children might compel him himself to leave the field. This he did not want; he would, he says, stay in the mountains as long as he was able. And yet, "The tax upon my strength, in these difficult mountains, is more than my system can bear, to say nothing of the responsibility and care that burden me. Every day brings some new anxiety, and all is increased, rather than relieved, by the prospect of others sharing these trials and privations."

And well he might worry, for the long-expected war seemed ready to erupt at any moment. Having failed to make peace with Nurullah Bey, Mar Shimun set about rallying his forces, but by then it was too late. In his bid for temporal power the patriarch had alienated all the maleks except his brother-in-law, Ismael of Chumba, and he could find little support among his flock. (Remember that only two years before, many of these men had signed a letter to Nurullah offering to betray Mar Shimun into his hands.) The wild men of Jelu, safe in the absolute pinnacle of the Hakkari mountains, showed little interest in him. The district of Tehoma, adjacent to Jelu, had long been at odds with Mar Shimun and his family. People in the tiny valley of Tal had already made their peace with Nurullah. And so it went. When Blind Mohammed of Rowanduz had invaded in the 1830s, everyone in the mountains—Kurds and Nestorians—united to repel him. Now disunity ruled. Raging at this, Mar Shimun resorted to his most potent weapon: the anathema. Excommunication in normal times meant disgrace and near-death, yet now it had little effect. Too many people were being cursed too often by the same ineffectual leader.

Forty men were working on the mission house when the news arrived: Bedr Khan's army was on the Khabur River, across the mountain barrier to the west. Construction ceased at once, as every man rushed for his gun. Eighty men ran off at once to reconnoitre, while others set out to bring in the flocks. Few people slept that night and the next, as warning shots rang out in the mountains, and in Asheetha and the rest of the Tiyari villages the residents buried their valuables and waited.

From the Khabur River, word came back: it was a false alarm. Two sentinel villages, already plundered earlier in the year, had sent in erroneous reports. At first the Asheethans were angry at this misinformation, and work resumed on the mission house. Then they found out that the Kurds had indeed been on the Khabur, but they were not on their way to Asheetha. Instead they had veered north and attacked the *zozan* of Chumba, where the previous year Grant had delivered the Syriac Psalms and suffered with his swollen face. At the *zozan*, evidently chosen because of Malek Ismael's consistent support of Mar Shimun, several people were killed and huge numbers of sheep driven off.

Mar Shimun, incensed at the lack of response from his people, returned to Asheetha. He now turned to Mohammed Pasha of Mosul, from whom he continued to expect help. The

Little Ensign brought him down to earth at once, saying that the price of succor would be complete submission to his authority. To this the patriarch sent a defiant reply. His people, he said, were not lesser animals but lions, and they would fight. This was not what the pasha wanted to hear. Several more notes were exchanged; from Mohammed Pasha no commitment was forthcoming. The most he would say was, If Bedr Khan Bey sends an army on that side, I will send one on this. The meaning of this he did not explain.

As the hills seethed with skirmishes and rumor, the time had come for Asahel Grant to make good on his promise to Bedr Khan, the emir of Bohtan. He had no desire to undertake a long ride through unknown mountains to meet a man planning to make war on his friends. Not even the midnight visit to Nurullah in 1839 could have been more daunting. But though he now regretted it, Grant had given his word. As would be expected, Mar Shimun opposed the visit, though not out of Christian concern for the doctor. Such a journey at this point, the patriarch thought, might look as if they were suing for peace. And the last thing he wanted was to look weak.

On June 8, at six in the morning, Asahel Grant and two Nestorian attendants set out for Derguleh. As they rode off, the people of the village gathered to bless the doctor and wish him well. His familiar reminder—that he could not and would not interfere in politics—did not prevent the people from hoping that he would do it anyway. Their pleas were echoed by shepherds, who left their flocks to greet him as he rode along the mountainside. These men and boys, isolated with their sheep, evoked his pity most of all. If invasion came, they would be utterly alone.

Though Grant gives a straighforward account of his journey to Bohtan, complete with descriptions of castles, towns, and encounters with ethnic groups, the dread that rode with him made his progress anything but ordinary. By then, in a vehement rush of color, spring had arrived. Snowdrifts withered in the grass; water gushed from the rocks; and on the oak twigs a billion tiny gall-wasps were burrowing. Across the mountainsides peasants were harvesting wild fennel, a major source of fodder for their animals. Through this riot of existence a pious fatalism guided Asahel Grant. Had he been a Buddhist he would surely have thought of himself as the lotus blossom floating above the world's stench and muck, drawing his strength therefrom. As a Christian physician he could only prescribe the medicines he had, avert his gaze, and move on. At this time, he gives no account of his health. Perhaps the sunshine had driven away the malaise. Perhaps he was sicker than ever.

Two hours out of Asheetha, Grant came upon the past and future fused in one place. Beside a stream, rows of poplars marked where a village should have been. Two years before, a Kurdish village had been there; now there was only a ruin of ashes and broken walls. The perpetrators, says Thomas Laurie, were those same Asheethans "who now trembled lest the same fate should befall their own." This was only one of several villages, both Kurdish and Christian, that the Tiyari men had burnt: the Kurd villages because war demanded it, the Christian to show that they were even-handed.

Soon Grant crossed a pass into the domains of the Hertushi Kurds, bitter enemies of the Nestorians and noted robbers in their own right. Here the waters fell westward toward the Khabur, a river which today, in its last miles before joining the Tigris, forms the border between Iraq and Turkey. On the opposite side and further upstream sat a castle occupied by the notorious Zeiner Bey, who was busy robbing villages in the district. Grant and his Nestorian guides stayed well away from this place. After spending the first night at a Nestorian village, where the howling of dogs prevented him from sleeping, Grant arrived the next afternoon at Zakho, an important town on an island in the Khabur. Here, where he spent two nights, people talked of nothing but Zeiner Bey and his depredations, deeds sponsored by the exiled Ismael Pasha, a man determined to do everything possible to vex the Little Ensign. Against this organized thuggery the Ottoman soldiers in the citadel, outnumbered and ill-equipped, could do nothing. Moving northwest from Zakho, Grant was soon in the territory of Bedr Khan, the emir of Bohtan. Everywhere he stopped, the doctor took time to treat the sick, and heard from them the same wearying tales of robbery and oppression. On the morning of June 13, having set out on the road at two in the morning to avoid the heat of the Tigris valley, Grant entered Jezirah ibn Omar (now Cizre), the chief town of Bedr Khan's territories.

By that time all hope of peace had expired. Everywhere the talk was of war; even the soil Grant's mule trod upon seemed drenched in history and strife. The town of Jezirah, desolate, fly-blown and deserted, enjoyed a reputation for violence and xenophobia which it has retained to this day. Immediately to the east, hemming in the Tigris, hunched the rocky shoulders of Judi Dagh, Noah's landing place. Here the Kurdish mountains crowded about the river and restricted travel to the north. This was where, in 401 B.C., Xenophon and the Ten Thousand Greeks, marooned in Mesopotamia and trying to fight their way home, spent seven desperate days forcing their way past a people called the Karduchoi—assumed to be the Kurds—enroute to the highlands of Armenia. The Karduchoi fought furiously to hold back the Greeks, rolling great boulders down upon them from the heights and using bows so powerful that the arrows could pierce body armor. It was an instructive episode. Now, in 1843, those same mountains formed the core of Bedr Khan's domain.

Derguleh lay eighteen miles northeast of Jezirah, across the Tigris (crossed by Grant on a goatskin raft) and up a rocky canyon green with terraces and cultivation. On the grassy slope before the Bey's castle, situated upon a bluff, the missionary spotted the tents of Nurullah and Ismael Pasha, and, at the castle gate, encountered Nurullah himself. The emir, his face clouded with suspicion, asked why the doctor had come. When Grant told him that Bedr Khan had requested his services, Nurullah relaxed and bade him welcome. But "Do not interfere with our plans," he warned, and with that he went in to announce the doctor's arrival to the bey.

At this place, and in the nearby *zozans*, Grant spent ten of the strangest days of his life. From across Kurdistan and as far north as Van, violent, thuggish men assembled, greeted him cheerfully, and made ready to kill his friends, friends whom he knew to be equally violent and thuggish. Except for a sharp stomach pain (wrongly attributed to poisoning) soon after his arrival, the doctor had no cause to complain. Bedr Khan and Nurullah vied to make him a guest, and in the end he compromised by staying with the former at night and the latter during the day. When he recovered from his stomach cramps, Grant spent days in the castle treating the sick. Of the bey's illness, real or feigned, there was little to say. Grant took the great man's pulse, listened to his complaints, and decided that Bedr Khan, known for his "voluptuous habits," was spending too much time in the harem with his thirty wives. As the strictest of Muslims, he could not be faulted for over-indulgence in alcohol, but sex was another matter. The man might simply have been worn out.

Grant gives little physical description of Bedr Khan Bey, except to say that he wore robes of Damascus silk, a richly-embroidered turban, and accented his eyes with kohl. Others have described his above-average height, hawk-like visage, and commanding presence. Some observers regarded him as the quintessence of fanaticism and cruelty, and it is true that Muslim law, *Sharia,* dictating severed limbs and extreme repression, ruled in his domain. At the same time, when Austin Wright and Edward Breath, responding to an appeal for medical help, rode from Urmia to Derguleh in 1846, they found Bedr Khan seated before his castle doling out money to the poor and lame of the district. They thought him severe but just, a ruler who prided himself on keeping his word. Indeed, despite all the atrocities attributed to Bedr Khan, and there were many, Grant conceded that this emir of Bohtan had kept his promises—at least, those made to Grant himself.

In the first place, he promised war and vengeance. The emirs of Hakkari and Bohtan had made an alliance, and having given his word, the latter was not going to back out. To Grant and his companions, the Kurds fully disclosed their plans, and the mullahs who advised the bey urged all within hearing to kill as many infidels as possible. But Bedr Khan promised Asahel Grant that if the people of Asheetha submitted, their valley would be spared, and no harm would come to the doctor or his mission house. Moreover, the bey repeated the emirs' principal demands: that the Nestorians should acknowledge Nurullah's supremacy in Hakkari, Mar Shimun should give up political power, and all temporal affairs must be left to the maleks. On these terms, they could have peace.

This sounds reasonable enough, but in 1843 reason carried even less weight in the Middle East than it does today. Tribal loyalties, religious obsession, and a cult of masculine honor generally combined to crush any compromising spirit. When Grant mentioned the possibility that Mohammed Pasha might march from Mosul to aid Mar Shimun, Nurullah merely scoffed. The doctor listened to the bey's offer and explained at length the American Board's policy of non-involvement in local politics. He told the emirs that he would inform the Nestorians of the offer but could not advise them to accept or reject it. The Kurds thought this "over-scrupulous," and well they might: to them it was inconceivable that a man could disentangle himself from those ties of kinship, tribe, and religion that we would call political life.

Grant had come a long distance to reach this impasse: attending a patient who was not really ill, living in the midst of a crowd of men preparing for war. He wanted to leave for Asheetha immediately, as did his two Nestorian companions, men whose terror at their surroundings we can only begin to

comprehend. As soon as it was seemly, Grant asked leave to
depart; but Bedr Khan would not hear of it. He was leaving the
next morning for his *zozan,* higher up in the mountains, while
at another *zozan* his chief officer, a Georgian who had converted to Islam, lay gravely ill. Grant had no choice but to give
in, and it was arranged that he should go to the officer, treat
him, and then rejoin Bedr Khan in a few days.

Asahel Grant made the best of this interlude, but his heart
lay elsewhere. The Georgian's illness ("deep-seated,"—probably
cancer) had advanced beyond treatment, and the spectacular
situation of the *zozan,* with views that stretched as far as Mosul
and the Jebel Sinjar, could not salve Grant's depression and fear.
Soon he returned to Bedr Khan Bey, this time at his *zozan* further to the north. The bey's army, now fully assembled, was
expected any day to leave for Julamerk and Diz. There Grant
lingered without purpose, a Presbyterian peg in a round Kurdish
hole. He had fulfilled his obligations as a man and a physician;
peace-making and conciliation were no longer possible. He might
as easily have held back the Tigris with his hands. Once again
Grant asked leave to depart, and this time Bedr Khan agreed.

20

Devouring Fire

"And he will stretch out his hand against the north, and destroy Assyria; and will make Nineveh a desolation, and dry like a wilderness.

And flocks shall lie down in the midst of her, all the beasts of the nations: both the cormorant and the bittern shall lodge in the upper lintels of it; their voice shall sing in the windows; desolation shall be in the thresholds: for he shall uncover the cedar work.

This is the rejoicing city that dwelt carelessly, that said in her heart, I am and there is none beside me: how is she become a desolation, a place for beasts to lie down in! every one that passeth by her shall hiss, and wag his hand."

—*Zephaniah 2: 13–15*

NOW BEGAN THE WAIT. By June 27, after three days of hard traveling, Asahel Grant was back in Asheetha. Amazingly, even at that late date the Christian tribes of Hakkari had done nothing to prepare for war. Sheltered behind their rocks and their legendary ferocity, they had always been invincible. But Kurds could scale rocks as well as anyone; and what was reputation in the face of overwhelming force? "Is there danger?" asked the

Asheethans as Grant and his companions dismounted from their mules. "Even unto death," came the reply.

For the next ten days Asahel Grant lived through a plague of speculation and rumor. The reports varied so wildly that no one knew what to expect. Some concerned Grant himself, saying that he was a prisoner of Bedr Khan Bey, that his hands had been severed, or that he had gone to Mosul. In truth the missionary went about his business as usual, preaching the gospel and dispensing medicine. Suleiman Bey at this point sent a message asking the tribes of Tiyari to surrender, threatening them with imminent invasion if they refused. The tribesmen came to ask Grant for advice. It is an indication of their desperation that they, men of action accustomed to mountain ways, should seek the counsel of an unarmed foreigner who knew nothing about warfare and politics. Grant told them that they should be unified in their councils and actions. Exactly what this would mean in terms of practical policies he didn't say.

The doctor knew that he would soon have to return to Mosul; yet any suggestion of such a desertion so panicked the villagers that he could not bear to do it. Long before, he had decided that an exit now would mean abandonment forever. Either the government of the region made it possible for mission families to live there as permanent residents or it did not; only if it did would he make the commitment to bring women and children to Asheetha. The brief season of hope was waning; he must have felt it in his blood and in his mercury-scarred guts. July 3 finds him writing to Thomas Laurie, implying that only the excitement of Asheetha is keeping him alive. He often feels ill and longs for the nursing of Laurie's wife when he realizes that he is alone. "I have a sort of premonition," he writes, "that I shall be an invalid as soon as I leave this exciting scene of toil; if, indeed, I am not before." Nothing could be less ambiguous: he was barely holding on. Only his faith helped him to withstand the hammer blows of reality. "A glorious day is at hand," he wrote to Dr. Rufus Anderson in Boston. "The deepest darkness precedes the dawn. Our faith may be sorely tried; but we will not despair."

At this point came a summons: yet another tribal leader in a remote village appealed for medical attention. Berkho, a malek in the district of Raola, east of the Zab, had taken sick. Could Dr. Grant come to him? Mar Shimun argued strenuously against this. No love was lost between himself and Berkho; in fact, the malek was well known to be an ally of Nurullah Bey. The patriarch told Grant that Berkho was trying to lure him into a trap, that he would kill him in order to gain favor with Nurullah. As usual, Grant didn't know which of these two to believe. He did not like the malek, but he thought if it were possible to reconcile these two enemies he should at least make the attempt. So on July 7, just ten days after his return from Derguleh, Asahel Grant left Asheetha. He did not know that he was leaving for the last time, and in fact he probably hoped to return. This was, after all, the place where he had hoped to die. But even at the brink of disaster the doctor could not refuse an appeal for medical aid.

The two-day journey to Salaberka d'Raola involved crossing the bridge at Lezan, driving the mules into the river, and riding for six hours after they had gained the east bank of the Zab. At Lezan two more urgent messages awaited from Malek Berkho, and the men of the village encouraged the visit in the hope that Berkho might join the council of war. By the time Dr. Grant reached Salaberka, both his mules had gone lame, their shoes torn off by the rocks. While a priest set to work repairing the damage, Grant tended his patient, who was in agony from a boil on his neck. The doctor's lancet soon drained the sore, to the malek's extreme gratitude. The next morning, the Sabbath, an exhausted Grant tried in vain to rest. No sooner had he risen from his bed than the sick began to gather. In the upper room of the malek's house, open to the summer air and sunshine, he spent yet another day seeing patients and telling them about the "Great Physician."

Malek Berkho would not leave his village to attend a council of war. Danger lay too near. One of Nurullah's sons, accompanied by a party of warriors, had taken up residence at the same mountain camp where only the previous summer Grant had received final permission to build his house. The son's mission was simple: intimidation and the prevention of alliances. Peace was on offer under the usual terms. Peace would even be offered to Tiyari, Berkho told Grant, if Mar Shimun would come to him in Salaberka. The malek argued this so strenuously that the American became suspicious. Moreover, Berkho detested his fellow Tiyarians. For example, he told Dr. Grant that if the Kurds did not destroy Asheetha he would go and do it himself.

All this eleventh-hour maneuvering was soon swept into irrelevance. Messengers began to arrive from the north bringing terrible news. Near Julamerk, Nurullah's army had poured across the Zab and fallen upon the villages in Diz, the principal residence of Mar Shimun's family. Diz lies deep in the Zab gorge, a cathedral of black rock opening into a lateral canyon, as impregnable, and nearly uninhabitable, as a place could be. At a meeting to talk terms, all its tribal leaders had been murdered, and after that the slaughter began. It was rumored that some 800 people had been killed, and many more taken captive. Priest Zadok, the patriarch's brother, and Grant's truculent, bibulous traveling companion, was slain along with his young son, Mar Shimun's designated heir. The patriarch's hoard of ancient manuscripts went up in flames. The body of his mother, who had welcomed Grant so often and taken care of his son Henry, was mutilated and thrown into the Zab.

No one, and certainly not Asahel Grant, could sleep after hearing such news, and the next morning brought worse. Hostile forces, reports said, were converging on Tiyari from three directions: Bedr Khan in the northwest, Nurullah from Diz, and on the southwest, to block any escape, the army of the governor of Mosul. Once and for all, the enemies of Mar Shimun and the Tiyari tribe were going to have their way. And after hearing the fate of those in Diz, no one was going to meet to talk about terms of surrender.

Dr. Grant set out at once for Lezan and encountered enroute a messenger bearing a letter from Thomas Laurie, telling the doctor that his friends in Mosul were afraid for his life; in the strongest language they urged his immediate return. Obviously, the mission's end had come, and a return to Asheetha was out of the question. Still, Grant hesitated. This was, he later told Laurie, the lowest point of his life. His heart was "crushed." For all their savagery, he had come to love the Tiyari people, and now the dream that had sustained him since Judith's death lay bleeding on the rocks. In Lezan the reports of catastrophe were confirmed, though back in Asheetha, Mar Shimun still had not been told the full extent of his personal loss. Before starting for Mosul, Asahel Grant sent the patriarch a farewell message. When Mar Shimun received this, he also learned the truth about his family.

From Lezan, Grant set out upon the same remote path he had taken on his first visit to Tiyari only four years before. All other roads were blocked by enemies. At Duree he stayed with his friend the bishop; at another village he was sheltered by Jews. After four days of hard riding, evasion, and fear, he crossed the Tigris to safety on July 15, 1843.

It was the worst possible time to be in Mosul; even the *serdabs*, eight feet below the scorching earth, offered no refuge from bad news. Every day, as the weight of a July sun crushed the town beneath it, reports of fresh horrors flowed with the refugees and travelers across the bridge of boats. Twelve days after Grant's return, Mar Shimun came with them.

When the doctor heard of the patriarch's approach, he hurried across the river to meet him near the ruins of Nineveh. The man he found was in far worse condition than the prematurely-aged prelate who had greeted him in 1839. Terror and grief had scored the patriarch's features, and he had no idea what he would do next. Tears flowed as the two men exchanged stories of the murdered and missing. Grant offered refuge to Mar Shimun and

his younger brother, who accompanied him, as well as to the rest
of his retinue. But soon, as they approached Mosul, the party
met Christian Rassam and George Percy Badger, who had also
come to bring greetings. Rassam told Grant that he had already
gone to Mohammed Pasha, and arrangements were in place for
the patriarch to stay at the consular residence. Mar Shimun's
dream—that he would be appointed the civil head of his people
in Hakkari—still had not been formally quashed—or even considered—by the Porte, and for the time being, having received
instructions from his ambassador in Stamboul, Rassam thought
it best that the patriarch should live under British protection.
Grant had no quarrel with this plan. It confirmed what he had
been telling Mar Shimun and his compatriots all along: that he
and his fellow Americans had no political influence whatever,
and were concerned solely with spiritual matters.

Besides, he had other duties to occupy him. As the mountains emptied of their refugees, the doctor's clinic filled with
patients. Each person who came to him had a story to tell, and
as the days wore on an outline emerged of the mountain war
and its progress. By that time, as observers described it, the
campaign had become little more than a series of massacres.
Out of all this horror at least two incidents, both related by
Austen Henry Layard, will suffice to tell the tale.

After the carnage in Diz, Nurullah's forces linked up with
those of Bedr Khan and followed the Zab south toward Chumba
in Upper Tiyari. There, despite a brave defense by Malek Ismael
and his men, the outcome was not in doubt. Wounded, with his
hip bone cracked by a musket ball, the malek was carried away
and hidden in a mountain cave. A woman of the village, threatened with death, betrayed his hideout. The ensuing events are
described by Layard, who visited the ruins of Chumba in 1846.
Traveling with him was Yakoub, the *rais,* or chief, of Asheetha.
In 1843, after Asheetha was spared by Bedr Khan, Yakoub was
taken hostage, and he stayed with the emir through the ensuing

massacres. Yakoub thus witnessed the scene as exulting Kurds dragged Ismael before their leader and threw the malek on the ground. Bedr Khan asked who the infidel was that dared to sit in his presence, and who, he asked, "has dared to shed the blood of true believers?" Malek Ismael, raising himself slightly, addressed the emir of Bohtan. "This arm," he told him, "has taken the lives of nearly twenty Kurds; and, had God spared me, as many more would have fallen by it." Hearing this, Bedr Khan Bey rose and walked to the river bank, motioning to his men to bring the Nestorian chief. There, as he was held over the water, the head of Malek Ismael was severed from his body with a dagger, and both were thrown into the Zab.

But there was worse. A week before this, Layard visited Lezan, and there he recorded one of the indelible images of the 1843 atrocities. After he had seen the burned houses, the ruined orchards, the felled and girdled trees, one of the survivors, an energetic mountaineer, offered to show him something else. Together the two men climbed out of Lezan toward the mountain wall above. Beyond the terraced gardens they entered a wasteland of broken rock and scree, almost perpendicular and rising toward the cliffs. For over an hour they struggled on this surface, sometimes clinging to the ragged shrubs in the rocks, and other times crawling on their hands and knees. It was not long before evidence began to turn up, and eventually there was so much that they couldn't move without walking on it. At first a solitary skull appeared, rolling downhill with the loose scree and rock; then many others. These were of all ages, from adults to the size of an unborn child. Bones appeared, and complete skeletons; heaps of rotten fabric mingled with the plaited tresses of women. Layard gave up his attempts to count the dead. But "This is nothing," his guide told him: it was only the remains of those who jumped or were thrown from the rocks above. "Follow me!" said the man.

When the Kurds swept through Tiyari like "devouring fire"—the missionaries' phrase—all who could escape fled before them. In Lezan a thousand men, women, and children streamed toward the mountain, taking refuge in a remote, almost inaccessible pocket amid the cliffs. There, with scant food and water, they hunkered down to hide from Bedr Khan Bey and his warriors. Yet the Bedr Khan who had managed to flush out Malek Ismael did not take long to find a thousand people, even on a ledge thousands of feet above the Zab. Rather than attack, he decided to surround them and wait it out.

This is the place that young Layard was climbing to see, and the task was anything but easy. Only mountain people could have accomplished such a retreat, and the Englishman, his leg bruised from a mule's kick four days earlier, began to falter. A ledge appeared in the cliff face; to their left they could barely discern the Zab thousands of feet below. Eventually the path narrowed, said Layard, to the width of his hand, and then it disappeared altogether. Though this made no difficulty for his guide, it was too much for Layard. In the end he had to be satisfied with a glimpse of the rock platform and its contents. But that glimpse was enough.

After three days of siege, exposed to the full force of the sun, the refugees had run out of water. Left with no choice, the Lezanis offered to surrender. The terms Bedr Khan offered were simple: their lives in return for their weapons and property. This bargain, Layard reports, Bedr Khan swore on the Holy Koran to uphold. Having surrendered, the Nestorians admitted their enemies to the rock ledge, and there, after disarming them, the Kurds waded in and commenced the slaughter. No one was spared, of any age or sex, and nothing was said about the emir's word of honor. When the killers wearied of using their knives, they let gravity do the work, as hundreds more fell or were thrown from the heights. Of the thousand who fled to the cliffs, only one escaped.

This was the sight that Layard glimpsed: an open platform covered with human remains, a trove of the grotesque. Then he delivers what could be Bedr Khan's epitaph, the sum total and metaphor of a ruler's legacy on earth—and our last look at this sorry episode. They had "little difficulty," Layard noted, in returning to Lezan, as "a moving mass of stones, skulls, and rubbish carried us rapidly down." He was riding, in other words, an ossuary in motion: a down escalator of the dead. It is a damning image, one which no amount of equivocation can retract. The moving mass writes, and having writ, moves on. Forget fairness, it says: forget reputation and honor. And certainly you may disregard fine robes of Damascus silk, solemn promises and public alms, piety and fearless leadership. All are subsumed in that cascade of bones.

21

A LONG, STEEP JOURNEY

"An innavigable sea washes with silent waves between us and
the things we aim at and converse with."
—Emerson: "Experience" (1844)

"Those who try to do the undoable must also think the unthinkable."
—Simon Jenkins, *The London Times,* 3 December 2003

THE EVENTS OF 1843 transformed the political landscape of
Hakkari, and they did so despite a narrow range of destruction. In all the Christian *ashirets* only three major districts
were hit: Diz, the home of the patriarch's family; Upper Tiyari,
the domain of Malek Ismael, and Lower Tiyari, Lezan and
Asheetha, and within those areas the devastation, though widespread, was by no means uniform. In Lower Tiyari, for example, Asheetha was spared (at first), as was Zawitha, home
of the young man whose sight Asahel Grant had restored in
the 1830s. Lezan, however, lay shattered, as did the Chumba
of Malek Ismael and scores of villages between. Other areas—
Jelu, Baz, Tal—had made their bargains with Nurullah or Bedr
Khan and were not affected. Tehoma, another powerful

Nestorian district, Layard found utterly untouched when he visited in 1846. Tehoma, in fact, had contributed warriors to the slaughter: they were, wrote Thomas Laurie, "the hand by which [Nurullah] smote Tiyary. It was they who slew their brethren during the war, as often and as mercilessly as he commanded them." Laurie and Azariah Smith, visiting Hakkari in the autumn of 1844, wrote a vivid account of the corpses left behind following a raid by the Tehomans, with some Kurdish allies, upon the Nestorians in the Raola valley. The Tehomans' turn would come later.

None of this lends itself to easy generalizations about "religious war" or the Good vs. Evil Armageddon that Grant so devoutly expected. For the Christian tribes, as well as the Kurds, this was the end of an era. Under the leadership of Bedr Khan, the Kurds had shifted the balance of power; but that fact, which may have seemed so important, made little long-term difference. What really mattered was that the outside world had taken an interest in their heap of rock. Indeed, it was that greater world which bore much responsibility for the upheavals of 1843, and if called upon one could trace a direct line from the reforms of Mahmud II to that pile of bones on the ledge in Lezan. Thirty years earlier no one in Europe or America would have known what a Kurd was, let alone a "Nestorian." Now readers of the *Missionary Herald*, whether in Boston or Illinois, could follow the intrigues of such people as Nurullah Bey and Mar Shimun, and every Western traveler who came to Turkey, no matter how unimportant, was sure to write—and easily sell to an eager publisher—his memories of the adventure. These agents of modernity, whether they sought knowledge, leeches, or righteousness, had irretrievably upset the political balance in Kurdistan. No longer could the tribesmen carry on with their petty insular quarrels: now ethnic rivalries were a matter of statecraft. The maneuverings of the Great Powers, and the extension of Ottoman power to meet the challenges of the modern world, had set up a chain of events that no one could control.

The 1843 attack upon Tiyari was the worst massacre suffered by the Nestorians since Tamerlane and his hordes drove their ancestors into the mountains at the beginning of the 15th century. First reports, repeated by Laurie, estimated that 10,000 people—some twenty percent of the population—had died in the Nestorian domains of Hakkari, and many more were sold into slavery. This number was no more than a guess, yet it is repeated to this day. Subsequent guesses revised the figure downward. After their visit to Bedr Khan in 1846, Breath and Wright put the number killed at 7000, though that, they said, "may be too high." Early in 1844, George Percy Badger, working with Mar Shimun, compiled a list of losses suffered by each village in the three stricken districts. His estimates put the number of dead at 4000. In the absence of reliable observers, no one could say for sure, and in the end we must acknowledge the fact that ugliness and horror are not adequately measured by raw numbers.

Strangely enough, the brutalities of 1843 seem to have surprised even the Kurds themselves. At Julamerk in 1844, several of the leading men of Nurullah's entourage spoke with the ever-present Da'ud, gall merchant and guide *extraordinaire*. "We had no idea the affair would turn out so disastrously," they said, in Laurie's paraphrase: "We only meant to frighten the Nestorians into obedience to our wishes." Before subjecting this statement to the Plausible Excuse Test, which it will surely fail, we must admit that among the Kurds who lived beside the Nestorians (as opposed to the outsiders, outlaws, and opportunists among Bedr Khan's forces) there must have been many who genuinely regretted the massacres. Both sides could be extremely rough and brutal, yet for centuries they had managed to avoid large-scale war. They traded commodities on a daily basis, whether salt, lead, or foodstuffs; their villages were commingled in many areas; they joined each others' raiding parties for fun and profit. These were not implacable blood enemies who killed each other every chance they could get. Yet, after 1843 their relations had changed profoundly, and as the century progressed they would only get worse.

For Asahel Grant, August of 1843 could scarcely have been a more heartrending time. Heat, sickness, and sorrow filled the days, as lines of refugees straggled in from the mountains. Before long the English and Americans were feeding and housing as many homeless Nestorians as they could find room for. Had he not been a doctor and a missionary, one who embraced every disaster as an opportunity for renewed effort, Grant might well have gone mad. Of his grief we have already caught a glimpse, in Thomas Laurie's memory of their solitary sunset walks on the roof of the mission house in Mosul. The venue is significant, for the rooftops of Mosul were special places, where the most private thoughts might emerge. On any summer night, an aerial view of the city would have disclosed some 30,000 slumbering people lying on these platforms under the stars. In his *Notes from Nineveh* (1850), J. P. Fletcher, Badger's lay associate, talks about the sanctity of that space. In every other room, visitors might intrude at any moment unannounced, but on the rooftop no visitor or servant would dream of disturbing Fletcher's privacy. If Grant had doubts about his past or future, it was on the roof at day's end that he would have expressed them.

But the most important medium for his thoughts remained the written word. By early 1843 a regular mail service had been established between Mosul and Constantinople, and of this the missionaries, especially Asahel Grant, took advantage. In the aftermath of disaster Grant's letters show bitterness, pessimism and confusion, overlain with the usual crusading zeal. He feels certain that he has given his all, yet he knows that some have criticized him for having risked his life in pursuit of unreachable goals. Even then, Nurullah had written inviting Grant to return to the mountains, and "at the risk, perhaps, of being deemed insane," the doctor had considered doing so. To Rev. Wayne Gridley, he writes asking not only for his personal opinion but for that of his fellow Christians. Had he done wrong to pursue the course he had taken? Should he go back and trust himself to the emir's protection, or should he stay? "Though great havoc has been made, the great mass of the population, some tens of thousands, still remain. The field is wide, and ripe for the harvest." It is a familiar metaphor, and as naïve as ever: the field of golden grain, with no rust or blight, no locusts or adulterating weeds, utterly removed from the imperfections and struggles of men.

In a letter of September 1843 to Dr. Rufus Anderson, Grant let forth a freshet of gall. His privations in the mountains, he noted, "could not be detailed without an appearance of boasting." Moreover, "To return there is in no ways inviting to flesh and blood. All the romance of that field—if there ever were any—is now sober reality. There is no poetry in winding your weary way over rocks and cliffs, drifted snows or dashing torrents. Neither is there any in appeasing hunger from their filthy wooden bowls or still fouler goat-skins, while tormented with smoke, insects, vermin, and a thousand nameless trials, among an impoverished and lawless people."

This is a stark admission from one who had lived so long with his "beloved" Nestorians. But love can co-exist with resentment and even disgust, especially within one who carried a steam engine called Duty forever chuffing in his breast. Though the importation of mission families was now out of the question, Grant remained ready to return to the mountains any time the Board directed. The Turks had no power to protect him; only the Kurdish chiefs could do that. It would be dangerous, and he might lose his life; but "I had rather go to judgment" he wrote Anderson, "with the approval of God, and the frown of the world, than, for the sake of a good name among men, meet that Judge, conscious of having betrayed my trust."

The most disturbing passages of Grant's letters are those in which he speaks of his mountain friends as if they were clay figures in a game invented by the vengeful Jehovah. So determined is he to see the hand of God at work in all things that he seems almost to welcome the summer's carnage. In a letter to Rev. Wayne Gridley, he quotes Hosea 5:15: "In their affliction they will seek me early." This, one of endless maledictions by that minor prophet, he takes as a hopeful sign, meaning that the Nestorians surely will now repent and be saved. "The Nestorians needed humbling," he adds, "and they may find it good to have been afflicted. Whom the Lord loveth, he chasteneth." The mind boggles when confronted by such statements, especially the latter. The final verb echoes 19th-century philosophies of child-rearing: the youthful delinquent struck hard and often as evidence of parental love. On this basis, says the missionary, the Nestorians "may find it good" to have been massacred. Had the statement been made a century later, and in a political context, we would call it Orwellian. The sentiment is difficult to understand, but in a century where physicians routinely drained the life blood of patients in order to cure them, nothing should surprise us.

Amidst the hard work and anguish, one thing had not changed: the resentment and machinations of George Percy Badger. For this, oddly enough, the Englishman had little time, for like the Americans, the Badgers and Rassams spent long hours working with the refugees. Of special concern were the thousands held captive by Bedr Khan or already sold into slavery. Letters went out to the British embassy in Constantinople pleading for help, which was forthcoming both from British and Ottoman authorities; it was largely due to their efforts that the captives were eventually freed. Despite these demands on him, Badger continued to make trouble.

Mostly the rivalry centered around a Syrian Jacobite youth named Micah, who had come to the Americans seeking instruction and who was eventually hired as a helper. When the mission, stymied by the mountain war, decided to expend more effort with the local Syrians, Thomas Laurie decided that he had to learn Arabic, the Jacobites' primary language. Micah became his teacher, and gradually the two became friends. After Laurie began to explain to Micah the Protestants' interpretations of Scripture, the young man became intensely excited, and experienced a religious conversion. Eventually Thomas Laurie opened a Bible class for Syrian youths, including Micah; it met regularly on the banks of the Tigris.

Badger soon found out about Micah's relationship with the Americans, and was of course displeased. He took the boy aside and, in his excellent Arabic, explained ecclesiastical history proving that the Americans were "out of the church," and "affectionately" (Laurie's adverb) warned him against the schism and dissent he was introducing into the Syrian Orthodox community. Much of this, it later turned out, the Americans learned from Badger's mother, who disapproved of his tactics. Micah, however, loved the Americans, and would not be swayed. When diplomacy did not work, Badger resorted to threats. Writing to the Syrian bishop of Mosul, who was then in Stamboul, he denounced Micah as a potential source of dissension. When the bishop wrote to Micah ordering him to leave the Americans' service, the boy wrote back a respectful letter full of Biblical citations showing that he was a true Christian. The Jacobite bishop, hearing from others that Micah was a good lad, decided to leave him alone. Badger's last attempt was the most blatant of all: he offered to double Micah's wages if he would come and work for the English mission. Even this did not work: Micah turned him down again.

All this quarreling and competition eventually attracted attention. Writing from Boston, the missionaries' superiors counseled them to pity Badger and pray for him, "and by your example show him a better way." In October Paul-Émile Botta came to Dr. Grant with a copy of the *Journal des Débats*, published in Paris on September 8. An article in the paper, of which Grant secured a translation, quoted a dispatch from the Stamboul correspondent of the *London Globe*. News of the Hakkari massacres had reached European capitals, and the correspondent—probably the young A.H. Layard, though Laurie does not name him—reported that the chief cause of the bloodshed could be found in the bickering and in-fighting among the missionaries at Mosul, for which the chief responsibility was Badger's; he held the Americans "blameless." According to J.F. Coakley, Austen Henry Layard, then a protegé of Sir Stratford Canning at the British embassy in Constantinople, wrote an identical letter to the London *Morning Chronicle.*

Grant's conscience would not allow this to go unanswered. These reports, we must remember, held him entirely without fault in the affair; only his nemesis, George Percy Badger, had been denounced. Nevertheless, he had to reply. On October 16, Grant sent a letter to the *New-York Observer,* at that time a Presbyterian publication, in which he laid out the history of events, as he saw them, that had led to the massacres of 1843. Mohammed Pasha of Mosul had, he wrote, been trying for years to subdue the Christian mountaineers. The struggle over Amadiyah had slowed down the process, but the idea was always there. Curiously, Grant omits the role that Nurullah, Bedr Khan, and Mar Shimun played in the affair. The controversy over his house, he says, was nothing but lies and exaggeration: the same thing had happened to Botta when he constructed a small mud-brick shelter for himself at Khorsabad. This too the Pasha of Mosul denounced as a "castle," spreading the same lies that were circulated about Grant's mission house. As for the "English Puseyites," the Americans had sought "by every proper means, to cultivate a friendly relation." Certainly they had done so with the Dominicans and other Catholics resident in Mosul. If they had failed, "the responsibility must rest with Mr. Badger for any evil arising from his opposition to us." But this quarrel, Grant states unequivocally, had nothing to do with the disaster visited upon the Nestorians. Despite this letter, the Englishman did not cease his efforts against the Americans.

As they approached the first anniversary of Abel Hinsdale's death, illness once again visited the missionaries. Of course, it had never left; but this was different from the bouts of malaria that had become a part of life. As October passed into November, Martha Laurie began to weaken, developing symptoms of what Dr. Grant called "quick consumption." Whether or not this was truly tuberculosis, no one can say. What is certain is that Martha was soon in agony.

Besides accounts of her deep piety, Thomas Laurie tells us little about his wife. In fact, he doesn't even tell us her first name, and it is left for the researcher to find it among marriage records on the Internet. In the *Missionary Herald,* she is simply "Mrs. Laurie," the name by which her husband refers to her. Not until the 1850s did the *Missionary Herald,* official publication of the American Board, begin to treat missionary wives as human beings possessing first names—a recognition that Judith Grant never received. This, of course, is typical of an era when females and their biological reality were treated with a delicacy that verged upon abhorrence. Justin Perkins, for example, gives a long, detailed account of the journey suffered by his wife Charlotte and himself in 1833, a trip which included virtual imprisonment by Russian authorities and a last-minute rescue by Dr. Riach of the British Legation. Within a week after their arrival in Tabriz, Charlotte Perkins gave birth to a baby girl, and no hint as to the imminence of this event was given by her husband. Rev. Horatio Southgate, visiting Baghdad in 1838, refers in one story to a woman "in a certain condition"; Justin Perkins could not bring himself to do even this, and Thomas Laurie is no different.

For a brief moment late in 1843, Martha Osgood Laurie of Westford, Massachusetts, emerged from anonymity to die. Her husband does not neglect the clinical details. The "quick consumption," was quick only in relation to the usual form of the disease. Her death was preceded by fifty hours of agony, "the most painful and protracted [Grant] had witnessed in a practice of fifteen years." At last, after countless expressions of gratitude, and protestations of her unworthiness to die for Christ in horrific pain, Martha fell into "quiet unconsciousness—her eyes fixed, her face and hands cold and clammy." To a last question, "Are you ready to rest on Christ?" she managed to say "Yes," before the "rattling in her throat" stifled the remainder. Just after midnight on December 16, 1843, Martha Laurie "sweetly fell asleep in Jesus."

One by one the missionaries had fallen, while in the mountains thousands of Nestorians had succumbed to torture, imprisonment, and disease. In this climate of uncertainty and grief, Asahel Grant received a letter from Hastings, his eldest son. The doctor was so affected by its contents that he wrote to colleagues asking for advice. By then news of the massacres had arrived in the United States. The boy's message, as summarized by Grant, was a heartfelt plea for his father to return home, not only for himself but for the sake of his younger brothers. Hastings must have been terrified at the thought of losing a father whom he had not seen since March of 1841, and the doctor's aging mother surely felt the same way. Torn by internal conflict, Grant now began to think the unthinkable.

As the New Year crept in, Death followed and claimed another character in this drama. Sooner or later even the thieves, liars, and impalers of this world must go to judgment, and in January 1844 Mohammed Pasha's time had come. With the Christian tribes subdued and the Kurds sated with plunder, the Little Ensign could well have made some rewarding moves in the coming year. But his luck was running out. Sir Stratford Canning, longtime British emissary to the Sublime Porte, was not called the Great Elchi (ambassador) for nothing. He was so effective in pressing the case of the murdered Nestorians to the Ottoman government that the Turks began to show a determination to investigate. This did not bode well for Mohammed Pasha; nor did the reports, which the Porte had been receiving for some time, of the pasha's vast hoard of ill-gotten wealth. An official indictment soon followed.

A commission consisting of a reform-minded Turk and an English consul was already enroute to Mosul when word came to the pasha of their approach. The Little Ensign, never one to deny himself the pleasures of the grape, had lately taken to drink with renewed ardor, and on January 13 he was seized by an "inflammation of the heart." The pasha's physician, an Armenian who had studied in Italy, called in Asahel Grant to consult. Grant saw immediately that the case was hopeless, and wisely declined to prescribe any new medicine. After five days of what was probably congestive heart failure accompanied by severe angina, Mohammed Pasha of Mosul expired.

With this news the city erupted. Men kissed in the streets; people donned their finest garments and set forth to make merry. The day of the pasha's burial became a carnival. "It was even feared," wrote J.P. Fletcher, "that they might attempt a riot in the exuberance of their joy. People in the East are so little accustomed to freedom that even the semblance of it produces a species of moral intoxication." Indeed, this soon happened. Before Mohammed Pasha's arrival, Mosul had been divided into warring neighborhoods, each with its hereditary feud against the other. With his demise, parts of the city again became scenes of riot and confusion, while outside Mosul, Kurdish bandits renewed their raids. The Arab proverb, "Better forty years of oppression than one day of anarchy," was proven once again.

Meanwhile, Asahel Grant went on with his life's work. Not a day passed that he was not besieged with patients, and the situation became steadily worse. Many of the Tiyari people had escaped the onslaught of Bedr Khan, but they could not escape winter. Without crops or animals to live on, they fled to the city and to nearby Chaldean villages, swelling the population even more. In the crowded squalor of the shelters, disease soon followed. Typhus, spread by body lice, broke out among the refugees.

There was a change in Dr. Grant that winter. His letters, normally so full of plans and expectations, took on a fatalistic cast, and he spoke little of the Nestorians. "Every earthly bond of interest in that people," wrote Thomas Laurie, "seemed to fade away." Mar Shimun remained under the roof of the British consul, safely removed from the doctor's concern. Other than tend to his patients, there was nothing more that Grant could do. Writing to the Board after Martha Laurie's death, Grant insisted that Mosul, despite appearances, was not a particularly unhealthy station and should not on that account be closed. He also, with amazing naïveté, saw in the Yezidis a people ripe for conversion. Still, neither point was argued vigorously, and he left it to his superiors to decide the Yezidis' fate.

Though no decision had been announced, the Mosul missionaries had good reason to believe that it would be forthcoming. Late in the year Dr. Rufus Anderson had arrived in Constantinople to consult his missionaries and tour ABCFM outposts. Though no one expected him to make the long journey to Mosul, it was still reasonable to suppose that a decision about the station would soon be made. In one sense there was good news, for at last, after nine months' wait in Constantinople, Azariah Smith, a new M.D. sent by the Board, had been granted permission by the Ottoman authorities to travel overland to Mosul. He was now, in fact, enroute. With this news Anderson could write to Grant and solve the doctor's dilemma.

After his son Hastings' pleading letter, Grant had written to the secretary and asked his advice. By the end of February the reply had come, and on March 1 Asahel Grant wrote to his eldest son with the news. Taking the decision out of his missionary's hands, Anderson had ordered Grant to "go home and look after your children." From the weary doctor there now issued a great sigh of relief. It was the best thing that could have happened. "On reading this," Grant wrote, "my heart was *full,* and I passed almost a sleepless night." Rufus Anderson's order had lifted the millstone of responsibility and guilt; Asahel Grant could now leave Mosul with his conscience clear. To his mother, he wrote: "Your son will soon return, if the Lord will, to cheer you in the decline of life." "My heart is too full," he adds, "when I think of my lone mother, to allow me to say much of myself. But . . . while my health is not at any time *good,* and while I feel the need of a respite from care, I am now in comparative comfort, and free from any great bodily pain." It is obvious that Asahel Grant was a sick man. But the important thing was that he was *going home.*

With winter now passing into spring, the typhus epidemic spread among the refugees, the townspeople, and the Turkish soldiers in their barracks. Those mountain Nestorians who had found shelter with the Chaldean Catholics of the plains were driven out as soon as the disease appeared among them. This happened, according to Thomas Laurie, because the Catholics would not allow them burial within their cemeteries. The Syrian Jacobites of Mosul granted them asylum in their church-yards, and Badger took in many as well, but neither effort sufficed. Grant, faced with meager funds and an impossible problem, was reluctant to take in more people, but when fifty of his friends from Asheetha showed up on the doorstep, he could not turn them away. A house was found nearby, and immediately he took up the challenge of feeding and caring for these new refugees, duties which included opening a school. Soon, however, they too came down with the fever, and the small, unventilated house became the worst kind of hospital. Of the ninety patients under Grant's care, twelve quickly died. The remainder were slowly recovering when another sick man, thrown out by the Chaldeans, was carried into the house and rudely dumped among the people. Grant, not wanting to endanger his patients once again, ordered the sick man to be taken back. In the end he was removed, to be put in a Muslim cemetery where he quickly died.

On March 29, young Azariah Smith, M.D., arrived in Mosul. Unlike his predecessors, he had traveled without illness or calamity of any kind. Smith, a graduate of Yale, where he studied medicine and theology, had celebrated his twenty-seventh birthday enroute from the capital. A New York native like Grant (from Manlius, a village near Syracuse), he was a welcome addition to the company. Just how welcome would soon be evident.

Asahel Grant seemed well when Smith arrived, though "not as rugged" as the newcomer would have liked him to be. But this was to be expected. Grant had been sick for a long time, and the mask of weariness only confirmed what he had said in his letters. Six days before Dr. Smith's arrival, Grant had written to his "precious mother," his heart "full" with the news that he would see her again soon, probably in the fall. On the same day he wrote to tell his brother Ira the news, and concluded with the same "end times" speculations that he had entertained for the past three years: "This is the last of the twelve hundred and sixty years of the Mohammedan era, when many of their own people have predicted the fall of their power." It would be the last time that this fantasy would occupy his pen.

Soon after Azariah Smith's arrival in Mosul, he noticed that Dr. Grant was paying "particular attention" to his food at table. On Friday, April 5, Grant complained of feeling unwell, and in his bath he began to sweat profusely. Saturday and Sunday found him well enough to eat with the rest of the missionaries, but after that he never left his room again. By Monday it was obvious that he had taken a turn for the worse. In consultation with Azariah Smith, Grant decided that they should begin to "treat his case actively, and, if possible, break up in its early stages the fever which had already commenced." Those who had followed this story from the beginning should be in no doubt as to what those "active" measures entailed.

Doctors had long known that typhus bred in the crowded conditions which followed natural disasters, but no one knew why. We now know that body lice, imbibing the bacterium when they bite infected people, leave it behind in their feces. When victims scratch these bites, the microbes left on the skin invade the bloodstream. With too many refugees and too little room to house them, Grant's makeshift hospital had bred the germs that would destroy him.

For three days Asahel Grant was able to collaborate with Azariah Smith in the treatment of his disease, but at length he gave himself up to the other's care. Fever, delirium, and confusion accompany typhus, and Grant showed all these symptoms and more. On the 11th, letters from his children's guardians arrived in the post, and he read them eagerly. In the aftermath of this excitement he became worse. On April 13 acute diarrhea struck, leaving him even weaker. News soon spread of *Hakim* Grant's illness. The people of Mosul, high and low, inquired anxiously after his health. Paul-Émile Botta came daily to visit, as did Turkish officials from the palace. Mar Shimun sat and wept.

It is fitting that the last days of Asahel Grant should have been drawn out and difficult, a rough journey to a hidden place. But he deserved the mode of transport: a deathbed, a soft, clean place, where he could lie back and migrate at his ease—far better than the flashing knife, the sudden fall, the freezing mountain air which might earlier have brought his life to an end. Here he was surrounded by friends who joined him in prayer. Sarah Hinsdale brought him towels and broth. The American physician whom he had known for two weeks did his best. But with each hour the sufferer drew further back from life. Visitors who came to see him received a warm handshake and greeting, but seconds later the patient could not remember who they were. Sometimes in his delirium he spoke Turkish; at other times Syriac. He conversed with his mother and his children. He spoke with his Savior. Often he was on a ship going home. But no matter where his mind took him, his kindly smile remained.

By now spring flowers had appeared in Mosul, on the mound of Nineveh and in the surrounding wheatlands. The mountain rivers were swelling as April storms battered Hakkari with hail. It was time to begin again; time to leave. On April 24, 1844, by the banks of the Tigris, the shattered tenement of Asahel Grant was vacant at last.

22

The Monument in Asheetha

The Worldly Hope men set their Hearts upon
Turns Ashes—or it prospers; and anon,
Like Snow upon the Desert's dusty Face
Lighting a little Hour or two—is gone.
        —Edward Fitzgerald: "The Rubaiyat of Omar Khayam"

Funerals, some say, should be happy occasions. The dead, after all, have gone home to a better place. Many even direct that their services feature cheerful songs, expressions of joy at the life they have been granted and their hope for the world to come. Then there is another approach that says grief is natural and should not be denied; its suppression helps neither the living nor the dead. A person should aim to live life so well, bring such kindness and happiness to others, that when he dies the very earth should cry out at the loss. This, they say, is what emotions are for.

Both views found expression at the funeral of Asahel Grant. Cries of grief rose in chorus as the coffin wound through the streets, and nothing could restrain the sobs of those who gathered when he was lain in the vault with Abel Hinsdale and Martha Laurie. Both Mar Shimun and the Syrian Orthodox bishop read the funeral rites. The Turkish governor attended, as did Botta and Rassam. George Percy Badger's mother was dying, a situation which allowed him to stay away. The Americans were rebuked, says Thomas Laurie, because in all Mosul they alone did not weep. Said Mar Shimun, "My country and my people are gone! Now my friend is gone also, and nothing remains to me but God." It was not the last tribute that the Great Hakim would receive. Thomas Laurie fills eight pages with testimonials. Far into the coming years succeeding missionaries would encounter Kurds and Nestorians who had known Dr. Grant, and who sighed at the memory of that "great and good man." Even Badger, returning a prayer book borrowed from Grant, managed a word of tribute in a note he left behind.

What followed was a spring of upheaval and death. Without Mohammed Pasha's iron hand, robbery and brigandage, the specialty of Arab and Kurdish tribes, were increasing in the nearby villages. The people of the province would soon regret the tyrant's departure. In May came his successor, Sherif Pasha, a man who would stay less than two years and prove ineffectual in controlling the town. George Percy Badger's missionary career was also over. His superiors in London, having heard enough of his activities, made it clear that they would no longer support him. On April 28, just three days after Grant's burial, Badger's mother died. Four days later, their mission funds cut off by the Anglican authorities, Badger and his associate, J.P. Fletcher, set off on the desert route toward Mardin and Constantinople. Not until 1850 would Badger return to complete the travels and research for *The Nestorians and Their Rituals.*

Though the Americans no longer faced sabotage from Badger, and though Azariah Smith carried on his predecessor's medical practice with the same energy and dedication, Grant's death wrenched the last bit of heart and purpose from the Mosul mission. The station on the Tigris had come into being as a staging post enroute to Hakkari and the Nestorians. That goal was now left where it had always belonged: in the realm of fantasy. Fate, as we have seen, had been equally unkind to the Americans themselves. Of the eight missionaries who had set out for Mosul—the Mitchells, Hinsdales, Lauries and Drs. Grant and Smith—only three remained. Of this sorrowful remnant, the most disappointed may have been Sarah Hinsdale, who wanted as soon as possible to take her little boy home to a healthier climate. Before Grant's death, she had fully expected that by June the three of them would be on their way to the United States. Now she and her son faced another summer in Mosul.

There were other loose ends, for the Grant affair had not spent itself. Rumors and rancor still abounded concerning the mission house. In a letter to Rufus Anderson posted the previous October, Justin Perkins reported that "The Nestorians, both in Persia and in the mountains are . . . now extensively in the habit of referring the late disasters in Tiaree [sic] to Dr. Grant's residing & building largely there, which they say drew the attention and jealousy of the Kurds." Grant had done everything possible to deflect these charges; but if we look at his plans in his own words, quite a different impression emerges. In May 1843, just before he left to visit Bedr Khan, Grant wrote a letter to John Porter Brown, American chargé d'affaires in Stamboul, reviewing the building project and refuting all accusations of castle-building and military preparation made against him. He had not, he wrote, sought the permission of the Ottoman authorities because they did not wield any power in the area; however, he had repeatedly secured the permission of Nurullah Bey, their nominal governor. He went on to describe the mission house—about sixty feet square: a large footprint, but it was meant for four families—and the outbuildings he was building or intended to build. These were "a school-room 20 ft. by 45; a dispensary 18 ft. by 25; stable 15 ft. by 35; forage room 15 ft. by 30, kitchen 15 by 22 ft., and three rooms for boarding scholars, teachers &c., two of them 13 1/2 ft. by 19 1/2 & one 19 by 25 ft., to which two or three rooms are to be added for wood storage &c."

Given this list, which begins as an afterthought and and soon swells toward infinity, the size of the mission house becomes irrelevant. Clearly, Grant envisioned a very large compound, almost a village within itself—and a substantial intrusion into a mountain world that, until 1839, had remained unreachable. Despite Grant's good intentions, one cannot be seriously surprised that his ambitious project should have attracted "attention and jealousy." In July of 1844 the kettle of controversy was still boiling. In a letter to Boston, Azariah Smith wondered how he was going to explain Grant's house to Kamil Effendi, the Ottoman commissioner who had been sent out to investigate the massacres, and he went on to repeat rumors which grossly exaggerated the actual size of the house. "It appears," he wrote, "that Dr. Grant's house was 200 ft. long by 60 ft. wide." This is laughable, as anyone who thinks about it will realize. A house this large would exceed the dimensions of a normal American building lot; it would enclose *12,000 square feet* (almost a third of an acre) on the first floor alone. Not until the end of summer would Smith get an accurate idea of the house's true size, but by then it would look far different from what Asahel Grant had intended.

In the mission compound at Asheetha, so arduously built and unfairly maligned, so completely misunderstood and yet perfectly comprehended, we can trace the magnitude of Asahel Grant's failure. Like a hero of tragedy, while he toiled blindly in one direction, Fate was dragging him in another. No one could have striven more ardently to remake the world nearer to his heart's desire; no one could have believed more in the universality of his message. Love, warmth, and kindness poured from him like a river. All the medical skill he possessed he gave away freely. His entire life was an attempt to embody goodness, to broadcast that goodness to the four winds, to create harmony where it had never existed before. But the more goodness he spread abroad, the more heartache he bequeathed to his children at home; and the harder he strove for God and His Love, the more discord he sowed among those who worshipped Him differently. And he did all this simply because he existed; because he personified the menace of Europe even as he avoided politics; because he chose to live among violent men whom he could neither change nor understand.

With Grant gone, the Mosul mission, wavering between viability and morbidity, limped along into the summer. In July, at their most vulnerable point, they took another blow. In his *Pioneers East* (1967), David H. Finnie refers to little Abel Abdullah Hinsdale as a curiously-named child. In fact, Abdullah is an excellent—and religiously neutral—name, and for this reason it was used by Richard Francis Burton whenever he traveled in disguise. Abel was the name of the boy's father (from the Hebrew *Hebhel,* and Assyrian *ablu,* son), and Abdullah meant "servant of God" in Arabic (the language of his birthplace), so the boy's name was quite appropriate. For her little boy Sarah Hinsdale chose the best and most life-affirming names she could find. Reality, however, outflanks hope, and in 1844 that Moloch which ruled the summer days in Mosul yawned again in expectation.

By the middle of July, Mosul residents had been sleeping on their rooftops for two months or more. To this day the practice is common throughout the region, and in the villages its people pay a heavy price when, with alarming regularity, sleep-walking children make their way to the edges and step off into nothingness. The Americans were no different from the rest of Mosul, and after a day of stone-warping heat they too would retire to the rooftops at sundown. Smith and Laurie took one roof while Sarah Hinsdale, her baby boy, and an Arab maid slept on another, separated from the men by a low wall. At that time Abel was seventeen months old. He had long been unwell, and now he "pined away . . . under the pitiless heat of summer," a heat which sent the mercury well over 100° F. in daylight and only slightly lower at night. We have no idea of Abel Abdullah's true illness. Today it would probably pass on with little notice, van-

quished by vaccine, clean water, or decent care. The little boy
was struck down by the bad luck of having been born in an
unhealthy century.

"I will not soon forget," writes Thomas Laurie, "the night
that he died." And no wonder. Beneath that limitless dome of
sky, anyone would have felt eternity sink into his bones. It is
not easy to imagine 30,000 souls, silent on their elevated en-
campment beside the great river, their buildings dim and unlighted under the stars. Perhaps a breathing murmur filled any
silence left between the cries of the pariah dogs; perhaps the
Tigris itself was whispering. At midnight they were awakened
by a shriek. It was the Arab girl, and both Smith and Laurie
quickly guessed the "long expected" reason for her cry. Azariah
Smith hurried over to the adjacent rooftop and listened for the
boy's heartbeat, but of course it had ceased. When he told her,
Sarah Hinsdale was serene and resigned. "The Lord can take
better care of him than I can," she said, and with that she turned
to comfort the Arab maid and quiet her "wild outburst of oriental grief."

After the baby's death, the three surviving missionaries retreated to the vale of Sheikh Adi, and there in the shade of its
sacred olives found a measure of repose. But this could last only
a few days, and once back in Mosul a final duty remained. At
the end of August, leaving Sarah in the city, Smith and Laurie
set out on a valedictory tour, a twenty-four-day trek into the
mountain territories that Asahel Grant had made uniquely his
own. Though they could expect nothing but danger and sorrow, it was a journey that had to be made, and by doing it they
became the first Europeans to survey Hakkari after the destruction of the previous year. It didn't take long to find the evidence
they were looking for. Besides the inevitable skeletons, including several of children, in all Tiyari Smith and Laurie saw no
more than fifty habitable houses. What had been flourishing

districts were now a wasteland of felled trees, charred beams, and ruined terraces. They talked to Tiyarians and Nestorians who had survived, and to Kurds who had conquered. In Julamerk they met Nurullah Bey and his nephew Suleiman, and witnessed the continuing mistrust between the two. Most important of all, they saw the house in Asheetha.

Smith and Laurie reached the place after nightfall on Friday, August 28. Few people were there to greet them, and knowing that the mission house was guarded, they gave a shout to prevent surprise. Some forty armed Kurds emerged and surrounded the two missionaries. They were anything but friendly. Official passports were scorned; ditto for *buyurultus* and a *firman* from the governor. Two Turkish soldiers, sent from Mosul to keep the peace, apologized to the missionaries for the Kurds, who were, they said, "beasts who knew nothing and suspected everything." Only when the Americans' mule train arrived, carrying a letter from the revered Ismael Pasha of Amadiyah, did the Kurds relent and allow them to spend the night in Dr. Grant's house.

These Kurds were followers of Zeiner Bey, the Asheethans' old enemy, who had taken possession of the village. Theirs was a dismal lot. They had been left behind without provisions to guard a wasteland of their own creation, and their mood was foul. With the people driven off and crops non-existent, they were starving. It was the fitting end to a brutal episode.

In July 1843, Bedr Khan Bey kept his promise and did not sack Asheetha. However, the villagers were spared only to be taken over by their worst enemy. Zeiner Bey spent the remainder of the summer ruling by thievery under the guise of taxation. In October, having put up with this for months, the Asheethans made their move. The Kurdish garrison, including Zeiner Bey, was subjected to a surprise attack and besieged in Dr. Grant's mission house. The Nestorians maintained the siege from the shelter of the schoolroom, stables, and other outbuildings. Before long the Kurds were low on food and water. At this point Zeiner Bey summoned the Nestorians' leader, a deacon from Lezan named Hinno.

Hinno was an enemy of Mar Shimun, and already a compromised man. Before the invasion he had made his deal with Bedr Khan and in return was given presents, including 700 sheep. In a muttered conference at the front door, Zeiner told Hinno that he was ready to surrender, that there was a great deal of valuable property in the house, and if the deacon came inside Zeiner would deliver these riches to him on condition that the Kurd and his men be allowed to depart in peace. With that special foolishness born of cupidity, Hinno believed him. Having gone inside, the deacon was immediately seized and threatened with death unless Zeiner Bey and his men received provisions. This Hinno ordered his men to hand over, and, with a valuable hostage and a plentiful supply of food and water, the Kurds had no reason to leave.

The issue did not remain long in doubt. At this point a force of Kurds was seen approaching from the northwest, and soon the besiegers were forced to flee. Zeiner Bey now proceeded to do what he had wanted to do from the beginning. Everything destructible in Asheetha was destroyed; everything movable was stolen; hidden stores and valuables were gouged from their hiding-places by torture and threats. And Hinno was impaled within the walls of the mission house.

Not until the following morning could Azariah Smith and Thomas Laurie get a good look at Dr. Grant's house, and when they did they could only grieve. What had been primitive before, a low, flat-roofed structure with a cellar below, had changed beyond recognition. The stone walls laid in mud were now strengthened with lime mortar, and they rose not one story but two. At each of the four corners loomed a watchtower. The windows, which had aroused the suspicions of Nurullah (Why did Hakim Grant make such large openings? Was he building a bazaar?) were filled in with rock masonry, leaving only loop-holes for defense. In the center a large cistern stored water for the residents. The mission house had become, in other words, what Grant's enemies had always accused him of building: a strong, fully-equipped castle. It was the ultimate in irony. Grant's lancet had grown into a sword; his pruning-hooks were beaten into javelins. The house built by an unarmed physician for pur-poses of healing and peace had grown into a consummate sym-bol of violence and power.

None of this was lost upon Smith and Laurie as they re-turned to Mosul. On October 22, with no prospects ahead, they, with Sarah Hinsdale, closed the mission and put the Tigris be-hind them. Others, too, perceived the obvious—at least one of them had seen it coming for a long time. Justin Perkins, Grant's oldest missionary companion, the scholar of Urmia who had spent his life teaching, translating, and publishing, proved to be the truest prophet in the end. On October 2, 1843, some two months after the Tiyari disaster, he wrote to Dr. Rufus Ander-son in Boston. The whole subject of the mountain mission, he told Anderson, was intensely painful to him, for it had long been a cause of disagreement. Though unstated, his implica-tions are obvious. He loved Asahel Grant and revered the memory of Judith, and only with regret could he bring himself to say, "I told you so." He had never, Perkins said, supported the mountain mission. The region was simply too volatile and dangerous; native preachers, educated in Urmia, should be sent as emissaries to the mountains. Only his affection for Asahel Grant could have led Perkins to acquiesce in the project.

Never was the line drawn more clearly between the dedi-cated scholar and the romantic man of action; and never was there such stark disparity in the scope of their achievement. "Concentrated action," Rufus Anderson had instructed Perkins, "is effective action. There is such a thing as attempting too much." Just so. Perkins spent the greater part of his working life at a desk. From his labors, and those of his Nestorian colleagues, Neo-Aramaic emerged as a written language, capable of reviving the national consciousness of a small but significant sliver of mankind. Perkins propounded no grand theories; he expected no imminent Apocalypse. He simply studied, taught, and learned, and established an American educational presence that endured in Persia through the darkest days of World War I and into the 1930s. In the end, the sad truth is this: in Urmia, in the Islamic Republic of Iran, there now stand an agricultural college and a medical college, both grown from seeds planted by Justin Perkins and a host of other American missionaries, including Dr. Grant. In Asheetha there is nothing: even its name has disappeared.

Epilogue

AFTER LEAVING MOSUL, Grant's colleagues scattered. Sarah taught in Constantinople, childless and unmarried, before returning to the United States in 1855. The vigorous Dr. Azariah Smith stayed in Turkey, and did not live even to Asahel Grant's young age. He died of typhoid fever in Antep (now Gaziantep) in 1852, at the age of thirty-five. Smith's Yale classmates donated the money for what Gaziantep still calls the "American Hospital," dedicated in his memory in 1879. Thomas Laurie, his health broken by life in the East, returned to America in 1846. There he recovered, settled in Massachusetts, and began a long life of preaching and writing. He died in 1897 at the age of 76.

THE KURDS FARED much worse. In the fall of 1844, the emirs of Bohtan and Hakkari had reached the very apex of their power, and there they remained for the next two years. In 1846, responding to an attack by the Nestorians of Tehoma—who had reportedly sacked a Kurdish village, killed twenty of its occupants, and, most importantly, refused to make compensation—Bedr Khan Bey invaded that district and laid waste to the land and its people. This was one retribution too many. Following strenuous appeals from Britain and the European powers, the Ottoman government took the opportunity to get rid of a troublesome character and extend their power into Kurdistan. After assembling a large army, the Turks besieged Bedr Khan in his castle at Derguleh. The emir soon surrendered and, accompanied by his harem and a multitude of children, was shipped to exile, first in Candia (now Heraklion) on the island of Crete, and later to Damascus where he is buried. The Hakkari Beys soon followed him in defeat: Nurullah to Persia, where he soon died; his nephew Suleiman expired of cholera in Erzurum enroute to exile in Trebizond.

MAR SHIMUN LIVED longer, but his were years of gall and disappointment. In 1847, still in exile from the mountains, he arrived in Urmia, where Justin Perkins found him as well-disposed to the American mission as he had ever been. By 1848, however, things had changed. In that year he commenced a bitter campaign against the missionaries, broadcasting anathemas across the Urmia basin and threatening violence, and even death, to any of his flock who consorted with the Americans or sent their children to mission schools. He even put a price on the head of his youngest brother, the formerly belligerent Isaac, when the latter accepted "the pearl without price" and began working with the Presbyterians. Despite much trouble and physical attacks by the patriarch's supporters, the people did not turn against the missionaries. In 1849, thoroughly defeated, Mar Shimun was allowed by the Turks to return to the mountains. There in 1853 Rev. George Coan found the patriarch, still embittered, inveighing against the missionaries and lamenting the world that he had lost. The seventeenth Mar Shimun died at his home in Kochanes in 1861.

ACKNOWLEDGMENTS

THIS BOOK COULD NOT have been written without the help of the Interlibrary Loan staff of the King County Library System. Special thanks are also due to Mary Cochran Moulton, the child of missionaries in Iran, as well as to Philippa Brown of Waterville, New York. Both helped immensely with vital materials and encouragement. J.F. Coakley of Harvard University graciously agreed to read the book in manuscript, and offered valuable comments and corrections. Two other readers, Jere Bacharach and Fred Moody, deserve thanks as well. Last, Elibron.com is an excellent source for obscure out-of-print travel books. They provide titles, scanned from holdings at the Russian State Libraries (Moscow) and made available as print-on-demand paperbacks. A search of their website is highly recommended to anyone interested in European history or Middle East travel.

Notes and Comment

General Sources. There are five main sources for the events in Grant's life: (1) Thomas Laurie's biography (*Dr. Grant*, 1853); (2) Grant's own *Nestorians*, 1841; (3) his unpublished "Life in Kurdistan" (ABC 35) in the Houghton Library, Harvard University; (4) the microfilm archives of the American Board, esp. ABC 16.8.7; and (5) the collected editions of the *Missionary Herald* (Salibi and Khoury, eds., 1997) published under the auspices of the Hashemite Kingdom of Jordan. These works inform every chapter of *Fever and Thirst*. Another book often quoted is the *Memoir of Asahel Grant, M.D.* (1847), a book of his personal letters, edited by Rev. A.C. Lathrop.

Missionary Herald. All the American Board missionaries wrote regular journals, which they posted to ABCFM headquarters in Boston. Often these were printed verbatim in the *Missionary Herald*, the Board's official publication. Thus the *Herald* is invaluable, especially to anyone who must decipher the missionaries' handwriting. Rev. Thomas Laurie, for example, wrote his letters to Boston using the smallest characters possible. Then, having covered one side of the tissue-thin stationery, he would turn the sheet over and fill the reverse. These markings, combined with blotches of ink that bled through from both sides, threaten blindness to anyone trying to read them on microfilm. Having avoided this fate, the author would like to express his gratitude to those Jordanian scholars who have reprinted the *Herald*'s "reports from northern Iraq" in their present form. Their work has made available a treasury of information concerning the region, its people, and its politics during the 19th century.

Works on the Nestorians. The best general interest work on the Christian tribes of Hakkari is also the hardest to locate. This is Michel *Chevalier's Montagnards Chrétiens du Hakkari* (1978). The book, without illustrations and produced (in a typewriter font only) at the Sorbonne, has gone out of print. A mine of information on the culture and economy of the region, it deserves to be translated, amended with maps and illustrations, and republished. Also of use, and much easier to find, is Wigram's *Cradle of Mankind* (1914). This book and a revised edition, *The Assyrians and their Neighbours*, brought the story of the Nestorians (whom he calls Assyrians) into the twentieth century and told of their fate in the Great War. (Both can be found, complete and downloadable, at www.aina.org). John Joseph's classic *The Nestorians and Their Muslim Neighbors* (1961), as well as its successor volume, *The Modern Assyrians of the Middle East* (2000), are still the best modern histories of this people. (Joseph, it should be noted, is highly critical of Dr. Grant's role in the events of 1843 and of the American missionaries in general.) For more about contemporary Assyrian culture and politics, the reader may consult the Assyrian International News Agency, www.aina.org, as well as the website for the Assyrian Church of the East, www.cired.org. For a history of the East Syrian church, including a remarkable look at their influence in China and Central Asia, see Baum and Winkler, *The Church of the East: A Concise History* (2003).

Works on the History of Medicine. Here readers will find many books to consult. Besides the *Companion Encyclopedia* listed in the bibliography, the most useful book I found was John Haller's *American Medicine in Transition*. Asahel Grant practiced medicine just as microscopy was being revolutionized, anesthetics brought into use, and old medical practices were about to be superseded by the great discoveries of Pasteur, Lister, and others. Haller's is a priceless introduction to the waning era, with its bleeding and purgatives. For a further look into the medicine chest, J. Worth Estes' *Dictionary of Protopharmacology* is exhaustive, rewarding, and thoroughly unappetizing. Even less appetizing, but equally fascinating, is the information found at www.biopharm-leeches.com. Leeches, as readers may know (see *The New Yorker*, July 25, 2005, p. 72ff.), have recently made a remarkable comeback as therapeutic agents.

Odds and Ends. For a wonderful look at **iron-gall ink**, its history and formulation, see Evan Lindquist's online "Notes on Old Ink" as cited in the bibliography. There is a great deal about **orpiment** in Guineau and Delamare, *Colors: The Story of Dyes and Pigments.* **Manna,** I am assured by a correspondent in Suleimaniyah, Iraqi Kurdistan, continues to be made and consumed. Another correspondent tells about buying it in Iran in the 1960s. To get a taste of "manna from heaven," consult the shelves of Middle Eastern groceries in major cities. There it is sold as either *ghaz* (in Persian) or *man-es-sima* (Arabic). Also of interest is the *deli bal*, the "mad honey" of the mountains near Trabzon, in Turkey. For an article about this psychedelic (and toxic) honey, see: http://leda.lycaeum.org/ ?ID=16834. Another article tells firsthand of its effects: (www.sonomapicnic.com/06/ravhoney.htm).

CHAPTER ONE: The Remedy

1–4: The account of Grant's swollen face comes from Laurie, *Dr. Grant* (p. 255), as well as Grant's unpublished "Life in Kurdistan" (ABC 35).

CHAPTER TWO: Utica and Beyond

6–7: Utica population figures, Bagg, *Memorial History of Utica.* "His piety was not of that spongy character"; Laurie, p. 18; "I cannot . . . I dare not"; Laurie, p. 26.

8: "You know, dear brother": Laurie, p. 34.

11: "nicknamed Stamboul": There are other theories about the origin of "Istanbul," but I believe that like any other polysyllabic place name, "Constantinopolis" could not withstand the erosion of time. For instance, in Turkey, "Neocaesarea" became Niksar, "Iconium" became Konya, "Nicaea" became Iznik, and "Sebastaeia" became Sivas. These are only a few examples.

12: Pushkin quote: *Journey to Arzrum*, p. 75.

CHAPTER THREE: Miasma

15: Isabella Bird quote: *Journeys in Persia and Kurdistan*, vol. II, p. 218.

16: "Urmia and its moat": Southgate, *Narrative of a Tour in Armenia* etc., p. 213. Hadith: "water that flowed nine feet": cited in Whipple, *Role of Nestorians and Muslims in the History of Medicine*, p. 74. For an excellent example of a 19th-century physician's thinking on fever, miasma, etc., see Humphry Sandwith, M.D., *Narrative of the Siege of Kars*, pp. 56–59.

18: "Nestorian" label: Badger, p. 223–4. The label survives even today. In an article about Assyrians living in northern Syria during the 1990s (Alberto Fernandez, "Dawn at Tell Tamir"), one young man describes his grandfather, who was born and raised in the Hakkari mountains, as a "real Nestorian" ("kan nasturi haqiqi").

23: "We *must not lose him*"; and, "The most distressing and alarming effect"; ABCFM Archives, (ABC 16.8.7).

26–27: "A Steinway piano": Coan, p. 87.

CHAPTER FOUR: The Last Dreams of Mahmud

28: "His mother was a French girl": Blanch, *The Wilder Shores of Love*, pp. 207–282.

29: "a mob assembled": Sir William Eton, *Survey of the Turkish Empire*.

30: "the merchandise of Chios": Howarth, p. 63.

32–35: Nizib. There are two contemporary accounts of the battle, in W.F. Ainsworth's *Travels and Researches* and Poujoulat's *Voyage dans l'Asie Mineure*. My narrative relies heavily on that of John S. Guest in his *Survival Among the Kurds*, pp. 79–80.

36–37: "Scarcely a man dared to leave": Grant, *The Nestorians*, p. 32.

CHAPTER FIVE: Mosul and Mesopotamia

39: "Mardin is a beautiful place": So formidable was the castle of Mardin that in 1259 a mixed force of Turks and Kurds was able to hold out within for eight months against the Mongols of Hulagu Khan.

40: "the Little Ensign": For more on Mohammed Pasha, see Guest, *Survival Among the Kurds*, pp. 81–82. Henry Augustus Homes: see Finnie, pp. 229–231.

41: "In view of these considerations": Grant, pp. 34–35.

42: Captain Conolly: Hopkirk, *The Great Game.*

43–44: "Mosul . . . I found the same foul nest": Sykes, *The Caliphs' Last Heritage*, pp. 337–339. Layard quote: *Autobiography and Letters*, p. 160.

44: *keleks*: The best account of a *kelek* journey to Mosul is in E.B. Soane, *To Mesopotamia and Kurdistan in Disguise*, pp. 60–88. Layard quote: *Nineveh*, p. 277.

46: Grant letters: Laurie, p. 118.

47: "the devil drives": see Fawn Brodie biography of Richard Burton.

CHAPTER SIX: Into Kurdistan

48: "The bridge of boats": Grant, p. 41.

49–51: Re. the complexities of Kurdistan, see Martin van Bruinessen, *Agha, Sheikh and State.* Also, McDowall, *A Modern History of the Kurds.*

52: Coan: "My very soul was made sick": *Missionary Herald*, March, 1852.

53–54: "For a mile before reaching the town": Grant, p. 53.

56: "The Nestorian priest": Grant, p. 63.

57: "There must be a final struggle": Grant, p. 63. For a full account of American anti-Catholic bigotry, including the August 1834 burning of the Ursuline Convent in Boston (only a month before Dr. Grant felt the call to missionary service), see Gustavus Myers, *History of Bigotry in the United States.*

CHAPTER SEVEN: Manna and Its Heaven

60: "To the borders of their country": Grant, p. 66.

61: "The country of the independent Nestorians": Grant, p. 70.

62: "I had been brought": Grant, pp. 71–72.

64: "Mirza tells me": Bird, *Travels in Persia and Kurdistan*, p. 314.

65: "We spent nine hours": Bird, p. 267.

66: "In the wildest part": Bird, p. 268. "Many a strange house": Bird, p. 271.

70: "The quantity of gall-nuts": Justin Perkins, "Journal of a Tour" etc., p. 71. Also, see notes on gall ink, above.

71–73: Manna: See notes above. "Lezan, the first village": Lezan is now the border town of Çukurca, in Turkey.

74: "The only person": Grant, p. 73.

77: "bleeding became the treatment of choice": See Haller, pp. 47–50. Includes account of Sir William Blizard.

78: "leeches": Perkins letter in ABC 16.8.7. Fletcher, p. 90.

79: "The Lord has been visiting us": Lathrop, *Memoir of Dr. Grant*, pp. 59–60. "Tolstoy, serving in the Russian Army": Henri Troyat, *Tolstoy*, pp. 88–89.

81: "It was the hour of afternoon prayer": Layard, *Nineveh*, p. 148.

82: "We called to aid": Kinglake, *Eothen*, p. 28.

83: "the Fowler Method": George Fowler, p. 295. The trachoma cure is described in Wigram, p. 146.

CHAPTER EIGHT: The Patriarch and the Kurd

85: Asheetha, or "avalanche": The official Turkish name for Asheetha is now Çığlı, which means the same thing.

87–88: "There is an abundance": William Goodell, *The Old and the New*, quoted in *Journal of Kurdish Studies*, vol. 15, 1&2, p. 90.

89–90: "On either side the prospect": Grant, p. 96.

91: "From the Zab we ascended": Bird, p. 286.

92: "The patriarch": Grant, p. 101.

93: "first inquiries": Grant, pp. 101–102.

94: "Their form of church government": Laurie, p. 147.

96: "As soon as the sister": Georges Bohas, *The Aramaeans at the Very Edge of the World* (Toulouse, 1994). Quoted in *Journal of Assyrian Academic Studies*, vol. 13, no. 2, p. 7.

97: "avalanches thundered down in winter": For example, on January 7, 2002, according to the Avalanche Group of Turkey's General

Directorate of Disaster Affairs, the Hakkari highway was closed by an avalanche that stopped the flow of the river Zab for two hours.

98: "All signs of cultivation" and following quotes: Layard, *Nineveh*, pp. 173–174.

101: "Most unexpectedly I found the chief": Grant, p. 109.

103: "The sentinels": Grant, p. 110.

104: "He rapidly recovered": Grant, p. 111.

CHAPTER NINE: The Arms of Urmia

109–111: "The American mission cemetery": grave markings and dates courtesy of Mary Cochran Moulton.

117: "The ascent from the river": Laurie, p. 160.

119: "Changes have occurred": Grant, p. 127.

CHAPTER TEN: Competition

121: George Templeton Strong: quoted in Jensen, Kerr, Belsky, eds., *American Album*, p. 21.

123–125: Letters quoted are from ABC 16.8.7.

129: "You are the forerunners": Ainsworth, *Travels and Researches*, p. 242.

132: Rassam and Palmer story from Coakley, *The Church of the East*, p. 23. "We . . . informed the patriarch": Ainsworth, *Travels*, p. 248–249.

134: "This sudden interest": Ainsworth, p. 255. "Christians of the Hakkari mountains were doomed": See works by John Joseph and W.A. Wigram. For a poignant look at Hakkari ca. 1960, and the remains of its Nestorian villages, see Denis Hills, pp. 159–173.

CHAPTER ELEVEN: Critics, Snipers, and Frauds

136: Among the passengers lost on the *President* was Tyrone Power, Sr., an Irish-born actor returning from an engagement in New York. Power was the first of four actors to bear this famous name. (From *Fireman's Fund Record*, December 1946.)

138: Ainsworth re. Grant's Ten Tribes thesis: Ainsworth, p. 256–257. For a deeper look at the Lost Tribes obsession, see Tudor Parfitt, *The Lost Tribes of Israel: The History of a Myth*.

143: Breath's editor, Elijah P. Lovejoy, was considered the first Abolitionist martyr. "The proof-sheet of our first tract": Perkins, *Eight Years in Persia*, p. 456. This sheet is preserved in the Houghton Library, Harvard University, and is available on its website: http://www.hds.harvard.edu/library/exhibits/online/bible/5.html.

144: Letter of March 31, 1841: ABC 16.8.7.

CHAPTER TWELVE: The Pilgrim

163: Letter to Wayne Gridley in Lathrop, *Memoir*, p. 116.

169: "The year 1844": This year would see, in Iran, the emergence of the Bab, the Shia mystic whose teachings and martyrdom led to the establishment of the Baha'i faith.

CHAPTER THIRTEEN: Inferno

173: "In July": Laurie, p. 202. "a man of 'superior powers'": Lathrop, *Memoir*, p. 127.

175: Theodor Kotschy: information from website of the Kunsthistorisches Museum in Vienna: www.khm.at.

183: Coan cited above, p. 54. "In these unsubdued tribes": a native preacher, quoted in *Missionary Herald*, October 1864. Rhétoré quoted in Chevalier, p. 217.

187: Savagery of the Tiyarians: Smith and Laurie, *Missionary Herald*, April 1845; Justin Perkins, *Missionary Herald*, March 1850.

CHAPTER FOURTEEN: "Inductions Dangerous"

193: As indicated, the main source for this analysis is Badger, though other sources—Laurie, Layard, John S. Guest, John Joseph—contributed to the final product.

CHAPTER FIFTEEN: Demons and Angels

203: "I existed before": Kitab al-Jalwah in Guest, *Yezidis*, p. 200.

205–213: The full story of the Yezidis is told in Guest, *Survival Among the Kurds*. This chapter relies heavily upon his work. The Satan story is told in Revelation 12: 7–9. "Giving him a bad name": Guest, *Survival*, p. 226. Bashiqa population: See Patrick Graham, "Iraq's 'Devil Worshippers,'" *National Post*, December 17, 2002.

214: The most famous visitor to Sheikh Adi was Agatha Christie, who went there with her husband, the archaeologist Max Mallowan, when they were digging near Mosul in the late 1930s. See *Come, Tell Me How You Live*: London, 1946, p. 100. "One must be strong": Freya Stark, *The Journey's Echo*, p. 199.

CHAPTER SIXTEEN: "Wars and Rumors of Wars"

215: Grant's supply requisition in ABC 16.8.7.

217: Conolly: see Hopkirk, *The Great Game*.

226: Albagh: After the Iranian Revolution, many refugees escaped from Iran through this region, and many froze to death trying. When Betty Mahmoody (*Not Without My Daughter*, 1987) was smuggled out of Iran by Kurds, it was over these mountains that she and her daughter were taken.

CHAPTER SEVENTEEN: The House in Asheetha

241: The facts on Eugène Boré, who later became superior general of the Lazarists (Vincentians), can be found in the *Catholic Encyclopedia*.

243: The *cherki*, from the Persian, meaning one-fourth, appears to have been a coin worth ten paras. In Ottoman coinage forty paras made up a piastre; thus, ten paras would be a fourth of that amount.

CHAPTER EIGHTEEN: Mr. Badger Drops In

253–261: The facts on George Percy Badger, like those of any historically notable Briton, can be found in the *Dictionary of National Biography*. I have relied heavily upon Coakley's *Church of the East*, as well as Badger's own *Nestorians*, for this section.

264–265: Visit of Smith and Laurie: *Missionary Herald*, April, 1845. Laurie quotes the Kurd's remark in *Dr. Grant*, p. 285–286.

CHAPTER NINETEEN: Holding Back the Tigris

269: Freya Stark quote: can be found also in her *The Journey's Echo*: New York, 1964, p. 195.

269–270: Coakley, *The Church of the East*, p. 40.

275: "a poor place for an ague-fit": Laurie, p. 307. Freya Stark: "All fragilities glow": *Perseus in the Wind*, 1947.

276: Judi Dagh. Here it must be said that few knowledgeable travelers take seriously the claims of "Mt. Ararat" in Turkey to be the resting place of Noah's Ark. In the Middle East, only the Armenians regard the "mountains of Ararat" (Genesis 8:4) to be this particular peak. The name "Ararat" in the Old Testament clearly denotes a country or geographical area, not a specific mountain, and the three A's in the name are an important indicator. During the early Christian era, when scholars were trying to translate Biblical texts in Aramaic, which does not have vowels, into Byzantine Greek, which does, they ran into problems with unknown words. When dealing with the story of Noah's Ark, they came upon a name they did not recognize: a place denoted by the symbols for -R-R-T. In the absence of a clear answer, they gave up and inserted -A- in the three slots indicated. Thus "Ararat" was produced. We now know this ancient country by its more accurate name: Urartu, a kingdom centered upon Lake Van and a rival to Assyria. Thus, an accurate translation of Genesis would say that Noah's Ark landed on the "mountains of Urartu," which is no more specific than saying "the mountains of Switzerland." (The Peshitta, the ancient version of the Bible used by the East Syrian Church, states that Noah's Ark landed on the "Turé Kardu"; i.e., the mountains of the Kurds.)

278: John Joseph's account of these events is classic. See Joseph, *The Nestorians and their Muslim Neighbors*, pp. 40–67.

279: "God is first preparing the way": Lathrop, *Memoir*, p. 157.

281: "I can only see the light": Laurie, p. 318.

CHAPTER TWENTY: Devouring Fire

292: "if the Kurds did not destroy Asheetha": quoted by Smith and Laurie, *Missionary Herald*, April 1845.

294–297: Layard's account of the massacres and their aftermath is in *Nineveh and its Remains*, pp. 156–165.

CHAPTER TWENTY-ONE: A Long, Steep Journey

299: "Good vs. Evil": Even today this episode is treated simply as a massacre of innocent Christians by the Kurds. See Robert Blincoe, *Ethnic Realities and the Church*, p. 45.

300: Loss figures: Breath and Wright, *Missionary Herald*, November 1846; Badger, pp. 366–367.

302: Letter of September 1843: In ABC 16.8.7; quoted by Laurie, p. 368.

303: "The Nestorians needed humbling": Lathrop, *Memoir*, p. 163.

305: Ref. to A.H. Layard in Coakley, *Church of the East*, pp. 372–373. Botta and Layard were in regular correspondence at the time; thus, it is only logical that Layard would have heard from him about quarreling among the missionaries. Letter to *N.Y. Observer* quoted in Laurie, p. 372–376.

308: "It was even feared": Fletcher, p. 339.

309: Grant's last letters, and a description of his death, are in Lathrop, *Memoir*, as well as in Laurie, *Dr. Grant*, and the *Missionary Herald*.

BIBLIOGRAPHY

Ahmed, Sami Said. "The Yazidis: Their Life and Beliefs." Ph.D. diss.: UCLA, 1975.

Ainsworth, William Francis. *Travels and Researches in Asia Minor, Mesopotamia, Chaldea, and Armenia.* London, 1842.

American Board of Commisssioners for Foreign Missions. Papers of the ABCFM (microfilm archives). Research Publications: Woodbridge, Conn., 1982–85.

———. Annual Reports of the ABCFM, 182–35. Boston, 1836.

Anderson, Rufus. *History of the Missions of the ABCFM to the Oriental Churches.* Boston, 1872.

Badger, George Percy. *The Nestorians and Their Rituals.* London, 1852.

Bagg, Moses. *Memorial History of Utica.* Syracuse, NY, 1892.

Bates, Marston. *Gluttons and Libertines.* New York, 1967.

Biopharm Leeches. "Clinical Uses of Leeches." http://www.biopharm-leeches.com/clinical.htm.

Bird, Isabella L. *Journeys in Persia and Kurdistan.* London, 1891.

Blanch, Lesley. *The Sabres of Paradise.* New York, 1960.

———. *The Wilder Shores of Love.* New York, 1983.

Blincoe, Robert. *Ethnic Realities and the Church: Lessons From Kurdistan.* Pasadena, 1998.

Bodenheimer, F.S. *Insects as Human Food.* The Hague, 1951.

Bonner, Thomas Neville. *Becoming a Physician: Medical Education in Britain, France, Germany, and the United States, 1750–1945.* Baltimore, 1995.

Broadway, Bill. "Direst of Predictions for Iraq: End-Time Interpreters See Biblical Prophecies Being Fulfilled." *Washington Post,* March 8, 2003.

Bruinessen, Martin van. *Agha, Shaikh, and State*. London, 1992.

Burnaby, Frederick Gustavus. *On Horseback Through Asia Minor*. London, 1877.

Bynum, W.F., and Porter, Roy, eds. *Companion Encyclopedia of the History of Medicine*. New York, 1993.

Chevalier, Michel. *Les Montagnards Chrétiens du Hakkari et du Kurdistan Septentrional*. Paris, 1985.

Coakley, J.F. Book Review: "John Joseph, *The Modern Assyrians of the Middle East*." *Hugoye*, Vol. 5, No.1.: http://www.syrcom.cua/edu/Hugoye/Vol5No1/HV5N1PrCoakley.html.

———. *The Church of the East and the Church of England*. Oxford, 1992.

Coan, Frederick G. *Yesterdays in Persia and Kurdistan*. Claremont, Calif., 1939.

Darwin, Charles. *The Autobiography of Charles Darwin*. London, 1876.

De Foliart, Gene R.,PhD. "The Human Use of Insects as a Food Resource: A Bibliographic Account in Progress." Chapter 21: " Southwest Asia." http://www.food-insects.com.

Dickens, Mark. "Church of the East Timeline." http://www.oxus.com/timeline.htm.

———. "The Church of the East." http://www.oxus.com/timeline.htm.

Dickson, Capt. Bertram. "Journeys in Kurdistan." *The Geographical Journal*, XXXV, No. 4, April, 1910. In *The International Journal of Kurdish Studies*, Vol. 15, No.s 1 & 2, 2001.

Duggan, T.M.P. "Friday, August 26, 1071." *Turkish Daily News*, 28 August 1999. http://www.turkishdailynews.com/old_editions/08_28_99/feature.htm.

Emhardt, William C., and Lamsa, George M. *The Oldest Christian People*. New York, 1926.

Estes, J. Worth. *Dictionary of Protopharmacology: Therapeutic Practices, 1700–1850*. Boston, 1990.

Eton, Sir William. *Survey of the Turkish Empire*. London, 1799.

Eyland, Peter. "History of the Church of the East." http://newt.phys.unsw.edu.au/~epe/4010/notes/4010.N16.html.

Fahmy, Khaled. *All the Pasha's Men: Mehmed Ali, his army and the making of Modern Egypt*. Cairo, 1997.

Felter, H.W., and Lloyd, J.U. "Galla.—Nutgall." *King's American Dispensatory, 1898.* http://www.iblio.org/herbmed/eclectic/kings/quercus-lusi_nutgall.htm.

Fernandez, Alberto. "Dawn at Tell Tamir." *Journal of Assyrian Academic Studies,* Vol. XII, No.1, April 1998.

Finnie, David H. *Pioneers East: The Early American Experience in the Middle East.* Cambridge, Mass., 1967.

Fireman's Fund Insurance Co. "Mysteries of the Sea." Fireman's Fund Record, December 1946. http://www.ffic-heritageserver.com/storbank/misc/m21.htm.

Fletcher, James P. *Narrative of a Two Years' Residence in Nineveh.* London, 1850.

Fowler, George. *Three Years in Persia; with travelling adventures in Koordistan.* London, 1841.

Frahya, Aris. "New Yezidi Texts from Beled Sinjar." *Journal of the American Oriental Society,* Vol. 66 (1946), No. 1, pp. 18-43.

Fraser, James Baillie. *Travels in Koordistan, Mesopotamia, and Persia.* London, 1840.

Gibbon, Edward. *The Decline and Fall of the Roman Empire,* abridge. D.M. Low. New York, 1941.

Glendinning, Victoria. *Trollope.* London, 1992.

Goodwin, Jason. *Lords of the Horizons.* New York, 1999.

Grant, Asahel. *The Nestorians, or, The Lost Tribes.* New York, 1841.

———. "Life in Kurdistan." Microfilm copy of an unfinished, unpublished manuscript (ABC 35) in the archives of the ABCFM. Houghton Library, Harvard University. n.d.

Guest, John S. *Survival Among the Kurds: A History of the Yezidis.* London, 1993.

———. *The Euphrates Expedition.* New York, 1986.

Delmare, Francois, and Guineau, Bernard. *Colors: The Story of Dyes and Pigments.* New York, 2000.

Guyer, S. *My Journey Down the Tigris.* New York, 1925.

Haley, Bruce. *The Healthy Body and Victorian Culture.* Cambridge, Mass., 1978.

Haller, John S., Jr. *American Medicine in Transition, 1840–1900.* Normal, Ill., 1981.

A Handbook for Travellers in Turkey, 3rd Ed. London, 1854. John Murray the publisher may also have been the editor.

Hasluck, F.W. *Christianity and Islam under the Sultans*. Oxford, 1929.

Haydn, Hiram C., ed. *American Heroes on Mission Fields*. New York, 1890.

Hills, Denis. *My Travels in Turkey*. London, 1964.

Hopkirk, Peter. *The Great Game*. London, 1990.

Howarth, David. *The Greek Adventure*. New York, 1976.

Huggler, Justin. "Yezidis: Hell's Angels." *The Independent*. 29 November 2003.

Issawi, Charles, ed. *The Economic History of the Middle East, 1800–1914*. Chicago, 1966.

Jackson, Monica. *The Turkish Time Machine*. London, 1968.

Jaubert, Pierre Amédeé. *Voyage en Arménie et Perse*. Paris, 1821.

Jensen, Oliver Ormerod, Joan Paterson Kerr, and Murray Belsky, eds. *American Album*. New York, 1970.

Joseph, John. *The Modern Assyrians of the Middle East*. Leiden, 2000.

———. *The Nestorians and their Muslim Neighbors*. Princeton, 1961.

Kaya, Ferzende. "Where will tribal votes head for?" *Turkish Daily News*. September 23, 2002.

Kinglake, Alexander. *Eothen; or, Traces of Travel Brought Back from the East*. London, 1844.

Kutschera, Chris, ed. *Le Kurdistan: Guide Literraire*. Favre: Lausanne (Suisse), 1998.

Lathrop, A.C. *Memoir of Asahel Grant, M.D.* New York, 1847.

Laurie, Thomas. *Dr. Grant and the Mountain Nestorians*. Boston, 1853.

———. *Woman and Her Saviour in Persia*. Boston, 1863.

Layard, A.H.. *Discoveries in the Ruins of Nineveh and Babylon*. London, 1853.

———. *Autobiography and Letters*. London, 1903.

———. *Nineveh and its Remains*. London, 1849.

Lewis, Bernard. *The Emergence of Modern Turkey*, 2nd ed. Oxford, 1968.

Lewis, Jonathan Eric. "Iraqi Assyrians: Barometer of Pluralism." *Middle East Quarterly*, Summer 2003. http://meforum.org/pf.php?id=558.

Lindquist, Evan. "Additional Notes on Old Ink." Last updated 7 July, 2005. http://www.clt.astate.edu/elind/oldinknotes.htm

Longrigg, Stephen H. *Four Centuries of Modern Iraq*. Oxford, 1925.

Maclean, Fitzroy. *A Person from England*. London, 1958.

Marsh, Dwight W. *The Tennessean in Persia and Kurdistan*. Philadelphia, 1869.

Maunsell, Capt. F.R. "Kurdistan." *The Geographical Journal,* Vol. III, February, 1894. In *The International Journal of Kurdish Studies,* Vol. 15, Nos. 1 & 2, 2001.

McCarthy, Justin. *Death and Exile: The Ethnic Cleansing of Ottoman Muslims, 1821-1922*. Princeton, 1995.

————. *The Ottoman Turks: An Introductory History to 1923*. London and New York, 1997.

McDonagh, Bernard. *Blue Guide: Turkey*. London and New York, 1995.

McDowall, David. *A Modern History of the Kurds*. London and New York, 1996.

Moulton, Mary Cochran. "A Mission Child in Iran." Privately printed; n.d.

————. Letter to the author, February 14, 2003. Including plan of the mission graveyard at Mt. Seir, Urmia, Iran, by George Moradkhan, 1957.

Murre-van den Berg, Heleen. "The Missionaries' Assistants: The Role of Assyrians in the Development of Written Urmia Aramaic." *Journal of the Assyrian Academic Society*. Vol. 10, No. 2. http://www.jaas.org/edocs/v10n2/heleen.pdf

Myers, Gustavus. *History of Bigotry in the United States*. New York, 1943.

Owen, Roger. *The Middle East in the World Economy, 1800-1914*. London, 1981.

Palmer, Alan. *The Decline and Fall of the Ottoman Empire*. New York, 1992.

Parfitt, Tudor. *The Lost Tribes of Israel: The History of a Myth*. London, 2002.

Peck, Ada Marie. *History of the Hanover Society*. Waterville, New York. N.D.

Pereira, Michael. *East of Trebizond*. London, 1971.

Perkins, Henry Martyn. *Life of Justin Perkins, D.D., Pioneer Missionary to Persia*. Chicago, 1887

Perkins, Justin. *A Residence of Eight Years in Persia*. Andover, 1843.

————. *Missionary Life in Persia*. Boston, 1861.

————. *The Persian Flower: A Memoir of Judith Grant Perkins*. Boston, 1853.

————. "Journal of a Tour from Oroomiah to Mosul Through the Koordish Mountains." *Journal of the American Oriental Society*, VII, 1851. In *The International Journal of Kurdish Studies*, Vol. 15, No.s 1 & 2, 2001.

Poujoulat, Baptistin. *Voyage dans l'Asie Mineure, en Mésopotamie, à Palmyre, en Palestine, et en Egypte*. Paris, 1840.

Pushkin, Alexander. *A Journey to Arzrum*, trans. Birgitta Engemanson. Ann Arbor, 1974.

Ralston, David. *Importing the European Army*. Chicago, 1990.

Research Institute of Regeneration. "About Leeches." http://www.frb.spb.ru/eng/leeches.htm.

Rich, Claudius James. *Narrative of a Residence in Koordistan and on the Site of Ancient Nineveh*. London, 1836.

Romney Marsh Countryside Project. "Medicinal Leech (*Hirudo medicinalis*) in the Romney Marsh Natural Area." http://www.rmcp.co.uk/MedicinalLeech.htm.

Salibi, Kamal, and Khoury, Yusuf, eds. *The Missionary Herald: Reports from Northern Iraq, 1833–1870*. 3 vols. Amman, Jordan, 1997.

Salt, Jeremy. "Trouble Wherever They Went: American Missionaries in Anatolia and Ottoman Syria in the 19th Century." Paper presented at Bellagio, Italy, August 2000. http://www.ciaonet.org/conf/mei01/saj01.html.

Sanders, J.C.J. *Assyrian-Chaldean Christians in Eastern Turkey and Iran: Their last homeland re-charted*. Amsterdam, 1998.

Sandwith, Humphrey, M.D. *Narrative of the Siege of Kars*. London, 1856.

Shaw, Stanford J., and Shaw, Ezel Kural. *History of the Ottoman Empire and Modern Turkey*. Cambridge, 1976, 1977.

Shiel, Lt. Col. J. "Notes on a Journey from Tabriz through Kurdistan via Van, Bitlis, Se'rt and Erbil, to Suleimaniyah, in July and August, 1836." *Journal of the Royal Geographical Society of London*, Vol. VIII, 1838. In *The International Journal of Kurdish Studies*, Vol. 15, No.s 1 & 2, 2001.

Shields, Sarah D. *Mosul Before Iraq: Like Bees Making Five-sided Cells*. Albany, 2000.

Smith, Azariah, M.D. "Contribution to the Geography of Central Koordistan." *Journal of the American Oriental Society*, Vol. VII, 1851. In *The International Journal of Kurdish Studies*, Vol. 15, No.s 1 & 2, 2001.

Southgate, Horatio. *Narrative of a Tour Through Armenia, Kurdistan, Persia, and Mesopotamia*. 2 vols. New York, 1840.

———. "A Letter to the Members of the Protestant Episcopal Church in the United States, from the Rev. Horatio Southgate, their Missionary at Constantinople." New York, 1844. http://justus.anglican.org/resources/pc/usa/hsouthgate/vindication.pdf.

Stark, Freya. *Riding to the Tigris*. London, 1958.

———. *Rome on the Euphrates*. New York, 1966.

Stearns, Peter, ed. *The Encyclopedia of Modern History*. New York, 2001.

Stoneman, Richard. *Across the Hellespont*. London, 1987.

Sykes, Mark. *The Caliphs' Last Heritage*. London, 1915.

Tchilingirian, Hratch. "The Armenian Protestants: A Brief History." *Window Quarterly* 2, 3, 1991; ACRAG c. 1991.

Toledano, Ehud R. *Slavery and Abolition in the Ottoman Middle East*. Seattle, 1998.

Troyat, Henri. *Tolstoy*. New York, 1967.

U.S. Department of State, Bureau of Intelligence and Research. *International Boundary Study: Turkey-Iraq Boundary* (JX 4111). Washington, 1964.

Walker, Joel, "Nestorians," and Gaddis, J.M., "Nestorius," in Bowersock, Grabar, and Brown, eds., *Late Antiquity: A Guide to the Postclassical World*. Cambridge, Mass., 1999.

Waterfield, Robin E. *Christians in Persia*. London, New York, 1973.

Whipple, Allen O. *The Role of the Nestorians and Muslims in the History of Medicine*. Princeton, 1967.

White, Paul. "Ethnic Differentiation Among the Kurds: Kurmanci, Kizilbash, and Zaza." http://members.tripod.com/~zaza_kirmanc/research/paul.htm.

Wigram, W.A., and Wigram, E.T.A. *The Cradle of Mankind: Life in Central Kurdistan*. London, 1914.

Wilmshurst, David. *The Ecclesiastical Organisation of the Church of the East, 1318–1914*. Louvain, 2000.

Xenophon. *Anabasis, or, The March Up Country,* trans.W.H.D. Rouse. New York, 1965.

Yana, George V. "Book Review: The Arameans at the Very Edge of the World, by Georges Bohas," Toulouse Cedex, France, 1994. *Journal of Assyrian Academic Studies,* Vol.13, No. 2. http://www.jaas.org/edocs/v13n2/review.pdf.

Zaken, Moti. "The Kurdish Jews in Israel." *The Sentinel,* May 16, 1991. www.israel-kurd.org.

Zirinsky, Michael. "Onward Christian Soldiers: Presbyterian Missionaries and the Ambiguous Origins of American Relations with Iran." Paper presented at Middle East Institute, Bellagio, Italy, August 2000. http://www.ciaonet.org/conf/mei01/zim01.html.

Zora, Subhi. "The Chaldean Christians: Their History, Liturgy and Status up to the Present Day." Farmington Reports, 1991. Farmington Institute, Oxford University. http://www.farmington.ac.uk/documents/old_docs/WR3.html.

Zürcher, Erik. *Turkey: A Modern History.* New York, 1998.

GLOSSARY

arzaleh: an elevated sleeping platform made of sticks and wooden poles, used in mountain villages.

ashiret: a self-governing tribe, esp. one that lies outside the power of the Ottoman government.

bey: an honorific title, similar to Sir or Mr., which is attached after a name; e.g., Ali Bey, Nurullah Bey, etc.

buyurultu: a written order of protection for travelers in Ottoman lands issued on the provincial level.

cherki: slang for a monetary unit among the mountain tribes, equal to approx. twelve and a half cents U.S. From the Persian for one-fourth, or, a quarter.

chiya: a mountain (Kurd.); e.g., Chiya Matinah.

dagh (gh silent or barely pronounced): a mountain (Turk.); e.g. Judi Dagh.

Ferenghi: Middle East slang for a "Frank," or European.

firman: a written order of protection for travelers issued by the Ottoman government in Constantinople.

hakim: a physician (Turk., Ar., Per.).

jabal, or **jebel:** a mountain (Ar.). Used before the name, e.g., Jebel Sinjar.

kelek: a raft made of logs and sticks, supported by inflated goatskins.

kellaita: a village meeting-house among the mountain Nestorians of Hakkari.

kharaj: a yearly tribute tax paid by non-Muslims in the Ottoman Empire in lieu of military service.

malek: a tribal chief among the Hakkari Nestorians; lit., a king.

Mar: a title meaning 'lord' in Syriac; used for religious leaders, bishops, or saints. Used before the person's name; e.g., Mar Toma.

millet: a recognized religious or national group within the Ottoman system; e.g., the Greeks, the Armenians, or the Jews.

mutesellim: governor or second-in-command to a ruler; e.g., Suleiman Bey was mutesellim to Nurullah Bey, emir of Hakkari.

pasha: an Ottoman general or governor of a province. Used as a title after the man's name; e.g., Kemal Pasha.

qasha: a priest of the Nestorian church. Used before the name; e.g., Qasha Zadok.

rayah: any village or group of people, whether Christian, Muslim, or Jew, who are subjects, or serfs, of a ruling tribe or person. (Compare with **ashiret**, above.)

serdab: a cellar, esp. those cellars of Mosul used as a refuge during summer heat.

zozan (also called **yayla** [Turk.] and **zoma** [Kurd.]): high-altitude pastures to which villagers take their flocks in summer.

Index